AF531791

# HINDU CUSTOMS AND TRADITIONS

# HINDU CUSTOMS AND TRADITIONS

*Editor-in-Chief*
**Swami Chidatman Jee Maharaj**

**ANMOL PUBLICATIONS PVT. LTD.**
**NEW DELHI - 110 002 (INDIA)**

**ANMOL PUBLICATIONS PVT. LTD.**
**H.O.:** 4374/4B, Ansari Road, Daryaganj,
New Delhi-110 002 (India)
Ph.: 23278000, 23261597
**B.O.:** No. 1015, Ist Main Road, BSK IIIrd Stage
IIIrd Phase, IIIrd Block,
Bangalore - 560 085 (India)
*Visit us at*: www.anmolpublications.com



*Hindu Customs and Traditions*


First Published, 2009
ISBN 978-81-261-3615-5



PRINTED IN INDIA

Printed at Mehra Offset Press, Delhi.

# Contents

# Preface

India colourful and vibrant, a land as diverse as its people. A mosaic of faiths, cultures, customs and languages that blend harmoniously to form a composite whole. One of the world's oldest living civilizations—which gave to the world—the concept of zero, the primordial sound Aum..., Yoga and Buddhism.

She is old. She is young. The two diametrically opposite, different yet unique and dynamic faces of India coexist even at this turn of the millennium. With a history of heritage, learning and civilisation dating back to almost 5000 years or perhaps even more, the modern India presents itself as an ideal country. From snow clad mountains to breezy sparkling blue sea side. From arid deserts with shifting sand dunes to lush green country sides. From ancient relics and architectural ruins dating back into antiquity to modern cities, India has it all.

To the north it is bordered by the world's highest mountain chain, where foothill valleys cover the northernmost of the country's maximum states. Further south, plateaus, tropical rain forests and sandy deserts are bordered by palm fringed beaches. Its southernmost tip is the meeting point of three Oceans.

India is a land of staggering contrast with a mingling of the tradition and modernity that is an unique experience to be in India. One will forever remember the stay in this wonderful Homeland-a land truly of mystery and enchantment. Only India can offer such an astonishing variety of contrasts.

She has given birth to numerous spiritual leaders and founders of some of the popular religions of the present day world. India probably has the most religious diversity in any country. It's the birthplace of Hinduism, Buddhism, Sikhism and Jainism and is among the few places to have a resident

Zoroastrian population. India with her veritable treasure trove of culture, mysticism, philosophy, art, music and architecture to name a few. Much of India's classical music is devotional and the North Indian Hindustani and South Indian Carnatic streams are distinct and both have a complex 'raga' framework. The legacy of dance in India is tremendous. The classical dances of India are numerous such as Kathakali of Kerala, Bharatnatyam of Tamil Nadu, Kuchipudi of Andhra Pradesh, Manipuri and Odissi from Orissa are the prominent dance forms in this country that sways to an altogether novel beat. The Yakshagana, nautanki and puppetry are ancient folk forms that live on till date. The earliest specimens of Indian painting are the ones on the walls of the Ajanta Caves dating back to 2nd century BC. The Mughals had a huge impact on Indian art. The influence of Persian art brought placid garden scenes, illustrations from myths, legends and history into Indian art. Word craft, handicrafts, architecture and sculpture all contribute to this rich and varied domain. Indian literature, both in English and in the vernacular, is ever more popular around the world.

The book aims at presenting perspectives of different aspects of Indian culture. It has topics on Indian classical music and dance, painting, ayurveda and yoga which are traditional and indigenous system of physical and mental wellbeing, language, philosophy and excellence achievements by Indian in the different branches of science and social sciences. It also includes our ancient religious and classic literature.

It is hoped that this book will be welcomed by the general readers as also scholars who are interested in the Indian heritage.

—*Editors*

1

# India—The Land of Unique Culture

## People of India

India is a fascinating country where people of different communities and religions live together in unity. Indian Population is polygenetic and is an amazing amalgamation of various races and cultures.

It is impossible to find out the exact origin of Indian People. The species known as Ramapithecus was found in the Siwalik foothills of north western Himalayas. The species believed to be the first in the line of hominids (Human Family) lived some 14 million years ago. Researchers have found that a species resembling the Austrapithecus lived in India some 2 million years ago. Even this discovery leaves an evolutionary gap of as much as 12 million years since Ramapithecus.

There are diverse ethnic groups among the people of India. The 6 main ethnic groups are as follows.

1. Negrito
2. Proto-Australoids or Austrics
3. Mongoloids
4. Mediterranean or Dravidian
5. Western Brachycephals
6. Nordic Aryans

***Negroids:*** The Negritos or the Brachycephalic (broad headed) from Africa were the earliest people to have come to India. They have survived in their original habitat in Andaman and Nicobar Islands. The Jarawas, Onges, Sentinelese and the

Great Andamanese are some of the examples. Some hill tribes like Irulas, Kodars, Paniyans and Kurumbas are found in some patches in southern part of mainland India.

***Pro-Australoids or Austrics:*** These groups were the next to come to India after the Negritos. They are people with wavy hair lavishly distributed all over their brown bodies, long headed with low foreheads and prominent eye ridges, noses with low and broad roots, thick jaws, large palates and teeth and small chins. The Austrics of India represent a race of medium height, dark complexion with long heads and rather flat noses but otherwise of regular features. Miscegenation with the earlier Negroids may be the reason for the dark or black pigmentation of the skin and flat noses.

The Austrics laid the foundation of Indian civilization. They cultivated rice and vegetables and made sugar from sugarcane. Now these people are found in some parts of India, Myanmar and the islands of South East Asia. Their languages have survived in the Central and Eastern India.

***Mongoloids:*** These people are found in the northeastern part of India in the states of Assam, Nagaland, Mizoram, Meghalaya, Arunachal Pradesh, Manipur, and Tripura. They are also found in northern parts of West Bengal, Sikkim, and Laddakh. Generally they are people with yellow complexion, oblique eyes, high cheekbones, sparse hair and medium height.

***Dravidians:*** These are the people of South India. They have been believed to come before the Aryans. They have different subgroups like the Paleo-Mediterranean, the true Mediterranean, and the Oriental Mediterranean. They appear to be people of the same stock as the peoples of Asia Minor and Crete and pre-Hellenic Aegean's of Greece. They are reputed to have built up the city civilization of the Indus Valley, whose remains have been found at Mohenjodaro and Harappa and other Indus cities.

***Western Bracycephals:*** These include the Alpinoids, Dinarics and Armenoids. The Parsis and Kodavas also fall in this category. They are the broad-headed people living mainly on the western side of the country such as the Ganga Valley and the delta, parts of Kashmir, Kathiawar, Gujarat, Maharashtra, Karnataka and Tamil Nadu.

***Nordics or the Indo-Aryans:*** This group was the last one to immigrate to India. They came to India somewhere between 2000 and 1500 B.C. They are now mainly found in the northern and central part of India.

## Languages of India

India is rich in languages. There are a quite a number of languages spoken in India. Some of these languages are accepted nationally while others are accepted as dialects of that particular region.

The Indian languages belong to four language families namely Indo-European, Dravidian, Austroasiatic (Austric) and Sino-Tibetan. Majority of India's population are using Indo-European and Dravidian languages. The former are spoken mainly in northern and central regions and the latter in southern India. Some ethnic groups in Assam and other parts of eastern India speak Austric languages. People in the northern Himalayan region and near the Burmese border speak Sino-Tibetan languages.

The written forms of language or scripts come from an ancient Indian script called Brahmi.

India has 22 officially recognised languages. But around 33 different languages and 2000 dialects have been identified in India. Hindi, in the Devanagari script is the official language of the Federal government of India. English is an associate official language. Sanskrit, the classical language of India, represents the highest achievement of the Indo-Aryan Languages.

The beginning of Sanskrit literature may be traced back to Rig Vedic period. It is the oldest literary language of India, which is more than 5,000 years old and the basis of many modern Indian languages including Hindi and Urdu. Its earliest dialect form, Vedic was spoken by the Aryans. All the classical literature and the Indian epics have been written in Sanskrit.

## List of Languages Recognised by the Indian Constitution

| Languages | Official Language of | Spoken by |
|---|---|---|
| Assamese | Assam | 15 million |
| Bengali | Tripura & West Bengal | 67 million |
| Bodo | Assam | — |
| Dogri | Jammu and Kashmir | — |
| Gujarati | Dadra and Nagar Haveli, Daman & Diu and Gujarat | 43 million |
| Hindi | Andaman and Nicobar Islands, Bihar, Chandigarh, Chhattisgarh, Delhi, Haryana, Himachal Pradesh, Jharkhand, Madhya Pradesh, Rajasthan, Uttar Pradesh & Uttaranchal | 180 million |
| Kannada | Karnataka | 35 million |
| Kashmiri | — | — |
| Konkani | Goa | — |
| Maithili | Bihar | 22 million |
| Malayalam | Kerala & Lakshadweep | 34 million |
| Manipuri (Meithei) | Manipur | — |
| Marathi | Maharashtra | 65 million |
| Nepali | Sikkim | — |
| Oriya | Orissa | 30 million |
| Punjabi | Punjab | 26 million |
| Sanskrit | — | — |
| Santhali | — | — |
| Sindhi | — | — |
| Tamil | Tamil Nadu & Pondicherry | 66 million |
| Telugu | Andhra Pradesh | 70 million |
| Urdu | Jammu and Kashmir | 46 million |

## List of Other Languages of India

| Languages | Official Language of | Spoken by | |
|---|---|---|---|
| Awadhi (sub-variety of Hindi) | | — | 20 million |
| Bhili | Bhil tribals | — | |
| Bhojpuri (sub-variety of Hindi) | | Bihar | 23 million |
| Bundeli (sub-variety of Hindi) | | — | — |
| Chhattisgarhi (sub-variety of Hindi) | | Chhattisgarh | 11 million |
| Deccani | — | 11 million | |
| Gondi | Gond tribals | — | |
| Haryanvi | Haryana | 13 million | |

*Contd...*

| ***Languages*** | ***Official Language of*** | ***Spoken by*** | |
|---|---|---|---|
| Hindustani (mixture of Hindi & Urdu) | | Northern part of India | — |
| Kannauji | Uttar Pradesh | — | |
| Kodava | Kodagu (Karnataka) | — | |
| Kutchi | Kutch (Gujarat) | — | |
| Magahi (sub-variety of Hindi) | | Southern Bihar | 11 million |
| Marwari | Rajasthan | 12 million | |
| Portuguese | Partly in Goa, Daman and Diu, Dadra and Nagar Haveli | — | |
| Sikkimese | Sikkim | — | |
| Tibetan | Tibet (Kashmir) | 6 million | |
| Tulu | Tulu people (Karnataka & Kerala) | | |

## Religions of India

India, the land of spirituality and philosophy considers religion as an integral part of its entire tradition. The worship of various religions and its rituals play a significant role in every aspect of human life in the country.

India is the birthplace of two great religions of the world, namely, Hinduism and Buddhism. It is also the birth place of one of the oldest religions of the world, Zoroastrianism, and home to an ancient religion, Jainism. Sikhism is another very recognisable religion which began here bringing together the best aspects of Hinduism and Islam. Followers of religions originated in other countries such as Islam, Christianity, Bahaism and Judaism also form a part of the population of secular nation, India.

Hinduism is the dominant faith. According to 2001 Census, 80.5 per cent of the population of the country are designated 'Hindu'. It is one of the ancient religions in the world, which began about 6000 years ago. Besides Hindus, Muslims are the most prominent religious group and are an integral part of Indian society. There are approximately 13.4 per cent Muslims (over 100 million), 2.3 per cent Christians (over 20 million), 1.9 per cent Sikhs (18 million) and others including Buddhists (6 million), Jains, Parsis (Zoroastrians), Jews, and Bahais, less than 2 per cent.

Hindus and Muslims are spread throughout the country. Muslims are found mostly in the states of Uttar Pradesh, Bihar, Maharashtra, West Bengal, Andhra Pradesh, and Kerala. They represent a majority in Jammu and Kashmir and Lakshadweep. Christian concentrations are found in the northeastern states like Nagaland, Mizoram and Meghalaya and the southern states of Kerala, Tamil Nadu, and Goa. Sikhs are a majority in the state of Punjab whereas Buddhists are found in large numbers in Arunachal Pradesh, Laddakh, Bengal and Sikkim. Though a tiny minority, Jains are found all over India. Majority of Jains live in the states of Maharashtra, Rajasthan, Karnataka and Gujarat.

***Buddhism:*** Buddhism stands on three pillars: the Buddha; its founder, the Dhamma; his teachings and the Sangha; the order of Buddhist monks and nuns.

Siddhartha, who was later known as the 'Buddha', the enlightened one, was the son of king Shuddhodana of Kapilavastu and his queen, Maya. He was born in 563 BC on the Vaisakha Purnima in the royal grove at Lumbini near Kapilavastu, Capital of the Sakyan republic. His family name was Gautama and he belonged to the Shakya clan. Hence he is sometimes called Shakyamuni (Shakya sage) or Shakyasimha (Shakya lion). Among his other epithets are Amitabha (infinite light) and Thathagata (he who has arrived at perfection).

Queen Maya died a week after delivering the prince. So the child was brought up by his step mother Gautami. At Siddhartha's birth, the royal astrologer prophesied that he would one day become disillusioned with worldly pleasures and go forth as a mendicant in search of the wisdom that can overcome suffering.

The king, remembering the astrologers prophecy, tried to save his son from unpleasant sights. The king found for him a lovely wife, Yashodhara. Yashodhara bore him a son. He named his son Rahula (impediment). But the seeds of disenchantment had already sprouted in Siddhartha's heart.

As prophesied, Siddhartha saw the three signs of suffering: sickness, old age and death. These sufferings touched his heart and he left his palace on the night of the full moon in the month of Vaisakha, at the age of 29, to seek mental peace in the homeless life of an ascetic.

With a view to finding a true solution, the Buddha endeavored for full six years. During this period, he searched, scrutinised and examined in detail the prevalent schools of thought. He realised that wisdom could not be attained through self-mortification. At last, meditating under a tree near Gaya, he attained Bodhi (Illumination). Prince Siddhartha became the 'Buddha', the fully awakened one and the tree which had sheltered him came to be known as the Bodhi tree.

After becoming enlightened, Gautama the Buddha could have immediately realised himself from the cycle of rebirths and attained 'Nirvana'; supreme liberation. But he decided to share his wisdom with others. His first sermon was preached in the Deer park at Saranath, near the ancient holy city of Varanasi. The five ascetics who had been earlier his colleagues became his first audience. Thereafter, for 45 years, the Buddha went about the country, from town to town, from village to village, disseminating the spiritual illumination for the benefit of suffering humanity. He attained 'Maha-Parinirvana' at Kusinagar in 483 BC at the age of 80. Just before his death, when his favourite disciple, Ananda started weeping, the Buddha said "All component things must dissolve. Buddha can only point the way. Become a lamp unto yourself, work out your own salvation diligently". These were his last words.

Besides being a great spiritual teacher and preacher, the Buddha was also a great social reformer. The Buddha revolted against oppressive social laws, and proclaimed his new philosophy of liberty, equality and fraternity for the common welfare of all. Lord Buddha was considered as the creator of the virtues like individual liberty, tolerance, fellow-feeling, and compassion, non-destruction of life (Ahimsa), moral character, benevolence, service and sacrifice.

***Christianity:*** The followers of Jesus Christ are called Christians. Christianity has the largest number of followers in the world. Jerusalem, the place where Christ lived and preached is considered to be the most sacred for Christians all over the world.

***Jesus:*** Jesus Christ was born in Bethlehem of Judea in 4 BC. Until he was 30, Jesus lived in Nazareth as an ordinary carpenter. Then he plugged into a very active public life for about three years. During these years he preached that God is a loving and merciful Father. Jesus insisted only on the necessity of showing our love towards God through loving our fellowmen without any distinction or reservation. He was the setting example for his own preaching. He treated both the sinner and the saint with the utmost love and respect. Jesus became a revolutionary figure among the Jewish religious leaders. They presented Gods as being always demanding, angry and ready to punish. They forced the ruling Roman Governor, Pontius Pilate to crucify and kill Jesus.

But the life of the Jesus did not end with his death on the cross. He rose from the tomb on the third day, thus proclaiming to the world the hope of universal resurrection after death. His disciples realised that Jesus was not an ordinary man, but the "Son of God" who really became man, in order to announce to the world, Gods love and concern for human race. He wanted to bring peace on earth. He strengthened his Apostles with the help of the Holy spirit, to preach his teachings and spread the good news about God the loving father to the entire human race.

***The Bible:*** Bible, the holy book of the Christians has two parts, namely "The Old Testament" and "The New Testament". The old Testament presents Gods dealing with men before Christ and gives the history of the Jewish people roughly for a period of 2000 years before Christ. The New Testament records the life and preaching of Jesus, his death and resurrection, the growth of Christianity in its early years and the message of the Apostles sent to various churches.

Bible is considered as the holy book of Christians because it is believed that bible was written under the guidance and inspiration of God. The Bible has a collection of 73 books. In 'The Old Testament' 46 books and in 'The New Testament' 27 books.

***Hinduism:*** Hinduism can be described as the 'museum' of religions. No other religious tradition is so eclectic, so diversified in its theoretical premises as well as its practical expression. Hinduism can be called as Sanatana Dharma or the religion Perenis. As the name implies ananta (without a beginning), it is eternal and ever-lasting (Shashvata). It is the only major religion which has not been traced to a specific founder and the only one which does not have a holy book as the one and only scriptural authority. A sacred text of Hindu religion consists of Vedas, Upanishads Bhagavad Gita, etc. Hinduism always absorbs anything that is good and valuable and at the same time, it shares its wisdom with whoever earnestly seeks it. Its doors are open to all.

Hinduism does not attempt at conversion. It is against any forceful conversion or inflictions on the non-believers. Its faith is that all men are born, children of Sanatana Dharma. Once people become aware of this inheritance and follow its universal principles, there is no need for any further conversion. Even the most uncompromising atheist finds a place in Sanatana Dharma and his philosophy and way of life are duly noticed and his arguments heard with all patience. This arises from the belief that even such a person may one day realise his fundamental values of life and become a follower of Dharma.

Hinduism has not only recognised the different aptitudes and temperaments of people but devised ways of life, catering to such needs. It has also divided individual life into different stages or ashramas. Thus a child is treated as an Anupanita or uninitiated, lives a life of discipline and study and acquires knowledge and virtue (Brahmacharya Ashrama). He leads a life of voluntary poverty, subjects himself to strict disciplining of his senses and mind and becomes a well groomed and highly cultured person. Then he marries and leads a family life (Grihastha Ashrama) and brings up his children in the right traditions. By learning the Vedas, offering sacrifices to gods and begetting a son, he pays off the three debts—debt to sages, to gods and the manes. As he grows older, he becomes a forest-dweller (Vanaprastha Ashrama) with all passions and prejudices removed. There perhaps is no better scheme of life, that harmonises the needs and the development of the individual and society in such a well knit fashion. Thus the Sanatana Dharma emphasises a comprehensive view of life which aims at the realisation of both Abhyudaya and Nishreyas-worldly prosperity and spiritual good.

Hinduism is not pessimistic. It has always exhorted men to realise the four Purusharthas or values of Life, namely Dharma (righteousness) Artha (wealth) Kama (desire) and Moksha (liberation). Only it has insisted that wealth and enjoyment should be based on Dharma and aim at Moksha.

One of the aspects of Hinduism that is considered to be not in keeping with the modern democratic tendencies is its "castesystem". The Brahmans (priests, teachers), Kshatriyas (warriors, rulers), Vaishyas (traders, merchants) and Sudras (unskilled workers) were four castes in the society. Originally in the Vedas it was conceived as a system for the proper division of functions in society and it was not rigid and birth-oriented. Later the system deteriorated and the original intention was totally lost. With the passage of time the caste system became over ridden with dust and filth. Birth became the determinative factor for establishing one's caste and the caste system led to social exploitation in Hindu society. Brahmans and Kshatriyas who were the high castes had certain privileges as compared to other low castes. The impregnable edifice of the caste barrier is crumbling. But caste system has never been a bar against God-realisation. Some of India's greatest saints, who were and are still being venerated even by the highest of Brahmans, have sprung from among the so called untouchables. Sanyasis, who are in the height of spiritual evolution, have no caste at all. Even when a Brahman takes Sanyas, he has to give up his caste.

Another important aspect of Hinduism is its free scope for philosophic thought. The six orthodox systems of Indian philosophy, namely, the Nyaya, the Vaiseshika, the Sankhya, the Yoga, the Mimamsa and the Vedanta, as also the heterodox systems like the Charvaka, the Buddha and the Jaina and many a religious movement started by synthesisers have allowed for a wide diversity of thought.

Everything that the Hindu does is God-centered. Hinduism believes in avataras or incarnations of God on earth in human or other form. The doctrine of 'avatara' is a perpetual reminder for a Hindu that he should not stick to outward forms but regard everything as manifestation of divinity and revitalise his life by the new energy from the surroundings.

In Hinduism, the ultimate goal is 'Moksha'; the liberation from the cycle of existence. There are many paths leading to this goal. Until Moksha is attained, all human beings are subject to rebirth. The conditions of life in each birth are determined by the cumulative results of the karma (deeds) performed in previous life.

A whole scheme of rituals is detailed for all and they are known as Samskaras, with them the man becomes a rounded, integrated personality, a 'Purna Purusha'. The rituals are so designed as to bring a harmony in the economic, educational, cultural and spiritual aspects of human life. In one sense what unites the wide and varying philosophic learning and devotional practices of Hindus are the common ideals which they all stand for...

***Islam:*** Islam is an Arabic word meaning both 'Submission to God' and 'Peace'. The followers of Islam who are called Muslims are found all over the world. There are over 100 cores (over one billion-1,147,494,000 Source: The World Almanac, 1999) of Muslims all over the world and out of this around one-eirth live in India alone.

Islam is not only a religion but also a particular way of life. The followers of Islam are governed by their religious teachings. Muhammad, the prophet of Islam, was born in Mecca in about 570 AD. In about 610 AD, God sent his first message to Muhammad. Messages came to him from god till his death in 632 AD. These messages were recorded by the companions of Muhammad. The collection containing these messages is called the 'Quran', the holy book of Muslims. The sayings of Muhammad which were distinguished from the words of god were collected and are known as 'Habit', the second most important source of Islam.

The Arabs called Muhammad, 'Al-Amen' or 'The trustworthy man' and respected him greatly. But when god sent through him the first message of Islam, there was stiff opposition against Muhammad from all sides.

The opposition kept mounting, so Muhammad was forced to leave Mecca in 622 AD. It is from this year that the Muslim calendar starts. Muhammad arrived in Medina where people listened to Muhammad and accepted him as a true prophet. The people in other towns challenged those who had already become Muslims and war became inevitable. However, when Muhammad died in 632 AD, not only the whole of Arabia had embraced Islam but also his religion called the Perfect Religion was fast spreading in many lands.

The death of the prophet of Islam posed the problem of succession. One group of Muslims wanted a person from the family of the prophet to be his successor. This group was known as the 'Shia'. The other group, the 'Sunnis', wanted the successor to be chosen by majority opinion. The majority went in favour of Abu Bark, who was chosen as Caliph. The Sunnis won, but this brought about two broad divisions of Muslims. After Abu Bark, two more caliphs'Omar and Othman'—were chosen. Then Ali, the son-in-law of prophet Muhammad and a candidate chosen by the Shia from the very beginning became the fourth Caliph of Islam. These four Caliphs are known in Islamic history as the Pious Caliphs.

Islam was revealed by god to the prophet of Islam at a time when Arabia was witnessing a period of ignorance and tribal wars. A common cause of wars was the dispute over which god was superior to the others. Each Arab tribe had its own god. Islam substituted one god in place of so many and brought the Arab tribes together under the supreme Islamic belief that there is only one god. From the belief in the unity of god, Islam went on to preach the unity of mankind.

The great force with which the message of the 'Quran' spread from Arabia to the whole of Mid-Asia and other far-off lands, gives proof that it had an easy appeal for the human beings.

It was the Arabs who went for trade with various countries, carried the message of Islam forward along with their merchandise.

The great increase in knowledge in all fields that followed the birth of Islam was a result of the great emphasis laid by the 'Quran' and by the prophet, on the acquisition of knowledge from whatever source, was available. The 'Quran' states clearly the importance of people who seek knowledge when it asks: 'Say, shall those who have knowledge and those who do not have it be considered equal?' The great contribution of Muslims to literature is to be seen in books like the 'Arabian Nights' and their contribution to art and architecture in many thousands of buildings, from the giant and majestic palace of Al-Hamra in Spain to the Taj Mahal in India.

The mystics of Islam, known as 'Sufis', played an important part in spreading the message of universal love and toning down the aggressive trends in Islam. Islam's spirit of brotherhood helped in loosening the rigidity of the caste system.

It will be observed that the cultures of the Muslims in various parts of the world have remained unchanged. This proves that Islam never attempted to uproot people from their own cultures. On the other hand, it has allowed them to nurture their culture within the broad framework of the basic beliefs and practices.

***Jainism:*** Jainism is primarily an Indian religion. There are more than 3 million Jains in India, forming almost the smaller sections among the various religious groups. In spite of its small number, the Jaina community has a strong influence on the Indian life. Jains belong chiefly to the mercantile class, spread mainly over central, northern and southern India. Splendid Jaina temples and statues can be found almost in all parts of the country. The Jains have also set up many trusts and charitable institutions in the country.

The theme of self-conquest, common to all religions is supremely important to the Jains. The very word Jaina is derived from 'Jina' conqueror. Carrying the idea of self-conquest to its extreme, Jainism has become the worlds most rigorously ascetic faith. God has no place in this system. The popular god's of Hinduism are accepted, but they are placed lower than the Jains who are regarded as the true recipients of worship.

Vardhamana better known by his title Mahavira (great Hero) was an elder contemporary of the Buddha. He cannot be called the founder of Jainism but rather its reformer. He is said to be the last of a line of 24 Jains. The first Risabha whose name is detected in the Vedas and hence Jainism can be claimed to be of great antiquity. The 22nd prophet 'Neminatha' (or Austanemi) who came from Kathiawar is very popular in Gujarat. He is supposed to be a kinsman of Lord Krishna, the Hindu god. Jainism belongs to mythology rather than history till the period of this prophet.

The 23rd Prophet Parsvanatha belonged to 8th century BC has been considered by the researchers and was therefore a historical personage. He was the son of Asvasena, the king of Benaras. He laid a normal life till the age of thirty and thereafter renounced all his worldly possessions, devoting himself to meditation and asceticism and attained supreme knowledge. When he was 70, he retired to a mountain now known as Parsanath near Bihar and went into meditation. He lived till 100 and died after a rigorous fast of one month. He had many followers. Mahavira was converted when he encountered a disciple of Parsvanatha and it is he who completed the doctrine. Therefore Jainism in its complete forms is not the work of one prophet, but Mahavira is held in the highest esteem as he completed the work and really set its principles and was also responsible for its growth.

Vardhamana was born in 599 BC at Kundagrama near Vaishali, about 27 miles north of Patna, in Bihar. He was born to an aristocratic parents of the Naya Clan. When he was about 30, his parents passed away and with his brothers permission, he distributed his worldly possessions and left house.

Mahavira imposed upon himself the life of a religious mendicant. After 3 months in the severe cold he renounced wearing cloths. He meditated for 2 years, undertook several fasts and began his journeys for 12 years across Magadh up to the western boundary of Bengal. He perfected his knowledge and elabourated the fundamental principles of the religious life which he preached later on. He attained Nirvana (omniscience) on a summer night of Vaisabha Sukla Dashmi under a Sal tree on the bank of the river Riyvalia near Jambhika grama. After leading the life of an ascetic for 42 years, Mahavira died or attained Nirvana at the age of 72, at Pavapuri near the present Patna.

Mahavira had 11 disciples, each entrusted with a band of about 300 to 500 monks to preach the religion. Bhadrabahu, contemporary of the great Mauryan king Chandragupta was the greatest propagator of faith. After Bhadrabahu's death, serious differences began to arise among the Jaina community. The group led by him migrated towards the west coast and Deccan, while others remained in the north. The group which remained in the north was chiefly led by Sthulabhadra, the last of the omniscient. The final break between the two groups came around AD 79. Jains divided into Digambaras (sky /air as their cloth), *i.e.*, naked who follow Mahavira and Swetambaras (wearers of white clothes), who follow Parshvanatha.

Most famous among the disciples were Gautama, Indrabhuti and Sudharman and they are said to have attained omniscience (knowing everything). Mahavira is said to have preached in Ardhamgadhi language. A fixed form was given to the Jaina Canon is the 5th century AD at Valabhi which consists of 45 works of varied content. Digambaras did not accept this canon. They believed mostly on the oral teachings of the monks and that liberation is impossible unless one renounced clothes, in the foot steps of Mahavira. They contest that Mahavira was married. Women can attain liberation and the omniscient can take ordinary nourishment. Finely they believe that the ancient texts have definitely been lost and do not believe in the authenticity of the scriptures which constitute the canon of Swetambaras. The Swetambara canon is called 'Agama' or 'Sidhanta' or even 'Gampidaha'. The other important Jaina religious texts are 'Devadashangas'; 'Upangas' and 'Mulashatras'.

Jains have made valuable contributions in many areas of Indian culture: philosophy, literature, painting, sculpture and architecture. Their poetry is often excessively didactic. Their sculpture is of a high quality and some of the images of Tirthankaras are technically perfect. Their faces are however devoid of any expression, as they are supposed to have transcended all human emotions.

The greatest glory of Jaina religious art lies in temple architecture, particularly at Ginar, Palitana and Mount Abu. These temples reveal a breadth of aesthetic sensitivity and a feeling for ornamentation reminiscent of the finest specimen of classical Hindu and Buddhist architecture.

***Judaism:*** Judaism is the religion of the Hebrews. It is a religion older than Christianity. Moses was the first prophet and law giver of the Hebrews. In order to save the Hebrews from the cruel Pharaohs of Egypt, Moses led them to the promised land of God. On the way, at Mount Sinai, Moses received the 'Ten Commandments' from Jehovah, the Supreme God. Thus around 1000 BC the Hebrews established themselves in Israel. Holy Books of the Law, the Prophets and the Psalms were put together and came to be known as the 'Hebrew Bible' or 'The Old Testament'. The 'Talmud' is the collection of detailed laws for the guidance of civil, domestic and social life of the Hebrews. According to Judaism right conduct is more important than right belief. Judaism does not believe in self imposed suffering or asceticism.

In India there are two ancient indigenous Jewish communities—Malayalam speaking Cochinites and the Marathi speaking Bene Israel (children of Israel). Ancestry of Cochin Jews dates back to the period when King Solomon's merchant fleet began their trade. As per scholars the Jewish settled along Kerala's Malabar coast soon after the Babylonian conquest of Judea in 586 BC. They were well received by the rulers and granted a small principality to Joseph Rabban, a Jewish leader. Their Synagogue at Cochin is one of the oldest in India and its interior is worth visiting.

Today migration to Israel and other countries has considerably reduced the Indian Jewish population. Now, only a few of them remain in Cochin.

***Sikhism:*** The word 'Sikh' goes back to Sanskrit 'Shishya', meaning disciple or leader. In Pali, Shishya became Sissa. The Pali word Sekh (also Sekha) means a pupil or one under training in a religious doctrine.

Sikhism had its birth in Punjab. The founder of the Sikh faith, Guru Nanak belonged to Punjab, a region where Hindus and Muslims had come in closer contact than in any other part of India. The Sikhs are recognised by their beards and turbans. They value these as the signs of their religious faith. These symbols are an essential part of the Sikh way of life. They are tall and well-built; the men all grow beards and wear turbans over their long hair which is never cut. Every Sikh considers it an obligations to wear a Kara (steel bangle). There are other religious injunctions, like abstaining from tobacco, which are obeyed rigorously.

The 'Guru Granth', the Holy scriptures, is the spiritual authority and is venerated as the living presence of the Gurus. It gives form and meaning to the Sikhs religious style and social customs. Their faith has a broad humanitarian base. Singly and in groups, in their homes and in congregations in their places of worship, the Sikhs conclude their morning and evening prayers, or prayer said at any other time as part of personal piety or of a ceremony, with the words: 'Nanak nam Charhdi Kala, tere bhane Sarbatt Ka Bhala'—May Thy Name, Thy Glory, forever triumphant, Nanak and in Thy will, may peace and prosperity come to one and all.

***Devoted Life of Guru Nanak:*** The first date in Sikhism is 1469, the year in which Guru Nanak was born. Guru Nanak's father, Kalyan Chand, who belonged to Bedi clan of the Kshatriyas and his mother Tripti, lived in a village of Talwandi Rai Bhoe, (now in Pakistan) and now named as "Nankana Sahib". According to the 'Janamsakhis' (traditional accounts of Guru Nanak's life) "Light flashed across the mud-built room in which the birth took place". The family priest, who came to cast the child's horoscope, told his father that his son would sit under Canopy. He further spoke: "Both Hindus and Turks will pay him reverence. He will worship and acknowledge but one formless Lord and teach others to do so. Every he will consider as god's own creation." Those early years of his life are described in 'Janamsakhis' in a variety of legends and miracles. Guru Nanak was the favourite of both Hindus and Muslims in the village, which was agreed by the early biographers.

Seeing that Nanak did not take to any useful calling in life, his father sent him to Sultanpur where his daughter, Nanaki lived with her husband. At Sultanpur, Nanak was put to work in the local Lodi chief's modihhana or stores, but he distributed things free to fakirs. So his father, at the age of 14 got him married to Sulakshna and they had two sons. But at the age of twenty seven, he left Sultanpur to embark on his long preaching odysseys called Udasis in the Sikh tradition.

The first words he uttered, after three days of silent communion were: "There is no Hindu, there is no Muslim". Guru Nanak thus rejected distinctions between man and woman by reason of creed or caste. He showed people the way to look beyond these barriers. His equal attentions to Hindu and Muslim identities and use of some of their religious vocabulary have led some to depict him as the reconciler of the two faith and to see Sikhism as "a deliberate mingling of Hindu and Muslim practices". Accompanied by a Muslim follower, called Mardana, Guru Nanak went to different parts in India and spread the message of love, faith and equality.

***Zoroastrianism:*** Zoroastrianism is one of the oldest Religion. It explains man's duties in this life and the high destiny which he can achieve by establishing his conduct in accordance with the eternal and immutable law of nature. Zarathushtra the founder of Zoroastrianism called it the law of Asha. Zoroastrianism is based upon the knowledge and illumination and its emblems are the Fire and the Sun.

***Zarathushtra:*** Zarathushtra is said to have been born around 6th century B.C in the town of Amui near Rae, on the salt lake Urumiah renamed Razsieh, in Azarbaijan province. He went up the mountains of that province for meditation and preached his faith for many years among hostile tribes. As a young boy, he was placed under able teachers, but they soon found that he was more advanced. Zarathushtra spent several years in meditation and study, pondering over the fundamentals of life and existence trying to find a rational explanation based upon the Law of nature, Asha. He discovers the perfection which lies in the absolute as possessing perfect power or energy and perfect wisdom, which reality he calls 'Ahura Mazda', Lord of Life and Wisdom.

The religion of the Iranian people of his time was a primitive form of polytheism of Indo-Aryan origin. It is partly based on the Rig Veda. There were many deities and each family had sacred idols. Each tribe had different rituals, sacred obligations and customs. To this eastern world, Zarathushtra brought a new universal concept of religion. His religion was not a set of superstitious rituals based on fears, but a universal call for a better life to be achieved with the aid of an invisible god of wisdom, truth, light and goodness.

Zarathushtra was the first man who gave a definitely moral character and direction to religion and at the same time, preached the doctrine of monotheism which offered an eternal foundation of reality to goodness an ideal of perfection. Zarathushtra showed the path of freedom to man, the freedom of moral choice, freedom from blind obedience to meaningless injunctions. He preached that the moral worth of deed comes from the goodness of intention and the value of his religion was upholding man in his life of good thoughts, good words and good deeds. Zarathushtra was the first prophet who emancipated religion from the exclusive narrowness of the tribal god.

At the age of seventy-seven, Zarathushtra was killed by a Turanian soldier during an attack on the city of Bulkh. The active heroic aspect of Zoroastrian religion reflects the character of the people. They had zest in life and confidence in their own, strength. They accepted the world in all seriousness. By force of will and deeds of sacrifice, they tried to achieve Haurvatat, wholeness, well-being, in this world and Ameretatat-immortality.

## Food Habit

Indian food is different from rest of the world not only in taste but also in cooking methods. It reflects a perfect blend of various cultures and ages. Just like Indian culture, food in India has also been influenced by various civilizations, which have contributed their share in its overall development and the present form. Foods of India are better known for its spiciness. Throughout India, be it North India or South India, spices are used generously in food. But one must not forget that every single spice used in Indian dishes carries some or the other nutritional as well as medicinal properties.

***North Indian Food:*** Food in the North India, to begin with, Kashmiri cuisines reflect strong Central Asian influences. In Kashmir, mostly all the dishes are prepared around the main course of rice found abundantly in the beautiful valley. Another delicious item cooked here is the 'Saag' that is prepared with a green leafy vegetable known as the 'Hak'.

But on the other hand states like the Punjab, Haryana and Uttar Pradesh show high consumption of chapatis as staple food. Again, these chapatis are prepared with a variety of flours such as wheat, rice, maida, besan, etc. Besides chapatis other closely related breads baked in these regions include Tandoori, Rumaali and Naan, etc. However in the northern region impact of Mughlai food is quite obvious.

***West Indian Food:*** In western India, the desert cuisine is famous for its unique taste and varieties of food. Rajasthan and Gujarat are the states that represent the dessert flavour of Indian food. Here an immense variety of dals and achars (pickles/preserves) is used that simply substitutes the relative lack of fresh vegetables in these areas.

In the states like Maharashtra, the food is usually a mix of both north as well as south cooking styles. Here people use both the rice and the wheat with same interest. Along the coastline of Mumbai a wide variety of fishes is available. Some of the delicious preparations include dishes like the Bombay Prawn and Pomfret. In Goa, that is further down towards south, one can notice Portuguese influence in the cooking style as well as in the dishes. Some of the major dishes of this regiun are the sweet and sour Vindaloo, duck baffad, sorpotel and egg molie, etc.

***East Indian Food:*** In the eastern India, the Bengali and Assamese styles of cooking are noticeable. The staple food of Bengalis is the yummy combination of rice and fish. Usually the Bengalis love eating varieties of fishes. A special way of preparing the delicacy known as 'Hilsa' is by wrapping it in the pumpkin leaf and then cooking it. Another unusual ingredient that is commonly used in the Bengali cooking is the 'Bamboo Shoot'. Various sweets prepared in this region, by using milk include the 'Roshogollas', 'Sandesh', 'Cham-cham' and many more.

***South Indian Food:*** In the southern India, the states make great use of spices, fishes and coconuts, as most of them have coastal kitchens. In the foods of Tamil Nadu use of tamarind is frequently made in order to impart sourness to the dishes. It simply distinguishes the Tamil Food from other cuisines.

The cooking style of Andhra Pradesh is supposed to make excessive use of chilies, which is obviously to improve the taste of the dishes. In Kerala, some of the delicious dishes are the lamb stew and appams, Malabar fried prawns, Idlis, Dosas, fish molie and rice puttu. Another famous item of this region is the sweetened coconut milk. Yet another dish is Puttu, which is glutinous rice powder steamed like a pudding in a bamboo shoot. Indian food is as varied as anything else in that country; there is no easy definition of an "Indian meal". Indian food is often thought of as very spicy, but there are some simple breads, sweet deserts, and milder 'one-pot dishes' that defy the norm. Many Indians are vegetarian, but then, some are not. There are regional specialities, different ways to serve the meal, and staple ingredients in each state. This combines to create a diverse cuisine that never becomes boring.

***Breakfast***

***Chappathi/Roti:*** Measure and sieve whole wheat flour and salt into a vessel. Slowly add three-fourths cup of water. Mix well. Knead into medium soft dough. Add more water if required. Cover the vessel and leave it for fifteen minutes. Divide into 14 equal portions. Make them into balls. Roll them out into six-inch rounds on a board by adding flour occasionally (So that they do not stick to the board). Cook on a griddle or a non-stick pan for about half a minute. Turn and cook on the other side for fifteen seconds. Cook till puffed and cooked on both sides. Turn over and press gently with a spatula or a cloth to puff up the chappathi/roti. Serve hot, topped with cooking oil or ghee (optional).

***Dosa:*** On a flat frying pan/skillet, the batter has to be poured and spread as a thin round. Add a teaspoon of cooking oil/ghee/butter to both the sides of the Dosa. When it turns golden brown, its ready to be taken off the frying pan and ready to serve too. Different types of Dosas can be made. The thinner and crispier the dosa, the better it tastes! Masala Dosa is another option.

***Idli:*** Grind the ingredients separately into a fine paste by adding sufficient water. Add salt to taste and blend the dough well and keep it overnight for fermentation. Next morning once again, mix the dough with a spoon and pour in scoops on the Idli tray and steam it for five minutes.

***Poori:*** Divide into small balls about golf-ball size, and roll out into 6" rounds with a roller, on an oiled board. Heat vegetable oil in a work or saucepan. Add a little salt to the oil to keep it from smoking. Fry the puri one at a time, holding them under the oil on the first side until they puff. Turn and fry till light brown; drain.

Serve as soon as possible; this bread is best had when its hot and is not as good, later.

Puris are traditionally served with Potato curry.

***India Meat Dishes***

- Kashmiri Gustaba
- Sag Paneer
- Fish Korma
- Tikya Kebab
- Prawn Curry
- Mughlai Chicken
- Malai Chicken
- Nargisi Kofta

- Pork Curry
- Mutton Curry
- Kashmiri Chicken
- Bombay Duck
- Mulligatawny
- Creamy Prawn Soup
- Cauliflower Chicken
- Chicken Makhani
- Chicken Pullao
- Coriander Fish
- Chicken Curry

***North Indian Style***

- Chicken Murga
- Tandoori Chicken
- Tandoori 2
- Lamb Vindaloo
- Indian Lamb with Spinach
- Prawns in Tomato Sauce

***Indian Vegie Dishes***

- Not strict vegie...some recipes have eggs, milk and cheese products
- Eggs in Spicy Almond Sauce
- Chick Pea Pancakes
- Dal Kofta Curry
- Bengali Eggplant

***With Mustard Seeds***

- Indian Chickpeas
- Gobi Aloo
- Masaledar Sem
- Vegetable Kurma
- Vegetable Curry
- Green Pepper Curry

- Sookha Aloo
- Nedar and Haaq in Yakni
- Alur Khosha Bhaja
- 3 Samosas
- Bandhakopir Ghanto
- Vegetable Biriyani
- Begun Pora
- Farashi Beaner Chochori
- Geela Kitchuri
- Tofu Cutlets

***With Pineapple-Ginger***

- Bengali Zucchini Curry
- Bengali Potatoes

***Indian Desserts***

- Kheer
- Kheer 2
- Besan Burfi
- Sewian
- Mango Ice Cream
- Carrot Halwa
- Kheer
- Shrikhand
- Benne Biscuit
- Rice Flour Pudding
- Gulab Jamuns
- Suji Halva
- Carrot Halva
- Rasgoola
- Sheera
- Seviyan
- Kala Jamoon
- Spicy Coconut Custard

***Indian Sauces***

- Garam Masala
- Bengali Garam Masala
- Coconut Chutney

***North Indian***

- Coconut Chutney (Thengai Thigayal)South Indian
- Tamarind Chutney
- Tomato Chutney
- Cashew Nut Chutney
- Cilantro Chutney
- Malabar Curry Powder
- Chile Mustard Relish

***(Bengali Kasundi)***

- Mango Chutney

***(Corom Chatni)***

- Mint And Coriander Chutney
- Spiced Fruit Chutney
- Ambarella and Raisin Chutney
- Anchovy Relish

***Eating Styles:*** Indian food is often eaten with the hands, however, this custom is guided by some basic rules. For instance, it is considered impolite to allow the food to pass the first joint of the fingers. The fingers should never touch the mouth directly. In addition, only the right hand may be used in eating.

Since most Indian meals include a kind of flatbread that is traditionally used to scoop or roll vegetables or rice. A spoon is provided for soup, but the bread may even be used to eat that! Meat, if served, may be eaten with a knife and fork, but it will more often be served pre-cut, so it may be easily managed by the fingers.

Indians usually eat their largest meal at mid-day, preferring to end with a light evening meal. People either bring their mid-day meal to work or use a lunch packing service called "tiffin" that delivers traditional hot meals to their workplace. If possible, many Indians like to come home for the mid-day meal.

***Regional Food***

***Punjabi:*** Possibly the most famous Punjabi contribution to Indian food is the tandoori style of cooking. This method uses large earthen ovens that are heated to high temperatures using coal fires. Once hot, many types of meat, breads, or vegetable dishes may be cooked inside. This method gives food a distinctive flavour and seals in the aroma of the item.

Many people in Punjab eat some meat. Thus, the state has developed many chicken and lamb dishes that are coated in spicy onion and mustard or sweet cream sauces. This is thought to be an influence of the Mughals during their time in India. Milk products such as yoghurt lassis and fresh cheeses are also an important part of the Punjabi diet, as are pulses and wheat.

***Gujarati:*** Gujarati food is mainly vegetarian. The staple grain of the area is millet, with wheat as a secondary grain. Other products include peanuts, sesame, and many types of vegetables. Pulses are very important in this region as a source of protein, whether as a side dish or made into soups called dahls, as the majority of the population does not eat meat.

Gujarati food is usually served as a "thali" meal, meaning that all items are served at once on a large plate. A traditional thali includes two vegetables cooked with spices, dahl, a flatbread, rice, pulses, and a sweet. There are also simple meals of mild rice and lentils known as "khichdi", served with a lightly spiced buttermilk or yoghurt soup called "kadhi".

***Maharashtrian:*** In contrast to the mainly vegetarian Gujarati food, Maharashtrians enjoy eating meat and fish with their meals. Fish may be stuffed or lightly fried, and meat is braised and spiced with sweet and sour ingredients. Peanuts and cashew nuts are widely used, as is the distinctive kokum berry, a sweet deep purple item with a slightly tangy taste.

On the coast, people eat crab, prawns, and shellfish. Maharashtrians also popularised fried rice-flour balls called "vada" (now eaten throughout the country) and a type of thin pancake called amboli made of semolina, urad dal, and fermented rice. A common sweet dish is puran poli, a flatbread stuffed with gram flour, brown sugar, and honey.

***Bengali:*** Bengal is known for its fish and its sweets. Located on the eastern coast of India, fish has become a staple of the Bengali diet. It may be sauted in yoghurt or marinated in Bengal's famous spice mixture. This region uses five basic spices, known collectively as "pachphoron". They are: aniseed, cumin seed, black cumin seed, mustard, and fenugreek. Even the oil that is used is mustard oil.

Many sweets eaten all over India originated in Bengal. Most are milk or cottage cheese based, including rasgolla, gulab jamun, and sundesh. Bengali sweets are often served with a sticky sweet syrup, and may even be found ending a traditional Gujarati or Goan meal.

***Kerela, Karnataka, and the South:*** Kerela food, from southern India, is traditionally served on a large banana leaf. The method is still used for feasts today. The staple food of southern India is rice. Different preparations of the grain may even be eaten for breakfast. The other staple is the coconut. Coconut is made into chutney, served as a refreshing desert, and incorporated into vegetable or fish dishes as a flavoring. This often gives Kerela food a surprising flavour that mixes sweetness with spices.

One can see the uses of these ingredients in many of the famous dishes of the south. For example, rice flour and urad flour are made into a batter and steamed to form rice cakes called "idli", eaten with a type of stew made of pulses and vegetables called "sambhar". Another dish, "appam", is a thin crepe made with rice flour and the sap of the cocomut palm. It is eaten with the "sambhar" mentioned above.

***Snack Food:*** Indian snacks may be salty, spicy, or sweet. Street vendors sell many different kinds, including warm dishes. Sometimes, they are substantial enough to serve as a light meal. The "pav bhaji" is a patty made of mixed vegetables that have been mashed and shallow fried and then served on a slice of bread. Another popular snack throughout the country is "bhel", a mixture of puffed rice, crunchy chickpea flour chips, onions, tomato, green peppers, and tamarind chutney.

"Pani puri" is small, hollow breads stuffed with a bit of potato, onion, or chickpea and topped with a "pani" of seasoned water. Nuts are another common choice, but they are roasted with a hot spice blend of turmeric, paparika, and cumin powder. Often a little lemon juice is squeezed on top.

***Drinks:*** The most common drink in India is tea. This is prepared with milk, sugar, and a blend of ginger, nutmeg, cinnamon, cloves, and cardamom. Most people will drink this tea, called "chai" with breakfast and in the late afternoon. In fact, it may be served at any time and is a popular refreshment for guests. An example of a common cold Indian drink is "lassi", which is a yoghurt or buttermilk drink that is sweetened and flavored with rose, mango, or served plain.

***Tea and Coffee:*** It is one of the favorites of Indians across the country. Be it Railway Station, Airports, Small Restaurants, you will always find people having Tea and Coffee. Tea is relatively more popular in North whereas Coffee is more popular in South.

***Water:*** Water is safe and chlorinated in large cities but it is always suggest carrying one bottle of mineral water with you. Mineral Water is normally safe to drink & is easily available throughout India.

***Soft Drinks:*** There is also good number of options for Soft Drinks in India. Majors like Coke and Pepsi offer various brands and tastes.

***Juices and Other Drinks:*** Popular juices like Apple and Orange juices are easily available & a safe alternate to normal water. Coconut Milk is also a popular drink in India.

***Alcoholic Drinks:*** Alcohol is normally expensive in India. Indian Beers are also very popular as alcoholic drinks and normally being sold for Rs. 25 to 160 depending upon the Restaurant and its facilities.

Indian imitations of popular brands are also available but it is advisable to stick to your brand.

## Indian Costumes

India is a land of colour and diverse cultures, so obvious in the varied dresses that adorn its people. Indian dressing styles are marked by many variations, both religious and regional with a wide choice of textures and styles. The many hued saris draped gracefully in different styles, brightly mirrored cholis, colorful lehangas and the traditional salwar-kameez have all fascinated the traveller to India.

The sari, simple, understated yet supremely elegant is increasingly becoming a fashion statement in urban India.

One of the most commonly worn traditional dresses, it is essentially a rectangular cloth measuring about 6 yards, though in Maharashtra, women wear the nine yard sari which is passed through the legs and tucked in at the back. The sari comes in a profusion of colours, textures and designs, determined largely by the region. There are several ways of draping a sari, which is first wound around the waist, before being pleated seven or eight times at the centre and tucked into the waistband. These pleats are called the patli. The remaining sari, called the pallu is then pleated again and draped across the left shoulder to fall gracefully behind. There are regional variations, like in Gujarat, the pallu comes from the back, and drapes across the front over the right shoulder. The sari is worn with a tight-fitting choli or blouse. The style and length of the choli varies according to fashion trends and from region to region.

The traditional dress for women in Rajasthan and Gujarat is the lehenga choli or ghagra choli. These cholis are brightly embroidered, waist-length bare-backed blouses. Ghagras or lehengas are gathered ankle-length skirts secured around the waist. The attire is completed by a veil-cloth called odhni or dupatta draped across the neck or over the head. The lehenga-choli or ghagra choli is extremely colourful, adding verve and colour to the surrounding landscapes. Tribal women in theses area bedeck themselves from head to toe with chunky silver jewellery.

Young girls in south India wear a half saree, somewhat similar to a lehenga choli. The only difference is that the dupatta is wound across the waist and draped across the left shoulder like the saree pallu.

A popular, comfortable and convenient dress is the salwar kameez or churidar kurta. This was traditonally the dress worn in Punjab, but is now worn almost everywhere, particularly among the younger generations. The kameez or the kurta is a knee-length flowing tunic worn over a salwar or churidar. A salwar is a pyjama-like trouser which tapers slightly towards the ankles, while the churidar is a tight-fitting trouser which gathers at the ankles. These gathers at the ankles look like bangles (churis) and hence the name. A dupatta generally completes the ensemble.

Western dressing styles are increasingly gaining popularity among the urban youth of both sexes, but women largely restrict themselves to fashion trends within Indian dressing mores. Young girls wear skirts and dresses, particularly to schools. After adolescence, and almost certainly after marriage, women are expected to wear traditional Indian clothing. This trend is changing with more women entering the urban work force, but this is confined to sections of society that are highly exposed to international lifestyles. Men are considerably less traditional when it comes to dressing.

In India, as elsewhere, accessories are an integral part of the ritual of dressing. The world over, Indian women are associated with the 'dot' in the middle of their forehead, called Kum Kum or bindi. Traditionally round, the bindi is now available in various colours, shapes and sizes. A bindi was traditionally a sign of marriage, or in some states, was worn as soon a s a girl reached young adulthood. Today it is for the most part an adornment. Vermilion or sindoor applied at the parting of the hair indicates a married woman.

A traditional Indian woman is rarely seen without jewellery. A mangal-sutra, a necklace made with black and gold beads is considered sacred, and in many areas is always worn by a married woman. Many women, particularly in the rural areas of Rajasthan, Maharashtra and Gujarat wear ornately crafted nose-rings. Gold, silver or colourful glass bangles are another favourite, dating from the tradition of never having your hands bare. Women in Rajasthan wear bangles that go all the way to their shoulders. Indian women generally have their ears pierced, and commonly sport ear-rings.

Men are considerably less traditional when it comes to dressing. In urban areas, they have adapted to a western style of dressing. In villages men generally wear kurtas, a knee length shirt-styled tunic, with lungis, dhotis or pyjamas. The lungi originated in the south but is now worn all over india. It is a piece of cloth wrapped around the waist. A dhoti is longer than a lungi, has sari style pleats and is draped through the legs.

In states like Rajasthan, Gujarat, Punjab and Maharashtra men wear a safa or turban on their heads. Elsewhere too, various kinds of topis are it is a long scarf which is wound round the head in different ways. The Pathani suit is very similar to the salwar-kameez and is generally worn by men in north India. The Achkan is a long collarless jacket worn over a churidar for formal occasions.

## The Family Customs

Family is important in India, and is what their life is centred around. It is common for several generations to live in the same house as an extended family.

When a woman marries, she leaves her birth family, many times without seeing them again, and goes to her husband's village and becomes part of his family.

There is significant discrimination toward girls and women. While young girls are expected to help with the women's work (which consists of fetching water, preparing meals, cleaning, and caring for animals) as well as care for their younger siblings; boys have it much easier.

They may be required to herd goats and other animals to and from the fields, but in general have it much easier than their female counterparts and this discrimination doesn't end with adulthood.

A simple draped cloth is still the basic attire for many Indians. The women wear a sari, which is worn with a blouse underneath, with the material ranging from cotton to silk. Men generally wear a dhoti, which can be worn full length or as "pants" depending on the region. In northern India, western clothing has replaced that of the traditional for men, while women still wear saris or other Indian styles of dress. In rare cases women will wear slacks and blouses, but that is generally among the elite.

***Clothing:*** To the foreign traveler, one of the powerful attractions in India is the colourful and diversified attire of its people. The silk saris, brightly mirrored cholis, colourful lehangas and the traditional salwar-kameez have fascinated many a traveler over the centuries.

***Attire for Women:*** For a single length of material, the sari must be the most versatile garment in existence. It is only one of the many traditional garments worn by women, yet it has somehow become the national dress of Indian women. A sari is a rectangular piece of cloth which is five to six yards in length. The style, colour and texture of this cloth vary and it might be made from cotton, silk or one of the several man-made materials. The sari has an ageless charm since it is not cut or tailored for a particular size. This garment can fit any size and if worn properly can accentuate or conceal. This supremely graceful attire can also be worn in several ways and its manner of wearing as well as its colour and texture are indicative of the status, age, occupation, region and religion of a woman.

The tightly fitted, short blouse worn under a sari is a choli. The choli evolved as a form of clothing in 10th century AD and the first cholis were only front covering; the back was always bare. Bodices of this type are still common in the state of Rajasthan.

Apart from the choli, women in Rajasthan wear a form of pleated skirt known as the ghagra or lehanga. This skirt is secured at the waist and leaves the back and midriff bare. The heads are however covered by a length of fine cotton known as orhni or dupatta.

Another popular attire of women in India is the salwar-kameez. This dress evolved as a comfortable and respectable garment for women in Kashmir and Punjab, but is now immensely popular in all regions of India. Salwars are pajama-like trousers drawn tightly in at the waist and the ankles. Over the salwars, women wear a long and loose tunic known as a kameez. One might occasionally come across women wearing a churidar instead of a salwar. A churidar is similar to the salwar but is tighter fitting at the hips, thighs and ankles. Over this, one might wear a collarless or mandarin-collar tunic called a kurta.

***Attire for Men:*** Though the majority of Indian women wear traditional costumes, the men in India can be found in more conventional western clothing. Shirts and trousers are worn by men from all regions in India. However, men in villages are still more comfortable in traditional attire like kurtas, lungis, dhotis and pyjamas.

The traditional lungi originated in the south and today it is worn by men and women alike. It is simply a short length of material worn around the thighs rather like a sarong. A dhoti is a longer lungi but with an additional length of material pulled up between the legs. Pyjama-like trousers worn by the villagers are known as the lenga.

Indian dressing styles are marked by many variations, both religious and regional and one is likely to witness a plethora of colours, textures and styles in garments worn by the Indians.

# 2

## Pooja and Rituals of Hindus

Prayer services and "Poojas" at home and at the Temples follow the traditions and rules established in the Agamas and in Bhakti form of the religion. The Temples are established as the palace of a manifestation of God in a form of the Incarnation that is represented at the Temple. Most Temples will have Sanctum for several forms of God, though it may have only one form as the Main Deity.

The temple worship has evolved over the years as a service to God as the King or the leader of the land. Here, an image of a likeness of a manifestation of God is consecrated after several days of Holy Rituals. Without these consecration rituals, the Image does not get the Divine powers or the respect more than a statue in a museum. Once so sanctified, all rituals are performed as done to a live King or leader of the land. The Deity is woken up every morning with a morning service with ceremonial bath with water, milk and other perfumed substances, dressing up with cloths and Jewelry.

The services are repeated four to six times or more every day, with offering of food as "prasadam" and singing prayers and songs in praise of the Deity and reading of the Scriptures. After this, "Aarti" of lighted camphor is performed for every one to see the Deity in a "Darshan." The service concludes with the offering of "prasadams" of fruits, flowers and food to the devotees attending the prayer services.

Often the services are individual and for the families rather than to a mass of congregation. The spirit of sacrifice and offering of ones belonging is stressed in these services. The devotees take what is given back to them as "Prasadams", let it be holy water, ashes, kumkum, a flower, a fruit or a full meal. The prayer services at home are also very similar in practice. Often there is a prayer room. Sometimes, a special area is arranged to perform the home prayer services. Here, prayer services are offered to a picture, small icon [vigraha] or a lamp which is sanctified by rituals for the occasion. The Divine powers of the form of God offered prayer on that occasion is represented in this. The rituals are simple and they first invite God as a guest to the house. Then, they perform a ritualistic bathing and offering of cloths. Then, there will be prayers and singing of songs and offering of food which is then offered to members of the family and friends.

Major part of Hindu Religious practice among the common people consists of ritualistic form of worship for God in the various forms of Deities of Saguna Brahma, called Avatara. It follows prayers offered to God in the devotional path as a worship to a Pratika [picture], Prathima or Vigraha [statue], Yanthra [a geometric drawing] or a Linga, following the rules and traditions established in the Agamas and Sasthras. Sri Adhi Sankara, in addition to the Advaitha Philosophy explaining that the Self as part of the Divine Nirguna Brahman, established a school for prayers to the Saguna Brahman is His six Forms called the Shanmatha Sthapanam. He established the rules for the six types of prayers to God at home as 1. Ganesha, 2. Kumara [Karthikeya], 3. Surya [Sun], 4. Shiva, 5. Vishnu, 6. Sakti. The main tenets of the practice are by prayers to "Ishta-Devatha." The methods of learning and doing the various types of prayers to the Ishta-Devata are governed by the rules of "Doctrine of Adhikara." By this doctrine, the religious teachings and methods of worship that is taught varies from person to person, according to the various schools they follow.

Special prayer rituals are usually taught and given specially to persons following certain tradition as a form of initiation to that form of worship practice. This is very much like speciality training and certification in modern day professions. One is not authorised to perform rituals of their choice unless trained and initiated in the same by a properly qualified teacher [Guru].

Accordingly, there are special rules and restrictions for pooja for Sri Shiva, Sri Sakti and Sri Vishnu in their various forms. Only a person who has received the religious teaching from a Sivacharya Guru shall perform pooja for Sivalinga. Similarly, only a guru who has understood the mantra of "Sri Viddhai" can teach the pooja methods of Sri Chakram to his Devotees. In the past, mostly men have been learning and performing these types of poojas. Very few women took these types of ritualistic worship. Most people performed prayers at home just by lighting a lamp for a collection of pictures and images of various Avatharas of God in their prayer room and recited some songs for prayer.

Karma, in addition to referring to our duty and activity for living, also refer to Vedic Karma or our spiritual duties. Thus study of the scriptures and performances of the Vedic ritual are as important as the performance of one's Dharma or duty to the community according to one's birth and profession and stage of life. Every one has to perform all their daily duties according to their Varna-Ashrama Dharma and their education and vocational training. They need to do the sandhya rituals and sanskaras and the yajñas to people, animals, ancestors, celestial bodies and to God. All these have an important effect on our family, our future births and ultimate liberation from the Samsara or cycle of rebirth. The daily Vedic rituals performed are called nithya karma like the sandhya rituals, various Yajñas and Sanskaras. Rituals of sandhya and sanskara are prayers offered to the gods through water, fire and Sun. Contrary to popular belief, a Karma Yogi also has duties of offering his prayers to the Divine through Nitya Karma. He also performs his work as a service to God, as he sees God in every one.

Sandhya are the most important rituals that a Hindu is expected to perform in the house every day, three times a day. These are rituals performed at dawn, noon and at dusk to God, to the Sun and to ancestors. Yajna rituals are offered to Vedic Gods such as Prajapathi, Indra, Varuna, Purusha, Rudra and the Deities of the nine planets. The Vedic gods are the custodians of our social well being and only from our sacrificial oblations in Yagnas they draw their sustenance. The Pancha-Maha Yajnas which are important include Brahma Yajna or sacrifices to Brahman, to Vedas and to sages, Deva Yajna to celestials, Pitri Yajna for ancestors, Bhutha Yajna to all creatures and Manushya Yajna to fellow men. There are fifty-two Sanskaras which are listed as rituals performed at home, of which ten are important. These Sanskara rituals like Simanthonnayana, Namakarana, Annaprasana, Chudakarana, Upanayana, Samvarthana and Vivaha, are for family events. There are also funerary rituals which are performed after death of a person and srardha ceremonies which are rituals to ancestors performed by family members.

## Soma Vara Vratam

One of the name of Lord shiva is soma-saha uma. For the Lord someshvara Who wears the soma, the moon crescent on the matted hair, on the somavara day (Monday), this festival is observed.

***When Observed:*** Though all Mondays can be observed as vrata there are speacial Mondays when it is much more emphasised to observe like the shravana somvar and karthika somavaram. According to skandha purana, on the Mondays of the month karthikai (mid Nov to mid Dec) this vrata is observed.

***Way of Observing:*** Getting up at the dawn one meditates on the Supreme shiva. After taking bath and having done the morning twilight salutation, praying the Auspicious and Graceful Lord shiva, worships the couples who are devotees of the Lord, chaste and loveful as the Divines couple Parvati-parameshawara themselves. Saluting those couples, offering them feast, the observer of this vratam eats only one time food that day. If unable to do the worship, then one would go to the temple and salute and pray the uma-maheshvara. Anointing the Lord with panychamritam and other pleasant substances, hailing the Lord offering bilva leaves, not being money-minded offering the nice food materials to the Lord, sharing the food with the kind hearted devotees one eats the food. One may fast also completely.

***Glory:*** One who observes this vratam would get to enjoy many pleasures in this world and finally would reach the kailasham. The moon observed this vratam and got his "moonness". He saluted the Lord Gauri-shankara and requested that this vratam be called somavara vratam (One of the names of the moon is soma. One of the name of Lord Shiva with goddess uma is also soma) and whoever follows this vratam should get their wishes materialised by the grace of the Lord and finally should get the liberation. God granted the boon.

Long ago a princess called sIman thini was observing this vratam regularly. Then two young boys cunningly came as if they were a married couple. The princess worshiped them. The young boys really became male and female couple ! The austerous sage vashishta got the chaste arun thadhi as his wife. One gets blessed by the shiva-shakti on observing this vratam sincerely.

## Uma-Maheshvara Vratam

***When Observed:*** This is one of the ashta maha vartams told in skandha puranam. It is observed on the full moon day when the sun is shining in the vruchchika rasi that is in the month of karthikai (Mid Nov to Mid Dec).

***Way of Observing:*** Getting up early in the morning on that full moon day, finishing the daily duties, one worships the form of shri uma-maheshvara made of gold or silver, with various sacred materials of worship and offerings. Later going to a temple one anoints the parvati-parameshvara with panychamrutam (fruits mixed with sugar) and other substances, salute with offerings and tambulam, pray the Lord making the gestures of salutations. Coming back home donating to the love hearted devotees of Lord shiva, one eats with them only once that day or may eat fruits and sweets along with them. The idol of the Lord uma-maheshvara is given to a shivanyani.

***Glory:*** One who observes this vrata sincerely, would get the material benefits of the world. Afterwards would get the liberation too. A sightless muni called dhiranabindhu observing this vrata got beautiful eyes. A lady by the glory of this vratam revived her dead husband, gave birth to a child and got to reach shivaloka. Vishnu following this vratam in krishnavataram got many children. Brahma got married to gayatri, savitri, Indra got the son jayantan, vashishta received kamadhanu for doing his yagnya, gautamar got the son sadananta maharishi, and janaka got the daughter sita. A dumb minded person called sudharman, mocked by the people about his stupidity, observed this vratam in devotion. By the Lord's blessing he got the grace of goddess Sarasvati and he became a pandit. The king sindhusenan was chased away by the enemies. He observed this vratam as per the advise of saint agastiyar. On the Lord's order kubera won back the kingdom for him and handed over to him. This vratam gets to the observer the wealths and takes to the path of liberation.

## Kedhara (Gauri) Vratam-Deepavali

***History of Deepavali:*** Kedhara Gouri vradham familiarly known as dipavali (Diwali) is celebrated throughout India in a grand manner. Without Caste creed, rich-poor differences people observe this festival. Infact very few people know that it is one of the important Saivite vratas. Brungi rishi is a great Shiva bhakta. When he prays to Lord, he prays only to Lord Shiva and ignores Shakti. Angered by his act Shakti devi removed the energy from his body. He was not able to stand. He prayed to Lord Shiva. God gave him a stick to support his body. Shakti wanted to become part of Lord's body. She observed the kedhara vrata, one of Gods favorite vratas. Pleased by Her austerities God gave the left part of His body to Shakti and became ardha narishwara. The vrata is then called kedhara gauri vrata since Gouri observed it.

***When Observed:*** This kedhara vratam is observed for twenty one days starting from shukla paxa dasami (Tenth moonday in its growing face) in the month of purattachi (mid Sep to mid Oct). The final day (dipavali) also should be observed in great devotion.

***Mantras to perform this Puja (Puja vidhanam):*** Install Lord Kedharishvara svami in a filled pot (calashes). Make a roof (mantapa) above the kalasham. Make vrata threads-21 fibers having 21 knots. The 16 courtasy worship has to be done for 21 days starting from the purattachi shukla paxa dasami to aipachi amarapaxa chaturdashi (dipavali) or amavasya. On the culmination day (21st) in a clean decorated area devotionally install the kalasham over the grains spread in a banana leaf and offer various food and fruits to the Lord as offering and donate to others.

***Glory:*** The glory of this vratam is very splendid as shri gauri devi observed this vratam in full devotion and got to be in half the body of Lord Shiva ! Vishnu became Lord of vaikunta observing this vratam. Brahma got hamsa vehicle, the guards of the eight directions got rid of the bane they got from brahma, bhagyavati and punyavati got lots of wealth all due to the glory of this vratam. One who observes this vratam with devotion pleases Lord shiva.

## Kalyana Vratam (Panguni Uththiram)

Kalyana vratam is one of the eight auspicious vratas. When the Sun is shining in the Pisces sign (mina rasi) that is in the month of panguni (mid of March to mid of April) on the uththara naxaththiram on the Moons growing face (shukla paxam), this vratam is observed. This is the day Shakti married Lord Shiva after a great austerity in the Himalayas, as the daughter of Himavaan. It is also observed as the auspicious day when Lord Muruga married devasena. This vratam is explained in the skandha puranam.

In the morning after getting up, the observer of the verbatim should meditate on the charming Lord shiva in the wedding posture with uma. After taking bath and through with other required deeds, should worship the Lord. The golden idol of the God and Goddess (who can afford to) should be anointed devotionally with holy substances. Then decorating them should make the wedding ceremony of the Goddess with the God. Making the nice and sweet offerings to the divine Parents, should salute them. Inviting the spiritual people who think of good to all the creatures, who have learnt the vedas and who are devotees of Lord Shiva, along with their wives, should host them a feast. Later should go to the shiva temple, worship, circumambulate three times and prostrate in front of the Lord. In the night should dine along with the kind hearted devotees of Lord Shiva and eat the sweet dishes like fruits and payasam.

Should sleep on the dharbai grass. The next morning after regular deeds, should donate the golden idol of God and Goddess to disciplined love hearted people who are the devotees of Lord shiva. Should eat only once that day.

Observing this vratam will get one the great boon of shri Lord Shankara's delight. It would bring much joy and comfort in life, lead to the abode of Lord shiva and give the liberation. Maha Vishnu got wedded to laxmi sincerely observing this vratam. Brahma wedded saraswati, Indra wedded indrani, moon wedded the 27 stars, and sage agastiya wedded lobhamudra observing this vratam. The two daughters of Vishnu namely amritavalli, saundaryavalli were married to the six faced Lord as devasena and valli. The daughter of vedanga Rishhi called sukesi got married to nandi devar. The two daughters of sage satyapurnar purna, pushhkalai were wedded to maha sastha. Kama got rathi, sita got Rama, jambhavati got Krishna, sage saupari got many princesses and so many more benefitted all in the glory of this vratam. The man who observes this vratam will get the girl he likes and the woman gets beautiful man as her husband. The couple who observe this will get good offspring. Anybody who observes with devotion will get His grace.

***Kalyan Sundarar:*** The beautiful (murti) in marriage (bhoga murti)

Shakti was born as parvati, the daughter of the king of Himalayas. As a young child, She was not interested in playing like the other children. She was more inclined towards meditating on Lord Shiva in the mountains. She desired to marry Lord shiva. For that she wanted to perform austerity in the snow covered Himalayas. Her parents hesitated, but finally had to subdue to the determination of parvati. Parvati performed austerity from an ashram. Lord Shiva who was happy with Her worship, came as an old devotee to her place. Parvati offered her respect to the Old bhakta of Her Beloved Lord. Now, He tried to convince Her that She shouldn't waste Her youth doing tapas, but should enjoy life getting married! He further suggested that she could get married to Him, instead of desiring for Lord Shiva Who dances in the cemeteries and wears skulls and bones! Parvati, without knowing that He is

God Himself, got very angry on hearing the Old man's words and told Him that she showed Him respect only because He seemed like a devotee and she would not want to hear any little blasphemy of God further. She asked the Old Man to leave the place immediately. The Lord, pleased with Her determination and devotion, revealed who He is. Parvati was surprised and begged the pardon of God. However God had accepted Her scolding as the most pleasant hailing. Didn't it come from a very deep love for God? He gave Her the boon She yearned for-getting married to Her.

The Himalayan king's family was delighted to see their beloved daughter's wedding. The region was decorated and shining with prosperity. The young beautiful parvati was decorated with chosen best ornaments for the wedding. Now came the Groom-Lord shiva—to the wedding place—on an old bull, with skull and bone ornaments, with the skin of the tiger as the clothing, accompanied by the roar of the buta ganas! The mother of parvati menai fainted to see the groom in such a form for her sweet daughter, softer than the flowers. Now the Lord changed to the form, glittering in a beautiful wedding robe-with golden ornaments and splendid clothing! When menai woke up and saw the Groom she was thrilled to see such a beautiful form and was very pleased that He is "the suitable" groom for her daughter. The play of the Lord has no bounds! Menai saw only the external appearance of the Groom. Other than the great parfait who knows the glory of that Groom? The enchanting Lord in the wedding robe got married to the Daughter of the mountains and this form of God is called kalyana sundharar.

## Shula Vratam

Shula Vratam is one of the eight maha vratam. The day when the Sun shines in the Makara rasi that is the thai (pushya) month new moon day is called the shula vratam day. On that day the observer of the austerity should pray the Lord holding three headed spear (shula) accompanied by Goddess shakti, after getting up. Then the worship of the God with anointment (abhishekam) and offerings (naivedyam), etc. should be done with devotion. Then should worship in the abode of Lord shiva. Donating to the devotees of Lord Shiva who wear rudraxa beads should be done. Only one time meal should be taken along with the devotees.

Observing this shula vratam would get one the victory over all the enemies, free from the terrific diseases, boon of having offspring and the prosperities. Finally the devotee would get the union in shiva. By observing this vratam maha Vishnu killed the cruel daemon kala nemi. Parashurama killed karta viryarjuna after observing this vratam. Maha Vishnu got rid of a worst head ache because of glory of this vratam. Brahma got relieved from his highly painful stomach pain. The highly powerful Lord virabhadra explained the greatness of this vratam to bhanu kambha.

## Vrishabha Vratam

This is one of the eight great austerities. In the time when the Sun is in the Rishabha rasi, that is in the month of vaikasi (mid May to mid June); on the eight moon day (ashhtami) in the growing lunar phase (shukla paxam) this vratam is observed. This vratam is described in the skandha puranam.

Getting up early in the morning, the devotee should think and salute the parameshavara with His consort uma on the bull. Later taking bath being purified, on should start the worship. Could do the worship to the Rishhabharudar form made in gold or silver. The Lord should be anointed with the substances like panychamritam and other holy things with the converging mind on the Lord. Offering to the Lord the rice and derived offerings like payasam on should pray to the God.

Then to the kind hearted devotees of Lord shiva material should be donated. Worshiping the Lord in the Lord shiva temple and making offerings there should return home in that happiness. Later along with the devotees, eat the rice, sugar-rice, fruits and sweets without spoiling the intent of the austerity. Listen to the glories of Lord shiva until late evening and then sleep on the bare floor relaxedly. The following day after saluting the Lord, donate the idol to a sincere love hearted of Lord shiva.

One who observes this vratam flawlessly would get long life, wealth, wisdom, health and the eight great treasures. Vishnu pleasing the paramashivam got lots of treasures and the garuda (one in the eagle family) as his vehicle. Indra got the elephant called airavatam, the deva of fire got the goat, deva of death the buffalo, north got human, deva of water got crocodile, deva of air got the deer, cudbear got airplane pushhpaka vimanam, Ishanar got the ox that resembles the justice, sun got the chariot of one wheel and seven horses, moon got the special ruby airplane as their vehicles by observing the vrata worshiping the Rishhabharudhar. The maharishi told once to the king of Maharashtra vishvasena the things that happened, happening and would happen. The astonished king asked how the maharishhi got to know these details. The sage told him that it was because of the glory of vrishhabha vratam. The king also observed the austerity and got to know these. The king santushhTa worshiping through this vratam got the eight great attainments (ashhta maha sidhdhi) and got the moxa. Vidhrutha king roamed around with the body in the seven down worlds and the worlds of Brahma, vishhnu and Indra, transpiring the knowledge of this vrata to his sons, observing this vratam for a long time, became shiva yogi. Such glorious is this vratam.

## Shiva Ratri Vratam

Shiva rathri is one of the most auspicious vratas. The puranas explain the significance of this vrata.

***History of the Shivaratri:*** Once when everything in all the worlds got reduced into Lord shiva, in that darkness of nothing present, the mother pArvati worshipped Lord shiva in the Agamic way with great devotion. The parameshvar pleased by Her prayer blessed Her. She asked for the benefit of all the creatures that in future whoever worships the Lord on the shiva ratri day with devotion, they should be blessed and should be given the ultimate liberation. The pashupati granted that showing way for all of us to get blessed easily.

When Brahma and Vishnu fought between themselves as "who is the greatest", Lord Shiva appeared before them as a pillar of fire. They were not able to find the starting and end of that pillar. This day is Thirukkaarthikai.

Then Brahma and Mahavishnu repented for their mistake and prayed to Lord Shiva for forgiving their sin worshiping the shiva lingam which is the form of the flame. In the night of Shiva ratri Lord Shiva appeared before them and blessed them. Devotees pray the God throughout the night of Shiva ratri by performing Abisheka, chanting and other holy deeds.

Every month in Krishna paksha chathurdhasi (fourteenth moonday) is called masa Shiva ratri. The one that comes in the month of "Masi" (mid February to mid March) is called Maha Shiva Ratri. This is considered as the most important vrata by the devotees.

There are many incidents told about the greatness of this day. Once a hunter in a jungle after searching throughout the jungle, was quite tired and could not get any animal. In the nightfall a tiger started chasing him. to escape from that he climbed a tree. That was a Bilva tree. The tiger sat under the tree waiting for him to come down. The hunter who sat on a branch of the tree was quite tense and didn't want to sleep. He was plucking the leaves and putting down as he was not able to be idle. Below the tree there was a Shiva lingam. The whole night went on like this. God was pleased with the Upavasa (hunger) and the Pooja the hunter and the tiger did even without knowledge. He is the peak of the grace. He gave the hunter and the tiger "Moksha".

In a Shiva temple on a Maha Shiva ratri day the lamp kept in the altar was very dim. That time a mouse which came take its prey touched the flame. Due to the heat it moved its head immediately. In the process it kindled the lamp and the altar was illuminated well. Lord Shiva, pleased by this deed made the mouse Mahabali, the renowned asura king.

There are many incidents like this told in our Puraanas. If we do the vrata with pure devotion and love there can be no doubt about getting the Grace of the Almighty.

***When is Shivaratri Observed:*** Skandha puranam describes about four shiva ratri. The first one is nitya shivaratri (daily shivaratri-every night). The second one is the masa shivaratri which is observed on the Krishna paxa chaturdasi (fourteenth moonday on the moons diminishing phase). The third one is the maga prathamadi shivaratri which is observed for the thirteen days starting from prathama titi in the month maga (masi) and on the chaturdasi night the Lord is worshiped throughout the night.

The fourth one is observed on the masi (maga) month Krishna paxa chaturdasi. This is the one observed in a widespread manner. It is also called maha shivaratri.

***Way of Observing Shivaratri:*** Getting up early in the morning one meditates on the Infinitely Auspicious, ornate with thousands of splendid garlands, who is in the form of the holy symbol of Shiva (maha lingam). Bathing and staying clean the worship of Lord Shiva in the form of shiva lingam is done in the four jamas of the night (four equal time intervals of the night). (Note that the linga worship is explicitly mentioned for this vratam as this is the time the God out of Its grace for the benefit of pashus appeared in a formless-form that is a symbol (lingam) from Its true nature of formlessness.)

## Nag Panchami

On the fifth day of the bright half of Shravan people worship the snake, or as snakes in India are known, the "nag".

The day is known as "Nag Panchami". The festival falls during the onset of the monsoons and is believed to counter the increased possibility of a snake bite during this time, especially since the rivers are in spate.

People visit temples specially dedicated to snakes and worship them. Shiva temples are also favoured places for veneration as snakes are considered dear to him. In South India, people sculpt images of snakes using cow dung, which are then placed on either side of the entrance to the house. This is done to welcome the snake god. In some other parts of southern India, figures of snakes are drawn with red sandalwood paste on wooden boards, or clay images of snakes coloured yellow or black are purchased. These are then worshipped and offered milk since snakes are believed to like milk. Some go to worship the snake which is believed to be hiding in the holes of anthills. Or else a five hooded snake is made by mixing "gandh" (a fragrant pigment), "halad-kumkum" (turmeric powder), "chandan" (sandal) and "keshar" (saffron) and placed on a metal plate and worshipped.

On this day, devotees pour milk into all the holes in the ground around the house or near the temple to propitiate them. Sometimes, a small pot of milk with some flowers is placed near the holes so that the snakes may drink it. If a snake actually drinks the milk, it is considered to be extremely lucky for the devotee.

Legend has it that the serpents are believed to have the capability to change their shape at will. When in human form, they are depicted as beautiful women and handsome men. The victory of Krishna over the Kaliya snake is commemorated on this day. For this reason Krishna is known as "Kaliya Mardan.

Naga Panchami is observed indifferent ways in different parts of India. One of the oldest festivals, many women fast on this day and in fact it even finds mention in the Puranas. It is believed to be one of the most auspicious days of the entire year. According to the Bhavishya Purana, when men bathe the snakes called Vasuki, Takshaka, Kaliya, Manibhadra, Airavata, Dhritarashtra, Karkotaka and Dhananjaya with milk on the fifth day of the bright fortnight of Shravan, they ensure freedom from danger for their families.

These are then worshipped and offered milk. Snake charmers wander about with all sorts of snakes, to which people offer milk. The snake charmers are paid some money for allowing this Serpent worship developed gradually from the fear of serpents that must have taken a heavy toll on life, particularly at the beginning of the rainy season. In the Ashvalayana Grihyasutra, the Paraskara Grihyasutra and other Grihyasutras, a rite called Sarpabali or 'offerings to serpents' was performed on the full moon night of Shriven. However the reason that it was moved from the full moon night to that of the fifth night of the bright fortnight is not apparent. It may be due to the slight change in the time of the onset of the rains.

## An Indian Pilgrimage

The old roads of Asia are the footways of the world's ideas. There is a camel-track that crosses the desert from Egypt into "Sooria," broken at the Suez Canal by a ferry. What road in Europe, Roman or barbarian, can compare in charm and pathos with this sandy path? On it we might yet see a woman carrying a child on the back of an ass, and an old man leading them, even as the legends picture the Flight of the Holy Family. By it long ago marched the armies of Egypt to meet those of Assyria in destructive conflict on the borders of Israel. By it Judea sent the streams of her burning thought and fierce ethical emotion to Alexandria, before Christianity was born.

Similarly, all over India, away from her ancient high roads, and thrown like a network across her proudest Himalayas, are little thread-like paths like this—ways made indeed by the feet of men, but worn far deeper by the weight of impelling ideas than by the footprints of the toil-stained crowds.

Such roads must once have connected China with Kashmir. Afghanistan, always a province of India, must by just such paths have sent its wandering merchants with nuts and raisins to the South, as long ago as the days of Solomon. Even now it is by ways unpaved, deep-trodden, that the long-haired goats scramble down with their loads through the snowy defiles from Bokhara and Tibet, to be sheared in the sunny valley of the Jhelum, and furnish wool for its famous shawls. Which comes first, we wonder, commerce or pilgrimage, the trade route or the palmer's path? Would it not appear that the utilities of exchange draw men from their homes to points organically related, and does it not seem reasonable to believe that associations of beauty, arising spontaneously at place after place on the line of march, give birth to the notion of religious privilege and obligation in making a return to particular spots?

***Benaras:*** At any rate, it is certain that behind sanctity of pilgrimage lies admiration of place, of art, even of geographical significance. Benaras in the North, and Conjeeveram in the South, are loved and visited in India for the same reason as Durham or Cologne amongst ourselves. They are cathedral cities, rich in architecture, in treasure, and in the associations of saints and scholars. Jagannath is placed where it is, for sheer beauty of the sea, and perhaps a little also for the old cosmopolitan grandeur of the port through which flowed the Eastern trade. Allahabad is sacred, because there two mighty rivers join their waters, making her the strategic key to two vast basins, inhabited by different races, with diverse traditions, hopes, and folk-lore. It is the solemn beauty of the Himalayas that makes them the refuge of holy men.

The four most meritorious pilgrimages of the Hindus are the four extreme points of India—North, South, East, and West—knowing which the country must be known. The worship of the Ganges, and the reverence that makes a Dekkan villager journey, as an act of piety, to look on the face of one who has seen any of the seven sacred rivers, amongst peoples less poetic, would be simply called the love of place. How large an element in Hinduism is the folk-lore of the country! To the student who is looking for this, it appears to be past all computing. The Mahabharata, the Ramayana, and the Puranas are to a great extent the outpouring of passionate fancy in local interpretation. In the story of Sati, the perfect wife, who can miss the significance of the fifty-two places in which fragments of the smitten body fell? "And one finger fell in Calcutta, and that is still the Kalighat.... And the tongue fell at Kangra (Jowalla Mukhi) in the North Punjab, and appears to this day as licking tongues of fire, from underneath the ground.... And the left hand fell at Benaras, which is for ever Onnopurna, the Giver of Bread." No foreigner can understand the crowding of associations into these few sentences.

Even the Pole Star has its Indian myth in the legend of the child Dhruwa, whose heart was the steadiest point in all the universe.

Nor is the historic element lacking, in this unconscious worship of country. Like that of some Indian Bernadette is the story told at a beautiful Southern temple of a cowherd who had one cow that gave no milk. He followed her into the jungle, and found a natural lingam in the rock, over which she poured her offering freely, of her own devotion. And, in proof of the occurrence, does the temple altar not consist today of that same lingam set in rough living rock? Of such stories the villages are full. Assuredly, a deep and conscious love of place pervades the whole of the Indian scheme. It has never been called patriotism, only because it has never been defined by boundaries of contrast; but the home, the village, the soil, and, in a larger sense, the rivers, the mountains, and the country as a whole, are the objects of an almost passionate adoration.

And nowhere are we more impressed by the completeness of Eastern idealism, than in this, its relating of itself to Nature. Norway, with her broken crags and azure seas and sombre pines, her glacier-crowned mountains, and her island-dotted fjords, is surely beautiful. But Norway's memories are always of the heroes, and we miss those voices of the saints that greet us at every turn in every part of India. Brittany, windy and grey, storm-tost and boulder-strewn, is beautiful. Here. too the miles are marked with rude Calvaires, and the tales of the saints lie like her own moorland mists across the whole Breton land. But this Catholic sainthood never reaches the stern intellectual discipline of Hinduism, and we long in vain for that mingling of mystic passion and philosophic freedom, where holiness merges into scholarship, that at once distinguishes the Orient, and weds its races and all their dreams to their own soil. It might almost have been S. Francis, but it is actually a Bengali poem of the people, that says:

*Oh, Mother Earth, Father Sky,*
*Brother Wind, Friend Light,*
*Sweetheart Water,*
*Here take my last salutation with folded hands,*
*For today I am melting away into the Supreme,*
*Because my heart became pure, And all delusion vanished,*
*Through the power of your good company.*

Beauty of place translates itself to the Indian consciousness as God's cry to the soul. Had Niagara been situated on the Ganges, it is odd to think how different would have been its valuation by humanity. instead of fashionable picnics and railway pleasure-trips, the yearly or monthly incursion of worshipping crowds. Instead of hotels, temples. Instead of ostentatious excess, austerity. Instead of the desire to harness its mighty forces to the chariot of human utility, the unrestrainable longing to throw away the body, and realise at once the ecstatic madness of Supreme Union. Could contrast be greater?

It is commonly said that Hindus derive the idea of pilgrimage from the Buddhist worship of relics. But the psychological aspects of the custom make this appear unlikely. Doubtless the great commercial nexus of the Buddhist period made transport easy, and thus strengthened and stimulated the tendency, just as railways have in modern times opened up the country, and created the possibility of a geographical sense amongst classes who in older days could not have aspired to travel far or often. But in its essence, the institution is so entirely an expression of love for the Motherland that it must have been anterior to Buddhism by at least as much as the Aryan occupation of India.

If one visits the Kennery caves, hidden amongst the jungles to the north of Bombay, this fact is brought home to one. Here are a hundred and eight cells, cut out of the solid rock. They are grouped in pairs; each pair has its own water-supply; and, wherever the view is finest, wherever a glimpse can be caught of the meeting-line of sea and forest, there a staircase and seat will be found specially carved in the stone, for purposes of contemplation. For Nature is the eternal fact, and the landscape from this point a thousand years ago was as beautiful as it is today.

***Ellora:*** Ellora shows at a glance that through century after century it has been a holy place. The Buddhist found it already so, and in due time the Muslim confirmed the ancient choice, by bringing his illustrious dead to lie in the mighty fane on its hilltop. But why was it first selected? None who has wakened to the dewy freshness of its morning, none who has gazed thence across the sea-like plain, can ask. To all eternity, while the earth remains what she is, Ellora will be one of the spots where the mystery of God is borne in, in overwhelming measure, upon the souls of men, whatever their associations, whatever their creed. But we are dominated more by the idea that is behind us than by the spontaneous impressions of our senses.

To the nomad of the desert, accustomed to the shifting of hot sands, and ceaseless moving of the camp, with what coolness and refreshment must rise the thought of death! Muslim piety has three motives—the glory of man, the charm of woman, and the holiness of the grave. In very early times we see the august pastor Abraham seeking out a cave in which to place the body of his wife. Death, the fixed, the still, the cold, must be shrined within the steady and imperishable. "The long home," a great rock in a weary land, endless rest, eternal cold and silence, all these are to be found in the grave. Is it not easy to understand that while the peasant, from the banks of the Ganges to the banks of the Tiber, turns naturally to burning of the dead, the wilderness-dwellers bury him deep in mother earth, or build him about with unyielding granite, and thenceforth make this dwelling-house of the beloved as the centre of their own wanderings?

Hence, what the sacred place of pilgrimage is to the Hindu that the Taj Mahal or the tomb of Aurangzeb, or the ever-memorable grave at Medina, is to the pious Muslim. Almost every Muslimised village in India, too, has its sleeping-place of some "pir" or saint; and I have seen a poverty-stricken God's acre, where the sole treasure of the people was a gnarled and scarcely-living stump, that marked the last home of a long-remembered holy man. For it is the ideal of the desert—rest from their wanderings and shadow from its scorching sun—it is this ideal, and not the natural dictation of their own birth-place, that has become the guiding-power behind the life and choice of these Moslemised Indian folk. And yet all their old poetry of soil comes out in the spot they choose! The tomb in the village-grove; the Taj at the river-bend; the iris-covered graves on the riversides and hillocks of Kashmir; what pictures do these make at dawn and sunset, or through the long Indian night, with its mysterious voices sighing and whispering about the dead! Surely, by thus adding the pastoral tradition to her own, India grows rich, not poor, in the things that form the true wealth of men.

***Pilgrim Camps:*** A pilgrim's camp is like some scene taken out of the Middle Ages, Or, rather, it would be like it, but that is so largely depleted of militant elements. The Nagas, or armed friars, are no menace to anything in the modern system, which indeed at this moment they do not understand; and the authority that actually protects and keeps order amongst the pilgrims is to be sought rather in the unarmed district officer, or tehsildar, than in anything that could be recognised as forceful by the naked eye. In the South, which is the home of orthodoxy, pilgrimage has gone out of fashion since the advent of railways. Fewer people, certainly fewer widows, visit Benaras, since it became easier to do so. And those who have seen a genuine crowd of shrine-farers, in some place remote from steam, cannot wonder at the shock which the pious imagination suffers at the sight of a locomotive. Amongst other things that the religious traveller has a right to expect is the opportunity of a flight from the New India to the Old, as an actual environment. From any point where many ways meet, and various streams of pilgrims converge upon each other, the road to the sacred place will be divided into regular stages of a day's journey, and at each halting-place a camp will be pitched for the night. Even these rest-camps will be situated as far as possible at spots peculiar for their beauty or interest. Is there a cluster of springs? The place is said to be "holy," and we must halt there for worship. Originally, this referred only to beauty and convenience; but in process of time one cannot doubt that a certain atmosphere of insight and devotion has really thrown its halo about the dust and water of the locality, and in the place where so much simple faith has spent its rapture, the highest love and prayer have become easier to all corners.

***Temples:*** But the temples are all visited, the bathing is performed, evening worship is over, and silence and sleep fall upon the pilgrims' camp. The moon grows to the full, for we must arrive at the goal on the fifteenth day. And again, it is the simple beauty of the world which determines the law, that under the young moon shall be the going forth, and with her wane the return home. The moon is near the full, and weariness sleeps sound. At what hour is the first tent struck? When does the first sleeper rouse himself, and take again to the road? Who can tell? Certainly not one who has never been able to rise so long before dawn that others were not up and afoot before her, their tents gone, and little heaps of white ashes from the cooking-fires the only sign of their twelve hours' tenancy of tree-shadow or stream-side.

On go the pilgrims, singly or in groups. Old women, bent double with age and toil, hobbling along by the help of the pointed alpenstock: Monks of all descriptions are to be seen. Some of them are covered with ashes, have long reddish-looking hair, wear only the yellow loin-cloth, and carry curious tongs and begging-bowls. These may be Yogis, of the order that believes in the mortification of the flesh; or Nagas, the militant monks, who were once ready to defend the Faith at any moment, and who to this day are powerfully organised to meet the shock of a world that has long ago, alas, passed away like a dream.

The sannyasin, often a man of modern education, decently clad in the sacred salmon-yellow, accepting no alms save food, refusing the touch of any metal, is here, doing the distance cheerfully on foot. Next comes an ascetic, with withered arm held aloft and useless this many a long year. Again, a proud mahunt, abbot of some rich foundation, master of elephants and treasure uncounted, is borne past. Or, as one climbs, having abandoned the open dandy that costs such intolerable labour to the bearers on a mountain march, one may be joined in kindly chat by some one or two of the "Naked Swamis"—men who wear neither ashes nor clothing beyond the necessary scanty rag, who wander amongst sunny deserts and snowy mountains alike indifferent to heat and cold, and of whom, when one talks with them, one remembers nothing, save that here are friends of the culture of scholars, and the breeding and rank of gentlemen.

But the crowd is still more motley. In camp, the strips of yellow cloth that so often do duty as a shelter for the religious, stand side by side with tents of all sizes and conditions. And here now are zenana-ladies carried in scarlet-covered palkees; other women, again, on horseback; men and women alike on foot, or in open dandies; householders, widows, sannyasinis in beads and yellow cloth; there are even some, too weak for walking or climbing, who are borne in straw chairs, strapped to the back of a man carrying a stout staff. On and on presses the irregular host, mixed up with Muslim baggage-carriers and servants, cooks, and food-vendors of all sorts.

Here the road is broken by a glacier. There it becomes a mere goat-path, running across dangerous crags. Here is the lake into which an avalanche, brought down by their hymn of triumph, once precipitated thousands of returning pilgrims. Now we have reached the heights where the ground is carpeted with edelweiss instead of grass. Again, we are wandering amidst wildernesses of flowers, while every few yards the dominant note in the composition is changed imperceptibly: first the yellow wallflower, then flame-coloured Iceland poppies, again the long-stalked single-headed Michaelmas daisy of the Himalayas. When the journey began, almost the only blossoms were the orchids on the tree-trunks in the region of maidenhair fern.

Now we have passed the last of the pine woods. Even the white birches, like smitten silver veining blown sharp and twisted against the mountain sides, are gone: and to-night, when the tents are pitched over purple and white anemones, there will be no fuel save the juniper scrub that clings to the face of the rock in sheltered niches. On the edge of the last glacier, growing beside the gentian, we find an evergreen forget-me-not, unknown to us hitherto, and making the third or fourth new species—from a large crimson and purple myosotis onwards—which our pilgrimage has bestowed.

Our neighbours in the tents about us are not amusing themselves by botanising, probably, but they are communing with Nature none the less truly than ourselves. On the last day, drawing gear to the shrine, we shall see them risk their lives to gather the great nodding columbines and the little Alpine roses growing on the rocks. Their talk is all of Shiva. As they are borne along, they are striving, doubtless, to fix their minds on the repetition of His name, or the contemplation of His form. But the awesome grandeur and beauty of the heights about them will always be remembered by them as the Great God's fit dwelling-place. They are in a church. Rocks and glaciers form the sanctuary. Snowy passes are the pillared aisles. Behind them stand the pine-forests for processions of singers carrying banners, and overhead are the heavens themselves for cathedral roof. It is the peculiarity of Eastern peoples to throw upon the whole of Nature that feeling which we associate only with the place of worship. But is their love less real, or greater, fcr this fact?

***Shries:*** The day of the full moon comes, the last and most dangerous points are surmounted, and the Shrine is reached. Happy the man or woman, who, on this journey to God, is snatched out of life! One false step, and the soul that was struggling to see may be carried up at once in a swift sure flight. Or death may come in other ways. "It is so beautiful! I must be one with it!" sighed a man who stood on a precipice, looking down at the valleys. And before any one could stop him, he was gone. Such things are not premeditated. There is a genuine ecstasy of the soul in which it hears the voice of the Eternities calling to it, and the poisoning body becomes suddenly intolerable. Is it a stain upon Hinduism that it has never called this "suicide while of unsound mind"?

But the Shrine itself—where is it? what is it? Perhaps a temple, placed above some gorge, on a beetling rock, with sister snows in sight. Perhaps the source of a sacred river. Perhaps a cave, in which continual dripping of water makes a stalagmite of ice, a huge crystalline lingam that never melts. One can picture how such a place would first be discovered. Some party of shepherds, losing themselves and their flocks amongst the ravines on a summer day, and entering the cavern by accident, to find there the presence of the Lord Himself. Men and beasts, awed and worshipping, how dear is such a picture to the Christian heart!

Worship! Worship! The very air is rent with prayer and hymns. From the Unreal to the Real! From the Many to the One! Lord of Animals! Refuge of Weariness! Shiva! Shiva! the Free! the Free!

Hours pass, and ere dawn next day the descent to the valleys is begun. Wonderful is the snowy stillness of the lofty pass, when, with our faces set homewards, the moon fades behind us, and the sun rises before. The pilgrims march with less regularity now.

All are anxious to return, and some push on, while others break off from the line of route. We reach our own village, and say farewell to the acquaintances of the pilgrimage, adding what comfort we may to the provision for their further journeying. The nights grow dark now, and the great experience becomes a memory, marked always, however, in the Hindu's life, by some special abstinence, practiced henceforth as the pilgrim's thank offering.

It is easy to believe that the scenes in which we have mingled are nowadays denuded of half their rightful elements; that once upon a time as many of the travellers would have been Tartar or Chinese as Indian; that the shrine represents what may have been the summer meeting of great trading caravans; that Nagarjuna and Bodhidharma, going out to the Further East with their treasures of Indian thought, were in the first place pilgrims on some such pilgrimage as this. Even now, many of the functions of a university are served by the great gathering. Hundreds, or even thousands, of religious men meet, in a manner to eliminate personal ties of friendship and affection, and emphasise and refresh the ideal and intellectual aspects of their lives.

At the vast assemblies of sadhus, which occur once in every twelve years at Hardwar, at Nasik, at Ujjain, and at Allahabad, there are fixed halls of learned disputation, where, for hundreds of years, Hindu philosophy has been discussed, determined, and expanded, something in the fashion of the Welsh Eisteddfod. Here come the wandering monks from every part of India. Here the householder finds himself in vigorous and renewed relation to his faith. Here fresh voices of learning and devotion are able to win for themselves ecclesiastical authority. Such opportunities must have been the means by which Sankaracharya asserted his undisputed mastery of the world of Hindu scholarship. Did it, we wonder, occur to Alexander that learned Greeks might be sent to such wandering colleges in order to hear and to tell new things?

Sanskrit is the *lingua franca* of this ancient learning. To this day the visitor to a Calcutta toll may hear the boys dispute with each other on timeworn themes in the classic tongue, and may picture himself back in the colleges of Thebes or Athens in the long ago. But here in the great melas are the crowning achievements towards which are directed the hardier ambitions of those Brahman boys. And we need not wonder at their enthusiasm for such distinction.

The great open competition, with its thousands of years of the prestige of learning, is like all the learned societies of a European metropolis thrown into one. The canvas city of a few weeks at Nasik or Allahabad serves all the purposes of Burlington House to London. But the system of culture to which Nasik belongs is no longer growing, it will be said. This is, indeed, its defect. The statement is not entirely true, for even now the test of a supremely national personality would still be, for the Hindu world, his power to add to their philosophy. But it is true to the extent that there is nothing left for collective thought to discover. The common mind of India has now to sweep great circles of intellectual exploration in worlds that as yet are virgin as the Polar ice, or India will die. Of this there can be no doubt.

Far away from the noisy throng of learned saints, or taking a humble place in white cotton garb as visitors amongst them, are the men whose lives are passed in the libraries of kings. For the system of patronage is part and parcel of Indian scholarship, and as the Japanese daimio or the Italian prince maintained his artists and artificers, so, under the old régime, did every Indian palace possess its staff of palace-pandits—men whose lives were made free of anxiety in order that they might heap up knowledge and pore over ancient texts.

The supreme privilege of the great is to foster piety and learning. But, on the other hand, Manu does not fail to point out that there is no crime for the Brahman like the acceptance of gifts from one who is not the lawful king. And it is not royal persons alone who are charged with the duty of supporting scholars. Never a wedding or a requiem can take place amongst the higher ranks of society without the distribution of money to tolls and pandits. For it is one of the postulates of ethical, and therefore of Eastern, economics, that all great accumulation is for subsequent great distribution.

It is a strange world that has been revealed to us in this camp of pilgrimage, and it is not easy to reach its full significance. Scarcely in any two tents do they understand each other's language, and we shall do better to ask for bread in Sanskrit than in English. Malabaris and Bengalis, Sikhs and Madrasis, Marathas and even Muslims, dwell side by side for the nonce. Could incongruity and disunion be more strongly illustrated?

Yet it was unity and not disunity that impressed us as we looked. From one end of the camp to the other the same simple way of life, the same sacramental reverence for food and bathing, the same gentleness and courtesy, the same types of face and character, and, above all, one great common scheme of thought and purpose.

The talk may be in different languages; but no matter at what tent door we might become eavesdroppers, we should find its tone and subject much the same—always the lives of the saints, always the glory of the soul, always fidelity to guru and dharma. By two formulae, and two alone, renunciation and freedom from personality, is all life here interpreted.

Other countries have produced art, chivalry, heroic poems, inventive systems In none of these has India been altogether wanting, yet none is her distinguishing characteristic. What, then, has she given to the world that is beyond all competition? Today her gifts are decried by all men, for today the mighty mother is become widowed and abased. She who has held open port to all fugitives is unable now to give bread to her own children. She with whom Parsi, Jew, and Christian have been thankful to take refuge, is despised and ostracised by all three alike. She who has prized knowledge above all her treasures, finds her learning now without value in the markets of the world. It is urged that the test of utility is the true standard for things transcendental, and that an emancipation into modern commerce and mechanics is a worthier goal for her sons' striving than the old-time aim of knowledge for its own sake, the ideal for itself.

And the modern world may be right.

But, even so, has India in the past given nothing, without which our whole present would be the poorer?

Who that has caught even a whisper of what her name means can say so? Custom kept always as an open door, through which the saints may dance into our company, thought sustained at a level where religion and science are one, a maze of sublime apostrophes and world-piercing prayers; above all, the power to dream rare dreams of the Word becoming flesh and dwelling among men that they may behold His glory—are these things nothing? If, after all the higher transformation of man be the ultimate end of human effort, which has more deeply vindicated its right to exist, the modern nexus of commerce and finance, or that old world on which we have gazed in the pilgrims' camp?

## The Story of the Great God: Shiva or Mahadev

*Thou that art knowledge itself,*
*Pure, free, ever the witness,*
*Beyond all thought and beyond all qualities,*
*To Thee, the only true Guru, my salutation,*
*Shiva Guru! Shiva Guru! Shiva Guru!*
*Salutation to Shiva, as the Teacher of the Soul.*

In India's great moments, the Himalayas have always been her highway, not her boundary. Those strings of pack-mules, with their sorry-looking rice-bags, that we meet on every hill-path, as we wander through the mountains, are the remains of a great continental traffic that once carried the religion into China. For beliefs, like diseases, do not travel alone. The pilgrim is accompanied by the peddler: the begging-friar dogs the footsteps of the merchant; the faith follows the line of trade. It may be that if Chinese silk and turquoise had not found their way to India many centuries before the birth of Buddha, the news of the Great Nirvana could never have reached the remoter East.

To this day, we find ancient capitals and their ruins, old fortresses, royal temples, scattered up and down the heights from Blochistan to Nepal, in regions long depopulated. And

Himalayan shrines and cities have an art and architecture of their own, which is more severely beautiful, because more directly related to the common early Asiatic, than the later styles, to be found further south. For the first culture-area of humanity had these mountains as its rim. Long before a local prepossession had named the Mediterranean, Asia was. And of that Asia, Egypt, Greece, Etruria, were outlying provinces. The Saracen and Moor, with all that they brought of art and chivalry, with all the intellectual vividness they conferred on Europe, were but the relic-mongers of its past. In the West, even now, we admit a people to be civilized only if we can trace its intellectual descent from this ancient Asia.

Above all, it is the broken voices of its primitive consciousness that are hailed today in every civilized country as divine revelations. India herself is no exception to this rule. For all the migrations of Asokan and other periods pale beside the memory of the still more significant era when for the first time there came to settle on the Northern Plain those little communities of people, already agricultural and industrial in their habits, who carried with them the culture of Central Asia. It was not a regimented immigration. The Lall Kaffir, or pale folk, dwelling to this day in the Hindu Kush, were not deserters, turning aside from the line of march. We must rather suppose a gradual overflow, through many centuries, of the Himalayan region. And yet, at some time or place, it must have been sufficiently consolidated and self-organised to become conscious of its great heritage of thought, to commit its knowledge to writing, and to give form and definition to the Aryan civilization.

Wherever and whenever it may have happened, this was the moment at which long ages of accumulating reflection and observation precipitated themselves into form as the Vedas. Even so are all Scriptures born. The Tartar herdsman, facing his unknown future as a peasant, records at once his ideals and his memories, and we have the Eki, or Book of Change, of the Chinese people. The austere self-isolation of a few tribes of Syrian shepherds fronts with terror the degradation of Babylonian cities, and the prophets pour out their sublime woes. The Latin Church carries to the Norse peasant with one hand the waters of baptism, with the other the script, by means of which he is to write down his magnificent sagas. The old order blossoms into complete self-consciousness at that very instant when every petal trembles to the fall.

So passed the Vedic age, for the Aryans settled down in India, and became Hindus. The process by which this was accomplished must have been complex and gradual. In some directions towards a greater luxury, it must have been fundamentally a simplification of life. The builders of the Himalayas had used wood and stone. The builders of the plains used bamboos, mud, and bricks; and their architectural designs began to approximate to those of pottery. The weavers of Central Asia had worked in wool, doubtless of marvelous dyes.

The craftsmen of the south were driven to cotton and silk. That system of ritual purification which was common to the whole of the Asiatic culture, and which is still retained by Europe in the form of sacraments and rubrics, must have been deepened and extended to meet the new climatic conditions. Natural metaphor underwent transformation. Coolness was exchanged for warmth as the qualification of friendship. Himalayan scenery was no longer present to give constant birth to grand myths and colossal imaginary. That gradual absorption of regional thought and worship began, which was to produce what in its latest phase would be known as Hinduism. But it was always to be absorption. It was always to be the play of the Aryan intellect upon the indigenous symbol; never the acceptance of a superstition that could not be rationalised. This wonderful continuity of thinking marks the solidarity of Hinduism as nothing else could. Every creed within its frontiers—and they are wide enough to include all types of religious thought—can prove the Vedas to be its authority. Even the image of the Goddess Kali is held to be foreshadowed in the sublime Anthem to Creation of the Rigveda:

> *We find in India, then, a classical nation like Egypt or Greece, which has been allowed to develop freely on the mental plane, and has held the thread of its thought unbroken to the present day. It may be said broadly that great culture and subjective philosophies are almost*

> *always continental in their origin, while the sense of nationality and insistence on the beautiful are insular. If this be true, it would explain the greater sympathy between Hellenic and Japanese developments than between Greek and Indian.*

For the Hindu imagination long ago detached itself from the cycle of physical beauty, to seek its fullest satisfaction in subtler realms. This fact is extraordinarily evident in Kalidas' poem of "The birth of the War Lord," where he depicts the wooing of Mahadev by Uma, the Himalayan princess. Here the poet places his heroine at the very acme of maidenly charm, kneeling in worship to lay flowers at the feet of the Great God, and having as her background the forest of plum and cherry and almond, all suddenly burst into blossom, because to them comes Spring, as the comrade of Love.

And then, with a single sweep of the brush, the picture is blotted out: the Great God has vanished from beneath his cedar; Eros is burnt to ashes; and the royal maiden kneels alone, while the bitter wailing of Desire, the beautiful wife of Love, fills the whole woodland. Uma's triumph is reached, and the Divine Spouse drawn to her side, only when, in the midst of unheard-of austerities, she gives supreme proof of courage and devotion as nun and worshipper instead of woman and lover. This touch lies far beyond the range of the Greek.

A similar tendency to use physical symbolism as a system of notation merely, instead of seeking in it the direct and adequate expression of spiritual conceptions, as did the classical genius of Europe, is to be found throughout the whole conception of Shiva or Mahadev, the Great God Himself. The tiger-skin in which he is clad, and some of the names of this deity, induce Tod in his "Annals of Rajasthan" to regard him as simply a new version of the Greek Bacchus.

It is a great deal more likely that behind the two, in the dim north, and in the distant past—in some Lake Manasarovar of thought, to quote Max Muller—there may loom up a common ancestor. But this probability only makes more significant the divergences between the two conceptions.

Any one who visits northern India must desire to know the meaning of the little black stones under every conspicuous tree, which are so evidently set up for worship. They are said by Europeans to be of phallic origin; but if so, Hindus are no more conscious of the fact than we of the similar origin of the maypole. Wherever one goes, one finds them, by the roadsides in cities and villages, on the river-banks, or inside the entrance to a garden, it there is a tree that stands alone. For in such places one is glad to think that the Great God, begging His handful of rice from door to door, may have seated Himself to bless us with His meditation.

The small stone pillar, called the lingam—the word lingam is literally symbol—may have been taken from the bed of a stream, and in that case is likely to be of a long egg-shape. But if it has been cut by the hand of man, it is short and slightly tapering, with a thimble-like top. Sometimes, in all good faith, the features of a human face have been more or less crudely marked on it, with white paint. In any case, it is only a question of time till some woman, passing by on her way from bathing, stops to pour a little water, or sprinkle a few grains of rice tenderly over the head of the stone, perhaps also to add bel-leaves, trifoliate like our clover; or a garland of white flowers; or, prompted by a heart more devoted and loving than usual, to touch it with a spot of sandal-paste, so cool and refreshing in this hot climate! Then the earth is touched with the head, and the worshipper passes on.

The simple act is not without its perplexities, and we seek for interpretation. At first in vain. Or the explanations given are more bewildering than helpful. Hindus are too conscious of the symbolistic nature of every faith, and too sensitive also to the scornful irreverence of most foreign inquirers, to speak out, or argue out, the heart of their heart with the passing stranger. Rather they will turn on one, with a strange pity. "Do you not understand," they will say, "that this is the Great God who is emblemed here? He can have neither visitor, nor history, nor worshipper. Such things are vain dreams of men. Only for our own hearts' ease, and to carry ourselves nearer to the inner vision, do we set up a stone whereon we may offer rice and water and lay a leaf or two!" It will be difficult in all India to find a woman so simple, or a peasant so ignorant, that to them worship is not, as some one has said, "a conscious symbolism, instead of a fragment of primitive personification." Yet by degrees the great myth leaks out. Little by little we learn the associations of the name.

The lingam, after all, is but a fragment of stone. Far better images of Mahadev are those who come and go yonder, amidst the passing crowd—the monks and beggars, some clad only in ashes with matted hair, others with shaven head, and clothed from throat to foot in the sacred yellow, but most of them bearing one form or another of staff or trident, and carrying a begging bowl. And finer still will these be, when, retiring into the forest, or climbing to the verge of eternal snows, they sit, even like this stone lingam, bolt upright in the shelter of tree or rock, lost to the world without, in solitary meditation.

About the whole conception there is a striking reminiscence of the Himalayas. Whether we will or not we are carried back, as we listen, to the great age of the Vedas, when the Aryan immigration was still taking place. It is a day of sacrifice, and at the forest-clearing people and priests are met, to heap the offerings on the mighty fire, chanting appropriate texts. Hour after hour, sometimes day after day, the mound of pure flame lasts, and long after it has ceased the hot white ashes lie in their immense bed, thrilling now and then to a faint trickling spark, sighing themselves out into the coldness of death. Who was it that first came and rubbed himself with those soft white ashes, in order to be clothed upon with the worship of God and separation from the world? Who was it that first retired into cave or jungle, and meditated, until his hair became a tangled mass, and his nails grew long, and his body emaciated, and he still pursued the sublime bliss of the soul? However the idea of such an exterior grew, the whole genius of India has spoken for many a century in just such a picture—the hermit clad in wood-ashes, with masses of neglected hair, piled on the top of his head, indifferent to the whole world, bent only on thought.

As the Aryans wandered in sight of the snow-mountains, with the fire-sacrifice for their central rite, an indissoluble connection arose in their minds between the two ideas. Were not the flames of the offerings white like the Himalayas, always mounting upward like the aspiring peaks, leaving behind them ashes for eternal frost? Those snowy heights, we must suppose, became the central objects of their love. Lifted above the world in silence, terrible in their cold and their distance, yet beautiful beyond all words, what are they like? Why, they are like—a great monk, clothed in ashes, lost in his meditation, silent and alone! They are like—like—the Great God Himself, Shiva and Mahadev!

Having arrived at this thought, the Hindu mind began to work out all sorts of accessories and symbols, in which sometimes the idea of flame, sometimes of mountain, sometimes of hermit is uppermost—all contributing to the completed picture of Shiva, the Great God.

The wood was borne to the sacrifice on a bull: Shiva possesses an old bull, on which he rides.

As the moon shines above the mountains, so He bears on His forehead the new moon.

Like the true ascetic, begging food at the householder's door, He is pleased with very simple gifts. The cold water of the bath, a few grains of rice, and two or three green bel-leaves, are His whole offering in the daily worship. But the rice and water must be of the purest, for they are presented to a most honoured guest. Evidently the bel-leaf, like the shamrock, refers to the Trinity. For, as we all know, this doctrine is Hindu as well as Christian and Egyptian.

To show how easily Shiva can be pleased, the people tell a pretty story. A poor huntsman—that is to say, one of the lowest of the low—once came to the end of a day's hunting without having snared or killed a single creature. Night came on, and he was far from home, in the jungle, alone. Near by stood a bel-tree, with branches near the ground, and he was glad to climb into it, to pass the night in shelter from wild beasts. But as he lay crouching in its branches, the thought of his wife and children starving at home would come to him, and for pity of their need great tears rolled down his cheeks, and falling on the bel-leaves broke them by their weight, and carried them to the ground. Under the sacred tree, however, stood a Shiva-lingam, image of Shiva, and the tears fell, with the leaves, on its head. That night a black snake crept up the tree, and stung the man. And bright spirits came, and carried his soul to Heaven, and laid it down at the feet of Shiva.

Then, in that holy place, rose the clamour of many voices questioning: "Why is this savage here? Has he not eaten impure foods? Has he offered right sacrifices? Has he known the law?" But the Great God turned on them all in gentle surprise: "Did he not worship Me with bel-leaves and with tears?" He said.

Looking closer at the flame, however, one thing was very clear. It was white, but it had a blue throat—we see it even when we light a match!—and in order to bestow a blue throat upon Shiva, the following story arose:

Once upon a time, all the splendour and glory of the gods seemed to be vanishing from them. (Are such tales, we wonder, a reminiscence of the period when the old gods, Indra, Agni, and the lords of the universe, found themselves growing unfashionable, because the Trinity, Brahma—Vishnu—Shiva, was coming into favour?) What to do, the gods did not know, but they determined to pray to Vishnu, the Preserver of the World, for advice. He told them, perhaps contemptuously, to "go and churn the ocean!" and the poor gods trooped forth eagerly to do his bidding.

They churned and churned. Many great and splendid things came foaming up, and they seized them with avidity, here a wonderful elephant, there a princely horse, again a beautiful wife for some one. Each was only greedy to be first in the handling of the next delight, when all at once something black began to come. Welling up and up, and then spreading over the whole ocean, it came. "What is it?" they asked each other in horror. It was poison—death to them, death to the world, death to the universe. It came to their very feet, and they had to retreat rapidly in fear. Already they were in the midst of darkness, and there was nowhere that they could flee, for this dense blackness was about to cover all the worlds. In this moment of mortal terror, all the gods with one voice called on

Shiva. He had taken no part in the receiving of gifts, maybe He would be able to help them now. Instantly, the great White God was in their midst. He smiled gently at their dilemma and their fear, and stooping down He put His hand into the waves, and bade the poison flow into the hollow of His palm. Then He drank it, willing to die, in order to save the world. But that which would have been enough to destroy all created beings was only enough to stain His throat, hence He bears there a patch of blue for ever.

Perhaps one of the most characteristic myths that have clustered round the name of Mahadev is the Legend of the Boar-Hunt. As we read it, we stand pan the snowy heights of the third range of the Himalayas, and seem to watch a mighty snow-storm sweeping through the ravine before us.

Arjuna, one of the principal heroes of the Great War, and the second figure in the dialogue of the Gita, had gone up into the mountains, to spend three months in worshipping Shiva, and invoking His blessing. Suddenly one day as he was praying and offering flowers before the lingam, he was roused by a wild boar, which was rushing forward to attack him. It was only an instant, and Arjuna, the practised archer, had seized his bow and shot the animal.

But at the self same moment a shout of warning was heard, and simultaneously with Arjuna's a second arrow pierced the body of the beast. The hero raised his eyes, and saw, coming towards him, a formidable-looking hunter and huntress, followed by an innumerable retinue of women, attired for the chase, and attended, at some distance, by a dim host of shadows—the armies of demons and hobgoblins. A second later, the whole hunt had come to a stop before him.

"The quarry was mine!" cried the Hunter—and his voice sounded like the winter-blasts, amongst the mountains—"the quarry was mine. Mine is the lordship of these forests! How dared you touch it?"

At this address, Arjuna blazed with anger, and picking up the bow and arrows that he had thrown aside before returning to his worship, he challenged the Hunter to a personal combat.

"Accepted," was the reply, and the duel began. But to the hero's dismay, he seemed to be attacking some terrible phantom, for, one after another, his good stout arrows disappeared into the person of his antagonist, working him no harm.

"Let's wrestle then!" shouted Arjuna, and casting aside his how, he flung himself upon his foe. He was met by the quiet touch of a hand on his heart, and fell to the ground stunned.

"Well, come on!" said the Hunter, as he recovered himself a few seconds later, and turned aside from the contest. But he seemed almost intoxicated. "I must finish my worship first," he said, in a thick voice, taking up a garland of flowers, to fling about the Shiva-lingam. The next moment the eyes of Arjuna were opened, for the Hunter towered above him, blessing him, and the flowers were about his neck.

"Mahadev! Mahadev!" cried the worshipper, Ringing himself on the ground, to touch with his head the feet of the God. But already the hunt had swept on down the valley, and the Hunter and Huntress had disappeared, with all their train.

Such are a few of the stories told of Shiva, so deeply loved by all his devotees. To them there is nothing in the world so strong and pure and all-merciful as their great God, and the books and poems of Hindus are very few in which he is not referred to with this passionate worship.

Sometimes He is entirely a personification of the Himalayas, as when the Milky Way is made to fall upon his head, wander round and round amongst the tangled locks, and issue from them at last as the Ganges. Indeed, the imagination of the people may be said to make of their northern ranges one vast shrine to Him; for it is far away, they say, across the frost-bound heights, where the Himalayas are at their mightiest and India passes into Thibet, that the Lake Manasarovar lies, at the foot of the great ice-peak of Kailash. Here is the reign of silence and eternal snow, and here, guarding the north, is the holy home that Shiva loves.

He is the very soul of gentleness, refusing none. Up here have gathered round Him all those who were weary of earth, having found no acceptance amongst the fortunate. The serpents, whom all the world hates and denies, come to Kailash, and Mahadev finds room for them in His great heart. And the tired beasts come—for He is the refuge of animals—and it is one of these, a shabby old bull, that He specially loves and rides upon.

And here, too, come the spirits of all those men and women who are turbulent and troublesome and queer, the bad boys and girls of the grown-up world, as it were. All the people who are so ugly that no one wants to see them; those who do things clumsily, and talk loudly, and upset everything, though they mean no harm, and the poor things who are ridden by one idea, so that they never can see straight, but always seem a little mad—such are the souls on whom He alone has mercy. He is surrounded by them, and they love and worship Him. He uses them to do His errands, and they are known as Shiva's demons.

But Shiva is more even than this. He is the Self-born, the eternally-existent postulate of freedom and purity and light. He is the great teaching soul of things. His function is to destroy ignorance, and wherever knowledge is achieved, He is. His name of "Hara! Hara!" ("The Free! The Free!") was. the battle-cry of the Marathas. More yet, He is Rudra, the Storm, the Terrible; and it is under this aspect that Hinduism raises to Him its daily cry:

*Evermore protect us,—O thou terrible!*

*From ignorance, by thy sweet compassionate face.*

For, after all, a human quality is always limited to one of two, the Divine must be lifted above good as well as evil, above joy as well as pain. We have here the Indian conception of same-sightedness, and perhaps its devotional significance is nowhere interpreted as in the Hindi song of Surdas, which is here repeated as a nautch-girl was heard to sing it in a Rajput Court:

*O Lord, look not upon my evil qualities!*

*Thy name, O Lord, is Same-sightedness,*

*By Thy touch, if Thou wilt, Thou canst make me pure.*

*One drop of water is in the sacred Jamuna,*

*Another is foul in the ditch by the roadside,*

*But when they fall into the Ganges,*
*Both alike become holy.*
*One piece of iron is the image in the temple,*
*Another is the knife in the hand of the butcher,*
*But when they touch the philosopher's stone,*
*Both alike turn to gold.*
*So, Lord, look not upon my evil qualities!*
*Thy name, O Lord, is Same-sightedness,*
*Make us both the same Brahman.*

## Samsara

In Hinduism, Buddhism, Jainism and other related religions, samsara or sacsara refers to reincarnation or rebirth in Indian philosophical traditions.

***Etymology:*** Samsara is derived from "to flow together," to go or pass through states, to wander. Mostly a great revolving door between life and death and a new life reincarnated cycle of life. Also known as a game in ancient India.

***Cycle of Rebirth:*** In most Indian philosophical traditions, including the Hindu, Buddhist and Jain systems, an ongoing cycle of birth, death, and rebirth is assumed as a fact of nature. These systems differ widely, however, in the terminology with which they describe the process and in the metaphysics they use in interpreting it. Most of these traditions, in their evolved forms, regard Sacsara negatively, as a fallen condition which is to be escaped. Some, such as Advaita Vedanta regard the world and Sacsaric participation in it as fundamentally illusory.

Some later adaptations of these traditions identify Sacsara as a mere metaphor.

***Sacsara in Hinduism:*** In some types of Hinduism, Sacsara is seen as ignorance of the True Self, Brahman, and thus the soul is led to believe in the reality of the temporal, phenomenal world.

In Hinduism, it is avidya, or ignorance, of one's true self, that leads to ego-consciousness of the body and the phenomenal world. This grounds one in desire and the perpetual chain of karma and reincarnation. The state of illusion is known as Maya.

Hinduism had many terms for the state of liberation like moksha, mukti, nirvana, and mahasamadhi.

The Hindu Yoga traditions hold various beliefs. Moksha may be achieved by love of Ishwar/God (see bhakti movement), by psycho-physical meditation (Raja Yoga), by discrimination of what is real and unreal through intense contemplation (Jnana Yoga) and through Karma Yoga, the path of selfless action that subverts the ego and enforces understanding of the unity of all. Advaita Vedanta, which heavily influenced Hindu Yoga, believes that Brahman, the ultimate Truth-Consciousness-Bliss, is the infinite, impersonal reality (as contrasted to the Buddhist concept of shunyata) and that through realization of it, all temporal states like deities, the cosmos and samsara itself are revealed to be nothing but manifestations of Brahman.

***Sacsara in Jainism:*** In Jainism, karma, anuva (ego) and the veil of maya are central. In Jainism, liberation from samsara is called *moksha* or *mukti*.

***Samsara in Surat Shabda Yoga:*** In Surat Shabda Yoga, the purpose is to realize the individual's *True Self* (Self-Realization), *True Essence* (Spirit-Realization) and *True Divinity* (God-Realization) while living in the human physical body. This *Journey of Soul* involves reuniting in stages with what is called the *Essence of the Absolute Supreme Being*, the Shabd. Attaining self-realization and above also results in *jivan moksha / mukti*, liberation/release from *samsara,* the cycle of karma and reincarnation while in the physical body.

Surat Shabda Yoga Cosmology presents the constitution of the initiate (the microcosm) as an exact replica of the macrocosm. Consequently, the microcosm consists of a number of bodies, each one suited to interact with its corresponding plane or region in the macrocosm. These bodies developed over the yugas through involution (emanating from higher planes to lower planes) and evolution (returning from lower planes to higher planes), including by karma and reincarnation in various states of consciousness.

## Tattva

According to the Indian school of Samkhya philosophy, the *Tattva* are a way of directly "experiencing" the 5 alchemical elements. So they are therefore the logical progression of the previous elemental grade where the elements were first discussed and symbolic ways of working with them described. The student is then taught a method of directly learning the "theoretical" structure of the elemental worlds.

***A Brief History of the Tattvas:*** There are six main schools of thought on Tattvic philosophy. The original *Tattva* system was developed by the Indian Maharshi Kapila as part of his Samkhya philosophy. This was about 700BCE, but the roots of Tattvic philosophy go back to at least 2000BCE. Kapila's Samkhya philosophy system divides the universe into five basic Tattvic shapes, which when countercharged become 25 Tattvas.

The word Tattva is comprised of two words, *Tat* (meaning *that*) and *Tvam* (meaning *thou*). Tattva basicially means *thatness*, that is, the real being of anything. It is generally translated as meaning *quality*. Further, *Tat* represents the Godhead and *Tvam* the individual, giving a meaning (which fits in well with Hermetic Philosophy) of "That (which is the Universe) art thou." This is similar to the Hermetic axiom of "As above, so below", and is directly related to the concepts of the Macrocosm (*Tat*, Godhead) and Microcosm (*Tvam*, individual).

The Hatha Yoga School of Tattvic Philosophy links the energy found in breathing (Prana) with the cycle of the five Tattvas. The eighth chapter of the *Shivagama* is *The Science of Breath and the Philosophy of the Tattvas*. It is written within this work that "The Universe came out of the Tattvas; it goes on by the instrumentality of the Tattvas; it disappears into the Tattvas; by the Tattvas is known the nature of the Universe."

The Tattvas are the five modifications of the Great Breath, Prana, which is described as the life principle of the Universe (macrocosm) and man (microcosm). Prana consists of an ocean of the five Tattvas.

The Buddhist texts of Indian Tantra describe 7 energy centres (chakras) in connection with the five Tattvas. This finds its ultimate refinement in the Tibetan Buddhist fivefold chakra system, which is part of their fivefold division of esoteric symbolism for categorising the Universe. The Tattvas correspond to the five lower chakras in the Indian scheme of energy centres, and to all five psychic centres of the Tibetan chakra scheme.

H.P. Blavatsky's Theosophical Society, based in Adyar, India, derived the bulk of their knowledge on Tattvas from Rama Prasad, who taught the Tattvic philosophy of the Hatha Yoga School. The Theosophists combined these teachings with those of the Esoteric Tibetan Buddhist tradition. On top of this they conjectured two more Tattvas, to make a total of seven, which allowed them to directly match the Tattvas to there sevenfold system, in particular to the seven Chakras.

The *Tattvas* they added were *Adi*, which is egg shaped, and *Anupadaka*, which is a crescent moon containing a radiant white sun.

The Hermetic Order of the Golden Dawn incorporated the Theosophical Tattva system, however discarding the sixth and seventh conjectured Tattvas, The Golden Dawn utilised Kapila's Sankhya Tattva system of 25 countercharges. This was the only Eastern concept that the Golden Dawn introduced into their system. It was perhaps influenced by the mention of Tattvas in Bulwer-Lytton's novel *Zanoni*, which was very likely the first mention of Tattvas in Western literature. In *Zanoni* the poisoning of the main character was neutralised by the magical visualization of the *Apas* Tattva.

The Golden Dawn system parallels the five Tattvas to the Western Doctrine of the 5 elements, the four primary elements and quintessence.

***The Tattvic Philosophy in Western Tradition:*** The neutrality of this section is disputed. Please see the discussion on the talk page.

The Tattvas are the astral form of the Elements, upon which the Physical elements are based. The process of how the Tattvic elements become manifest is a complex process, which will be described briefly below. In the Tattvic model a solar wind constantly streams forth from the Sun.

It is a partially electro-magnetic nitrous gas, which is very subtle and non-physical in nature (experiment show that the solar wind is mostly composed of high-energy electrons and protons). This is the Prana (*Life Matter*) of the Eastern Mysteries. The Earth's magnetic field captures this incorporeal nitre as the wind streams past our planet. This unmanifest substance circulates around the planet in a series of fivefold waves, each of which comprises five sub-waves. These waves are constantly rising and falling. It becomes more and more physical as it passes through our atmosphere. A salt is formed as this nitre passes through water vapour. This is "a most subtle virgin earth," the Prima Materia of the alchemists. Chemically if you could isolate pure $NO_3$ it would not form a salt on contact with water.

The Tattva flows start at sunrise and flow from Spirit, to Air, to Fire, to Water, to Earth. Each sub-Tattva takes four minutes and 48 seconds to transit a given spot, meaning it takes a total of 24 minutes for each main Tattva. Thus it takes a total of two hours for a primary flow of all five Tattvas to transit. The Earth's electromagnetic field and ley lines are vitalised by these currents. Current Scientific models suggests that earths magnetic field is best explained by Dynamo theory.

All five Tattvas are considered to be *aethers*. The atoms of the *aether* bring the atoms of the atmosphere into the necessary state of vibration for us to perceive it. Each of the Tattvic aethers is related to one of the five senses. Rama Prasad gives the example that Light is the manifestation of the Tejas Tattva (the luminiferous aether) within the atmosphere, that is, matter is brought into the correct visual vibration for us to perceive it. However, physicists and biologists have shown that vision works through a process of photons reflecting off objects and being detected by cells in the eye.

In *Nature's Finer Forces*, Tattvas are defined as the following: "a mode of motion; the central impulse, which keeps matter in a certain vibratory state; a distinct form of vibration.

Also, "every form and every motion is a manifestation of these Tattvas singly or in conjunction."

The first statement reflects what hermetic science states of the nature of the alchemical processes, that is, "*to raise the vibrations of matter*" and thus bring it into the condition of harmony, Quintessence. Modern Physics concurs with this ancient knowledge that all matter is energy at various vibratory rates.

The second statement, that all matter and motion is a manifestation of the Tattvas is a direct parallel with the Western Doctrine of Elements, which also asserts that all matter is comprised of varying proportions of the subtle elements.

The other direct parallel between the Eastern and Western systems is that Tattvic philosophy asserts that *Akasha* is the most important Tattva. *Akasha* is what Western Tradition calls *Spirit*, or Quintessence, and like the four base elements all deriving from *Spirit*, "it is out of Akasha that every form comes, and it is in Akasha that every form lives."

The Western Tradition's Doctrine of Elements is exemplified by the Enochian system of magic. Compared with the Tattvas, the Enochian system has been more intellectualised. This seems only natural in that (in psychological terms) the Western tradition is one of "thinking" and the Eastern tradition is one of "feeling."

Modern Enochian magicians have proposed a direct correlation between the Elements and the Forces of modern science. This is perhaps very relevant to the Tattvas, in that as "aethers" they are subtle and intangible, something that gives form to matter. Akasha/Spirit is correlated to the hypothesised "Superforce" of the Grand Unified Field theory of Relativity. Air and Fire are in juxtaposition in Enochian, compared to the Vayu and Tejas of Tattvic Philosophy, but are equated to the weak and strong nuclear forces of physics. Water/Apas is linked to electromagnetism and Earth/Prithivi is linked to Gravity.

***Symbols and Colours:*** Each of the Tattvas has a corresponding symbol and colour. These symbols differ from traditional Western symbols in shape and colour, and also vary slightly between the various Tattvic philosophies. Each of the Tattvas and their attributes will be described separately below.

Akasha The Akasha Tattva is associated with the spirit of Western Tradition and is the sonoriferous aether (sound). It is represented by some as a black or indigo Vesica Piscis, which is almond shaped. It represents the womb of the Universal Mother. In other versions, such as the Golden Dawn tradition, Akasha is symbolised by an oval or egg shape. Akasha is "every colour" or "clear." Black can also be seen as the absorption of all other colours, and its "flashing" (complementary) colour is luminous.

The quote given before, that Akasha is the most important Tatva, in that all forms come from and live in it, is of particular importance. The Akasha Tattva, when used as a "doorway" for scrying can allow one to scan for information within what Theosophists have termed the Akashic Record. The Akashic record contains, as the quote states, all forms. It could be compared with the "collective unconscious" of Jungian psychology. It contains all memories of human experience, but beyond it contains all future "history" in seed form.

Vayu or Pavan Vayu or Pavan is the tangiferous aether (touch). It is associated with the element of Air in Western Tradition. It is represented by a sky-blue circle.

Agni or Tejas Agni or Tejas is the luminiferous aether (sight/light/colour). It is associated with the element of Fire in Western Tradition. It is represented by a red equilateral triangle. The Fire of Tejas is considered to be Agni, which is the Vedic sacrificial fire and the interior fire of Kundalini Yoga.

Aap Aap is the gustiferous aether (taste). It is associated with the element of Water in Western Tradition. It is represented in the Tibetan version as a purple half circle. The Golden Dawn depicted Apas as a white or silver crescent, with the two points up.

Prithvi or Bhumi Prithvi or Bhumi is the odoriferous aether (smell). It is associated with the element of Earth in Western Tradition. It is represented by a yellow square.

The sub-Tattvas are represented by placing a smaller Tattvic symbol within the larger main Tattvic symbol. This gives a total of 25 Tattvas: Spirit of Spirit, Air of Spirit, Fire of Spirit, Water of Spirit, Earth of Spirit; Air of Air, Fire of Air, Water of Air, Earth of Air, Spirit of Air; Fire of Fire, Water of Fire, Earth of Fire, Spirit of Fire, Air of Fire; Water of Water, Earth of Water, Spirit of Water, Air of Water, Fire of Water; and Earth of Earth, Spirit of Earth, Air of Earth, Fire of Earth, Water of Earth.

Clairvoyance and the Tattvas Within the Western Tradition, the Tattvas are primarily used to help develop the faculty of astral clairvoyance.

The symbol of the Tattvas is placed upon cards. Sub-Tattvas are placed within the larger Tattva image. The process of scrying is started by sitting comfortably and gazing fixedly at the Tattvic symbol until it is thoroughly assimilated. The edges of the Tattvic symbol will appear luminous after several minutes, as the flashing (or complementary) colour appears on the retina. This complementary colour is considered to be the astral counterpart of the actual colour. While meditating on the chosen Tattva, one should also "feel" the attributes of the associated element, letting the entire consciousness be filled with the appropriate sensations. For example with the Vayu Tattva, one could imagine a breeze blowing around and through them, concentrating on how this airy breeze feels, smells, tastes and sounds.

Once the Tattva has been completely assimilated the card can be set aside and the eyes closed. The Tattvas symbol should appear in its flashing colour. This symbol serves as a doorway through which one travels. When entering through the symbol one should feel themselves pass through a 'veil' or membrane. Once on the other side, one should take a moment to adjust to their new surroundings, taking note of what the new surroundings consist of.

A guide can be summoned to accompany you on your exploration of the surroundings, who can explain aspects of the environment to you, and take you to important entities who live within the realm (According to 'safety' and 'protocol' various esoteric groups insist on the following: when first met, a guide should be tested with elemental signs, and the highest magickal names associated with the element. If the guide responds correctly to the signs, then it can be followed in good faith.) It is important to show all due courtesy to a guide, and thank it for its time and co-operation and bid it farewell. It is also of benefit to ask its permission to summon it again when you next return to this Tattva.

This initial entry point is also where one departs from, stepping backwards through the portal. Once back on the other side, one should visualise the portal closing.

This process is intended to allow one to enter into the actual element (Tattva flow), initially via "active imagination" and eventually by spontaneous clairvoyance. By scrying the astral current we are attempting to see beyond the material manifestation of an element by transmuting the physical Element into its astral state.

The intent is to learn about the vital principle, which the element represents. Within the astral this vital principle becomes perceptible to us as living beings of approximately human form. Everything within this astral environment is of a form and appearance that is highly symbolic of the meanings and intentions of what it represents. On the physical plane humans have obscured this process of dressing in a ways not symbolic of their true natures. Most animals however still retain a degree of symbolism, such as bright colours often representing the dangerous nature of the animal (especially in the case of tropical fish, tree frogs, and spiders).

On the astral, Elementals may masquerade for a while in deceptive form, buts its true form is always constant with its Element and character. (More from the 'traditions': To try and 'force' them into assuming their true form one can test them by using God Names, Grade/Elemental signs, Invoking/ Banishing forms of the Elemental pentagrams). Deep scanning of an entity's core ideals and feelings allows one to compare how it "feels" with how it "appears," and if the feelings don't match with its outward appearance then deception can be detected.

## Trimurti

In Hinduism, the Trimurti (also called *the Hindu Trinity*) is a concept that holds that God has three aspects, which are only different forms of one God. The three aspects of God, or "Parabrahman," or God's *personae* are as Brahma, Vishnu and Shiva. This Trimurti concept is a tenet most strongly held in Smartism, a denomination of Hinduism and rejected by other denominations of Hinduism, such as Vaishnavism. For example, the Dvaita school holds Vishnu alone to be the supreme God and Shiva as subordinate to Vishnu and interpret the Puranas differently. For example, Vijayindra Tirtha, a Dvaita scholar interprets the 18 puranas differently. He interprets that the Vaishnavite puranas as satvic and Shaivite puranas as Tamasic and and that only satvic puranas are considered to be authoritative.

- Brahma-the Source/Creator
- Vishnu-the Preserver/Indwelling-Life
- Shiva-the Transformer (Destroyer-Creator)

The Trimurti itself is conceived of as a deity and artistically represented as a three-faced human figure. Brahma is no longer as relevant as He once was in Hindu writing; some would say that focus on the aspect of the all-in-one Devi or of Shakti, the Divine Mother or God's Power personified, has replaced focus on the Source/Creator as Brahma.

According to the Trimurti belief, these three personae of God are simply different aspects of the one and the same God. In this manner, such beliefs are similar to some interpretations of the Christian Trinity such as Sabellianism.

Swami Sivananda, in his book, *All about Hinduism*, noted that "Brahma represents the creative aspect; Vishnu, the preservative aspect; and Shiva, the destructive aspect of Paramatman. These functions are akin to wearing different garbs on different occasions. For example, when you do the function of a judge, you put on one kind of dress. At home you wear another kind of dress. When you do worship in the temple, you wear another kind of dress. You exhibit different kinds of temperament on different occasions. Even so, the Lord does the function of creation when He is associated with Rajas Guna, and He is called Brahma. He preserves the world when He is associated with Sattva Guna, and He is called Vishnu. He destroys the world when He is associated with Tamas Guna, and He is called Shiva or Rudra."

A widely accepted belief is that it represents earth, water, and fire. The earth, or Brahma, is seen as the originator of all life and hence is regarded as the Creator. Water is the sustainer of life and hence is the Preserver and is represented as Vishnu. Fire transforms or consumes life and hence is the Destroyer and is represented as Shiva.

The Trimurti can also represent three individual forms on the different planes of consciousness. On the spiritual plane, the spiritual element is represented by Brahma, the mental/psychic element by Vishnu, and the physiological element by Shiva. On the mental/psychic plane, Brahma is the intuitive and creative thought, Vishnu is intelligence, and Shiva stands for emotions and feelings. The Sky as Brahma, the Sun as Vishnu and the Moon as Shiva form the earthly/physiological plane. Another representation by Adi Shankara, Shiva represents the Nirguna Brahman, Vishnu represents the Saguna Brahman and Brahma the Cosmic Mind.

Various phases of an individual's life are said to be represented by the Trimurti. The first of these phases, that of celibacy and studentship, (Brahmacharya Ashram) – is represented by Brahma. During this phase, knowledge is the individual's constant companion. Knowledge, in this conception, is represented by Goddess Saraswati, who is said to be the consort of Brahma. The second phase of adulthood and household (Grihastha Ashram) is represented by Vishnu. During this phase, the individual fulfils all religious and family obligations by involving oneself in generating wealth, which one uses to sustain oneself and one's family. During this phase wealth is the individual's companion and is represented by Vishnu's consort, Goddess Lakshmi. The third phase is that of old age (Vanaprastha Ashram) and is represented by Shiva. This phase marks the renunciation of one's worldly life for a life void of material pleasures, dedicated to the pursuit of true knowledge.

In ancient days, this typically marked the time when a householder, along with his wife, left their worldly belongings to spend their life in a forest, just like Lord Shiva leads a homeless life with only the essential belongings. The final phase (Sanyasa Ashram) the individual seeks to merge oneself with the Supreme power (Ishwara). One completes the process of renunciation and he along with his wife lead a life completely untouched by any attachments. The only occupation becomes deep meditation, leading to the individual becoming Ishwara Himself, with his wife as Ishwara's consort becoming the Universal Mother. The three phases of life, represented by the Trinity thus culminates into One underlining the fact that the three are in reality one and the same Ishwara.

In philosophical terms, Brahma is said to be associated with Divinity's Creative Ground of Being, Vishnu is said to be associated with Divinity's Emanated Idea (Logos, Wisdom, or Word), and Shiva is said to be associated with Divinity's Transformative Energy (Flame, Breath, or Spirit).

### *Evolution of Theology on the Hindu Trinity*

The definite settlement of the caste system and the Brahmanical supremacy must probably be assigned to somewhere about the close of the Brahmanas period. Division in their own ranks was hardly favorable to the aspirations of the priests at such a time; and the want of a distinct formula of belief adapted to the general drift of theological speculation, to which they could all rally, was probably felt the more acutely, the more determined a resistance the military class was likely to oppose to their claims. Side by side with the conception of the Brahman, the universal spiritual principle, with which speculative thought had already become deeply imbued, the notion of a Supreme Personal Being, the author of the material creation, had come to be considered by many as a necessary complement of the pantheistic doctrine.

But, owing perhaps to his polytheistic associations and the attributive nature of his name, the person of Prajapati seems to have been thought but insufficiently adapted to represent this abstract idea. The expedient resorted to for solving the difficulty was as ingenious as it was characteristic of the Brahmanical aspirations. In the same way as the abstract denomination of sacerdotalism, the neuter brahman, had come to express the divine essence, so the old designation of the individual priest, the masculine term brahma, was raised to denote the supreme personal deity which was to take the place and attributes of the Prajapati of the Brahmanas and Upanishads.

However the new dogma may have answered the purposes of speculative minds, it was not one in which the people generally were likely to have been much concerned; an abstract, colorless deity like Brahman could awake no sympathies in the hearts of those accustomed to worship gods of flesh and blood. Indeed, ever since the symbolical worship of nature had undergone a process of disintegration under the influence of metaphysical speculation, the real belief of the great body of the people had probably become more and more distinct from that of the priesthood. In different localities the principal share of their affection may have been bestowed on one or another of the old gods who was thereby raised to the dignity of chief deity; or new forms and objects of belief may have sprung up with the intellectual growth of the people.

In some cases even the worship of the indigenous population could hardly have remained without exercising some influence in modifying the belief of the Aryan race. In this way a number of local deities would grow up, more or less distinct in name and characteristics from the gods of theVedic pantheon.

There is, indeed, sufficient evidence to show that, at a time when, after centuries of theological speculations, some little insight into the life and thought of the people is afforded by the literature handed down to us, such a diversity of worship did exist.

Under these circumstances the policy which seems to have suggested itself to the priesthood, anxious to retain a firm hold in the minds of the people, was to recognize and incorporate into their system some of the most prominent objects of popular devotion, and thereby to establish a kind of creed for the whole community-subject to the Brahmanical law.

At the time of the original composition of the great epics two such deities,Shiva or Mahadeva (the greatgod) andVishnu, seem to have been already admitted into the Brahmanical system, where they have ever since retained their place; and from the manner in which they are represented in those works, it would, indeed, appear that both, and especially the former, enjoyed an extensiveworship. As several synonyms are attributed to each of them, it is not improbable that in some of these we have to recognize special names under which thcpeople in different localities worshipped these gods, or deities of a similarnature which, by the agency of popular poetry, or in some other way, came to be combined with them. The places assigned to them in the pantheistic system were coordinate with that ofBrahma; the three deities,Bráhma,Vishnu andShiva, were to represent a triple impersonation of the divinity, as manifesting itself respectively in the creation, preservation and destruction of the universe.

It is worthy of note that when theVedic triad of Soma, Agni and Vayu was still recognized, attempts are made to identifyShiva with Agni,-in one passage in theMahabharata it is stated that the Brahmins said that Agni wasShiva.

Although such attempts at an identification of the two gods remained isolated, they would at least seem to point to the fact that, in adapting their speculations to the actual state of popularworship, the Brahmans kept the older triad distinctly in view, and by means of it endeavoured to bring their new structure into harmony with the ancientVedic belief.

As regardsVishnu, thisgod occupies already a place in theVedic mythology, though by no means oneof such prominence as would entitle him to that degree of exaltation implied in his character as one of the three hypostases of the divinity. This belief is not universally held as there are many Vedic verses that utter the oppositive view, *i.e.*, Vishnu's supremacy as a personal supreme God. Moreover, although in his general nature, as a benevolent, genial being, the Vedic god corresponds on the whole to the later Vishnu, the preserver of the world, the latter exhibits many important features for which we look in vain in his prototype, and which most likely resulted from sectarian worship or from an amalgamation with local deities. In one or two of them, such as his names Vasudeva and Vaikuntha, an attempt may again be traced to identify Vishnu with Indra, who, as we have seen, was one of the Vedic triad of gods. The characteristic feature of the elder Vishnu is his measuring the world with his three strides, which are explained as denoting either the three stations of the sun at the time of rising, culminating and setting, or the triple manifestation of the luminous element, as the fire on earth, the lightning in the atmosphere and the sun in the heavens. This three strides corresponds with the events that took place when Vishnu incarnated as Vamana.

The male nature of the triad was supposed to require to be supplemented by each of the three gods being associated with a female energy (Shakti). Thus Sarasvati, the goddess of speech and learning, came to be regarded as the Shakti, or consort of Brahma; Sri or Lakshmi, beauty, fortune, as that of Vishnu; and Uma or Parvati, the daughter of Himavat, the god of the Himalaya mountain, as that of Siva. On the other hand, it is not improbable that Parvati, who has a variety of other names, such as Kali (the black one), Durga (the inaccessible one), Mahadevi (the great goddess) enjoyed already a somewhat extensive worship of her own, and that there may thus have been good reason for assigning to her a prominent place in the Brahmanical system.

A compromise was thus effected between the esoteric doctrine of the metaphysical and some of the most prevalent forms of popular worship, resulting in what was henceforth to constitute the orthodox system of belief of the Brahmanical community. Yet the Vedic pantheon could not be altogether discarded, forming part and parcel, as it did, of that sacred revelation (Sruti), which was looked upon as the divine source of all religious and social law, and being, moreover, the foundation of the sacrificial ceremonial on which the priestly authority so largely depended.

The existence of the old gods is, therefore, likewise recognized, but recognized in a very different way from that of the triple "revelation" of divinity. For while the triad represents the immediate manifestation of the eternal, infinite soul while it constitutes, in fact, the Parabrahman itself in its active relation to mundane and seemingly material occurrences, the old traditional gods are of this world, are individual spirits or portions of the Brahma-like men and other creatures, only higher in degree.

To them an intermediate sphere, the heaven of Indra (the svarloka or svarga), is assigned to which man may raise himself by fulfilling the holy ordinances; but they are subject to the same laws of being; they, like men, are liable to be born again in some lower state, and, therefore, like them, yearn for emancipation from the necessity of future individual existence. It is a sacred duty of man to worship these superior beings by invocations and sacrificial observances, as it is to honour the pitris (the fathers), the spirits of the departed ancestors.

***Turiya:*** In early Hindu philosophy, turiya (also called caturtha) is a state of pure consciousness, or the experience of ultimate reality and truth. It is a fourth state of consciousness that underlies and at the same time transcends three common states of consciousness: (i) the state of waking consciousness (jagrata), (ii) the state of dreaming (svapna), (iii) and dreamless sleep (*susupti*).

***Advaita Concept:*** The first two states are defective as experiences of reality and truth because of their flawed dualistic natures of subject and object, self and not-self, ego and non-ego. In the third state, dreamless sleep, one is not conscious of external or internal objects. But that does not mean consciousness is not present there. It is like saying 'I don't see anything in darkness'. The recognition that I don't see anything is what I 'see'. So also in dreamless sleep, one is not conscious of anything and the very fact that this statement is true proves the existence of consciousness during deep sleep.

In other words consciousness is the constant factor in all the three states and it is unaffected by the presence or absence of objects. Consciousness itself does not require to be revealed by another consciousness. It is self-revealed. While everything is presented to consciousness and is revealed by it, consciousness itself is not presented to anything else. It is never an object in relation to another subject. It is that which underlies both subject and object. It is the fourth, the turiya, the brahman. The Mandukya Upanishad defines turiya as follows:

*"The fourth state is not that which is conscious of the subjective, nor that which is conscious of the objective, nor that which is conscious of both, nor that which is simple consciousness, nor that which is all-sentient mass, nor that which is all darkness. It is unseen, transcendent, the sole essence of the consciousness of self, the completion of the world."*

***Four States of Consciousness:*** Turiya represents consciousness free from material influence. The idea is that consciousness, of which the atman is constituted, exists in our wakeful state of material experience, as it continues during sleep. In sleep we dream and experience the mental realm, whereas during our waking state the physical plane has more bearing on our lives.

Upon awakening from deep dreamless sleep one remembers existing in that condition. This is evidenced by the common expression, 'I slept well!' One cannot remember something one has no experience of. Thus in deep sleep when intelligence is transformed by tamo guna, the self continues to exist, as it does when intelligence is transformed by rajo guna during the dream condition and during the wakeful condition when intellect is transformed by sattva guna.

The self is thus independent of the body and mind. If the physical and mental realms were to shut down, the self would continue to exist. This we know from our experience in deep sleep. Realizing this involves entering the turiya.

***God as Turiya:*** Bhagavata Purana 11.15.16 describes Bhagavan with the words *turiyakhye* (the fourth), the meaning of which is found in the Bhagavad Gita 7.13:

*tribhir guna-mayair bhavair ebhih sarvam idam jagat*

*mohitam nabhijanati mam ebhyah param avyayam*

*"Deluded by the three [gunas], the whole world does not know Me, who am above them and inexhaustible."*

## Fifth State in Gaudiya Vedanta

The fourth dimension is the ground of our existence and the goal of all transcendentalists. For the Vedanta philosophers it is perceived variously, either as undifferentiated consciousness or a relationship with the divine. Regarding the latter, Gaudiya Vaishnava Theology concludes that love is greater than ourselves, and it is the greatest aspect of God, one that he himself is motivated by. For them, the nondual consciousness of Vedanta philosophy is realized when we know that we do not belong to ourselves, what to speak of anything belonging to us. If there is any time at which we can accurately say that something belongs to us, it is when, having given ourselves in love to God, we can say that "he is ours." Thus Gaudiya Vaishnavas are interested in *turyatitah gopala* (Lord Gopala beyond fourth dimension, Gopala-tapani Upanishad 2.96). This is the fifth dimension, in which one comes face to face with Gopala Krishna in Braj (Vraja Dhama), from adhoksaja to aprakrta, from God consciousness to Krishna consciousness. Jiva Gosvami elaborated on the turiya state in his Sandarbhas.

### *Guru-shishya Tradition*

The guru-shishya tradition (also guru-shishya *parampara* or lineage) is a spiritual relationship found within traditional Hinduism which is centered around the transmission of teachings from a *guru*. The term *shishya* roughly equates to the western term *disciple*, and in some parts of India is synonymous with the term *chela*. In a Hindu context, the term *guru* signifies one who teaches or imparts knowledge. Such knowledge, whether it be Vedic, Agamic art, architecture, music or spirituality, is imparted through the developing relationship between guru and disciple. The principle of this relationship is that knowledge, especially subtle or advanced knowledge, is best conveyed through a strong human relationship based on ideals of the student's respect, commitment, devotion and obedience, and on personal instruction by which the student eventually masters the knowledge that the guru embodies.

The guru-shishya relationship is a practice which has evolved into a fundamental component of Hinduism, since the beginning of the oral traditions of the Upanishads (c. 2000 BC). The term Upanishad derives from the Sanskrit words *upa* (near), *ni* (down) and sad (to sit)—"sitting down near" a spiritual teacher to receive instruction in the guru-shishya tradition.

An example of this dynamic can be found embodied in the relationship between Krishna and Arjuna in the Bhagavad Gita portion of the Mahabharata, and between Rama and Hanuman in the Ramayana. In the Upanishads, gurus and shishya appear in a variety of settings (husband answering questions about immortality, a teenage boy being taught by Yama, or Death personified, etc.). Sometimes the sages are women and at times the instructions(or rather inspiration) are sought by kings.

In the Vedas, the *Brahmavidya* or knowledge of Brahman is communicated from guru to shishya by word of mouth, bringing about the traditional guru-shishya *parampara*, or lineage.

The word Sikh is derived from the Sanskrit word shishya.

***Common Characteristics of the Guru-shishya Relationship:*** Within the broad spectrum of the Hindu religion, the guru-shishya relationship can be found in numerous variant forms including Tantra. Some common elements in this relationship include:

- The establishment of a spiritual teacher/student relationship between the guru and shishya.
- A formal recognition of this relationship, which usually assumes the form of a somewhat structured initiation ceremony. In this process the guru both accepts the initiate as a shishya, and also agrees to assume some level of responsibility for the spiritual well-being and progress of the new shishya. During this initiation process a meditation mantra is often taught to the new shishya.
- Sometimes this initiation process will also include the teaching of other esoteric wisdom and/or meditation techniques.

- Gurudakshina-The *shishya* giving a valuable to the *guru* as a token of gratitude, often, apart from his services, the only monetary or otherwise fees that the student gives. Such tokens can be as simple as a fruit to as serious as a thumb as given by *Ekalavya* to his *guru Dronacharya*.

***Guru-shishya Relationship Types:*** Amongst Guru-shishya relationships, there is a certain range of variation of the levels of authority that may be attributed to the guru. This level of authority ranges from the highest levels of authority as most often found in bhakti yoga, such as the Sathya Sai Baba movement, to the lowest levels, as found in the Pranayama forms of yoga such as in the Sankara Saranam movement. Between these two ends of the spectrum there are innumerable variations in degree and form of that authority.

***Advaita Vedanta:*** Advaita vednta requires anyone seeking to study advaita vedanta to do so from a Guru (*teacher*). The Guru must have the following qualities (see Mundaka Upanishad 1.2.12):

1. Srotriya — must be learned in the Vedic scriptures and sampradaya
2. Brahmaniþha—literally meaning *established in Brahman*; must have *realised* the oneness of Brahman in everything and in himself

The seeker must serve the Guru and submit questions with all humility in order to remove all doubts (see Bhagavad Gita 4.34). By doing so, advaita says, the seeker will attain moksha (*liberation from the cycle of births and deaths*).

## Sruti Tradition

The Guru-shishya tradition plays an important part in the continuation of the Shruti tradition in Vaidika dharma. The Hindus believe that Vedas are handed down through the ages from Guru to shishya. The Vedas prescribe for a young brahmachari to be sent to a Gurukul where the Guru (referred to also as acharya) teaches the pupil the Vedas as also the Vedangas. The pupil is also taught the prayoga to perform yajnas. The term of stay varies (Manu Smriti says the term may be 12 years, 36 years or 48 years). After the stay at the Gurukul the brahmachari returns home after performing a ceremony called samavartana.

The word Srauta is derived from the word Sruti meaning that which is heard. The Srauta tradition of handing the Vedas down the generations consisted in solely of oral tradition from Guru (teacher) to the Sishya (student). But of late many Vedic scholars make use of books in order to teach the Vedas to their students.

**3**

# National Righteousness

What is an akhara? It is a place of recreation for youth. It is a shrine of strength where earth is turned into gold. It is a sign of masculinity and the assembly hall of invigorated youth. Strength is measured against strength and moves and counter moves are born and develop. An akhara should be in an open area where fresh air and sunshine mingle. It should be away from dirt and filth and in a place where the earth is soft. It should be set off by a boundary of some sort and surrounded by thick foliated trees. There should be water nearby.

One should enter the akhara after paying obeisance and offering up incense to the Lord. An akhara is where one prays and where offerings are given and distributed. Its earth is saluted and taken up to anoint one's shoulders and head. And then one wrestles and the sound of slapping thighs and pounding chests fills the air. Grunts and groans of exertion echo ominously. One trounces and in turn is trounced. Exercise is done. Laziness and procrastination are drowned in sweat. The earth is mixed and finally one salutes the pit and leaves.

## Aesthetics

The spatial layout of an akhara is important insofar as it produces a geomantic aura of invigorating peace and tranquility. The ideal location for an akhara is a cool, clean, quiet area where one can get away from both an atmosphere of domestic obligation and an environment of work. One can well imagine the importance of such a place in the crowded environment of urban India. However, the aesthetic ideals apply equally to rural as well as urban akharas. On entering the compound of a number of different akharas, I was asked if I could sense an aura of shant (peace and tranquillity). Indicating the shade of a tree, the aroma of freshly moistened earth and the coolness of a refreshing breeze, wrestling friends would abandon themselves to a reverie of cathartic relaxation. Indeed, it seemed that many who came to Akhara Ram Singh and the other akharas I visited regularly did so in much the same way that one might visit a health spa. Older men came to relax before going to work and younger boys would rest on their way to school. People with minor ailments-constipation, arthritis, backaches, skin infections, bruises, and sprains-came to the akhara hoping to effect a cure. Wrestling-pit earth and akhara well water are both regarded as tonics which help to cure a host of common ailments. In many ways the earth pit functions much like a mineral bath that has a reputation for healing. Many wrestlers I spoke with claimed that they had at one time or another suffered some debilitating illness-rheumatism, consumption, heart weakness, high blood-pressure, kidney stones and that after visiting an akhara and lying in the earth had been restored to perfect health.

Akharas have a definite aesthetic appeal. Their visual tone is picturesque. Consider, for example, Akhara Bara Ganesh in the Lohatia bazaar of Benaras. The akhara is not visible from the main street, but its location is marked by the bright green leaves of a tall pipal tree and the thicker darker mass of a young nim.

As the name implies, Lohatia bazaar is a metal market and the main cobblestone road which runs through the market is lined with encroaching shops that sell thick-slatted parrot cages, buffalo tethering spikes, drum-sized cauldrons for boiling milk, and ladles whose size would match the cutlery of Ravana's kitchen. Anvils, arc-welders, and rivet wrenches spark, flash, and grind as contractors turn out dozens of bathtub-size feeding troughs, evaporative air-coolers, and meter upon meter of chain link.

Heading towards Maidagin and the old central post office, one turns left off the main road down a gali (narrow lane) which leads toward Bara Ganesh temple. A high river-rock retaining wall parallels the left side of the gali which leads directly up to a niche-shrine dedicated to lord Hanuman. Seated in the niche, a man reads verses from Tulasi Das's epic poem Ramacharitamanasa and dispenses Ganga river water and Prasad (ritually blessed food offerings) to men on scooters on their way to work and to women returning home with bottles of milk, who stop to pay homage to the Lord. Hawkers of marigold garlands, incense, jasmine flowers, and other ritual paraphernalia line the small path that turns left at the niche shrine and winds its way to the gates of Ganesh's temple. Beggars mirror the hawkers on the opposite side of the path and benevolently accept alms from those in search of grace. The path continues a short way beyond the temple gates until a short flight of stairs leads one up to the left, through an arch, and into the akhara grounds.

*Bara Ganesh Akhara* is situated on a flat bluff twelve meters above the main Lohatia bazaar and some six meters above Ganesh's temple. The retaining wall demarcates two edges of the compound, and buildings set off the other two sides, making a rough rectangle some forty meters long and seventeen meters wide. Although the akhara is raised above the street and the temple gate, buildings, spires, and crenellations frame the grounds and shade the pit from all but the mid-day sun.

Walking up the stairs and through the arch, one directly faces the main Hanuman temple of the akhara complex. The temple building itself is new: a modern, square, flat-roofed brick and concrete construction, lime-washed yellow. The image of Hanuman—who is serviced by a semiresident priest-dates back to antiquity; I was told, "There is not another one like it in Benaras." The grounds of the akhara are ample, and since the guru of Akhara Bara Ganesh is both a dairy farmer and a purveyor of sheet metal, the area in front of the temple is used as a buffalo corral and a storage area for tin tubs, water tanks, buckets, roofing material, and sundry other items. Lallu Pahalwan, the guru of the akhara, can be found every morning sitting on his cot among his buffalos dispensing fresh milk from two polished tin buckets. Just beyond the buffalos and tin tubs is a brick water drain, which marks an important spatial boundary. On the temple side of the drain the ground is covered with stubbly grass, bits of old metal, buffalo dung, sleeping dogs, and playing children. In sharp contrast, the opposite side of the drain is smooth, flat, hard-packed earth from which playing children and wandering dogs are unceremoniously chased. This is where the akhara precinct begins.

The akhara precinct is almost completely shaded by two large trees: a thick, broad nim that hangs low over the pit and a tall pipal that rises above the well. Under the shade of these trees, in the shadow of bazaar buildings, set against the temple skyline, stands the pit. It is the focal point of the akhara complex. Seven by seven meters square and a quarter-meter high, the soft red earth forms a large raised arena. Six cement columns stand at the four corners and at the center of two sides, supporting a tin roof which creates a canopy under the heavy branches of the nim. The columns are thickset, made of poured concrete and painted yellow. Each one is decorated with a mural drawing: a thickset wrestler lifting a nal (stone weight) over his head; another wrestler swinging a pair of joris; two wrestlers locked together measuring each other's strength; Lord Hanuman flying through the air carrying a mountain in one hand and a mace in the other; Shiva bedecked in peacock feathers holding a flaming jori in either hand. Vases of flowers supported on the backs of jumping monkeys decorate the inner face of the four corner columns. Intertwined blue cobras drinking from bowls of milk are juxtaposed on the centre posts.

On the temple side of the akhara, overlooking the lane where mendicants and lepers beg for alms and under the thickest branches of the nim, stands a short, thick, stone dais. Lallu Pahalwan can often be found reclining on the cool, hard stone holding audience with merchants, mendicants, and members of his family while casting a benevolent yet critical eye on his practicing disciples. As Lallu reclines and his wards grapple, rhesus monkeys, in their haste to get a share of Prasad at the temple, occasionally abandon the branches of the nim and race thunderously across the tin roof of the pit beating a tattoo matched only by the labourers in the gali below, who pound sheet metal into popsicle molds, leaf springs, and saw blades. The sound of monkeys on the roof, the gali, horns and bicycle bells on the road, prayer gongs in the temple, and ubiquitous loudspeakers broadcasting popular film songs and praises to the gods all blend into a distant cacophonous refrain that both envelopes and sets the akhara apart, if only by contrast and juxtaposition.

Across the pit from the guru's dais is a larger, wide stone bench used by the elder members of the akhara, who come to relax and watch the younger members practice. Behind this, and raised up half a meter, is a one-room cement building used to store exercise equipment, house visiting wrestlers, and change clothes, and to exercise and massage when the monsoon rains turn the hard-packed earth to mud. Rooted at the opposite corner of the pit from the nim, the pipal tree is set in tiered, concentric circles of poured concrete. Built onto this in the lee of the trunk is a small, brightly painted shrine dedicated to the memory of a neighbourhood saint. As the story goes, even after the saint's death his form could be seen wandering around after dark. Once a curious neighbour followed the form and saw it disappear into the trunk of the pipal. A shrine was erected in propitiation, and a few devotees come regularly to make offerings and ask for boons. The figure of the saint, who stands behind the iron gate of the shrine in a pose of contemplative prayer, is blessed, on occasions, by the akhara priest.

The akhara well is sunk behind the pipal. Being on high ground, the well is deep and the water cool. A large bucket suspended from a cantilevered pully is used to draw water. Set into the edge of the well and along the base of the pipal is a large, green, moss-lined cement trough used to hold water drawn from the well. A spigot at the base of the trough allows the water to drain into the bathing area, and from there out through the drain that marks the boundary of the akhara precinct and into the toilet at the far edge of the compound.

To appreciate the aesthetics of the space I have described above, it is necessary to take the perspective of an akhara member. Consider, for example, Amru Dada, who owns an extensive gold and silver business with a shop in the heart of the crowded Chauk Bazaar area of old Benaras. The shop is set in a narrow, busy gali off the main road. Though large as such shops go, it is cramped and confined. It is hot, and the air is redolent with incense, smoke, raw sewage, and dust. Amru Dada tends the shop from ten in the morning until eight or nine at night.

The clean, cool air, soft earth, shaded light, and cold, fresh well water of the akhara stand in sharp contrast with the thick, dense smells and harsh sounds of urban life that waft and resonate in the back galis. For Amru Dada the akhara is a retreat. It is also a much-needed escape for other wrestlers who labour as dairy farmers, clerks in government offices, cooks and waiters in hotels and sweet shops, dry-goods merchants, policemen, railway personnel, hotel managers, military recruits, and pan hawkers. The akhara is, as many were fond of telling me, eagerly in animated tones and pointed gestures and, at other times, in hushed, dreamy, relaxed voices, "a world unto itself," a place set apart from the world of work and family, a peaceful place from which to draw strength. Atreya describes the aura of his akhara at Kuthal Gate, Dehra Dun district: "Upon arriving at this place one will feel a mood of self-reflection. Thoughts will turn from instinct and mundane concerns to more philosophical questions. The place is charged with an atmosphere of metaphysical reflection".

Earth, air, water, and trees are the essential features which give an akhara its aesthetic appeal. The ambiance of an akhara, however, is greater than the sum of these individual parts. Although there are no rules that govern the spatial layout and geomantic ordering of trees relative to earth, air, and water, there is a sense that together they must comprise a picturesque integrated whole: a tableau of mutually dependent elements. The roots of the trees mingle with the water of the well; the air is cooled by the shade of the trees and is scented by their leaves. The earth is bound by the roots of the trees and, like the water, it draws on the ineffable essence of the trees and imparts to them the resources of growth. The water dampens and cools the earth, and the earth keeps the water fresh. The interdependence of natural elements reinforces a notion of the akhara as self-contained, an aesthetic world unto itself.

Malla Purana (Sandesara and Mehta 1964) describes in some detail the exact dimensions of various types of wrestling pits-square, rectangular and round. This text also elabourates upon the quality of the pit earth, emphasising that colour and texture are important and that it must be "pleasing to see and as soft as that required for seed laying" (ibid: 21). Sandesara and Mehta note that the mallas (wrestlers) of contemporary Gujarat mix various substances-buttermilk, oil, red ochre-into the earth to enhance its quality and texture (ibid: 26). At various akharas I have heard wrestlers talk of times when baskets full of rose petals and bottles of fragrant perfume would be added to the pit. Turmeric is often mixed into the earth to enhance its healing properties (Vaishya 1975). The earth of the pit is the nexus of the akhara complex as a whole: it is the distillate of the compound's physical elements and of its cultural meaning as well. The earth is the essence of strength.

The balance of earth, wind, water, and trees is best exemplified by *Akhara Bari Gaivi*. Bari Gaivi is as much a "therapeutic" akhara as it is an active wrestling gymnasium. Most people who come to the akhara do so to drink the tonic water of the central well, which has a national reputation for curing gastrointestinal maladies. In addition to a wrestling pit and exercise area, Bari Gaivi has a well-established temple complex.

The akhara used to be outside the city limits in a thick forested area. Now the city has encroached on the akhara, drawing it into a more urban environment. Nevertheless, the akhara grounds are clearly demarcated from the surrounding area. On the periphery of the grounds is a broad, sandy plain dotted with low scrub bushes. This plain serves a very important function in defining the akhara space, for it is the disha maidan (open area) where people go to defecate before exercising or drinking the well water. Defecation has a very positive aesthetic appeal in the routine of akhara attendance. It puts one in the mood to exercise or relax, I was told, by marking off both time and space. In effect, defecation is a form of socio-somatic punctuation that indicates a transitional pause between the world of work and the world of the akhara. On a number of occasions when I visited akharas I was asked whether I would like to defecate. Such inquiries were made in a very matter-of-fact manner, much as one might expect to be asked if a cup of tea would be in order at 4:30 in the afternoon. The sandy band of ground around Akhara Bari Gaivi thus serves as a topographical boundary and as a place to move from one state of body/mind to another.

Moving in concentrically from the band of sand, one finds five or six small ponds of swampy water that encircle the akhara precinct. The water in these marshy ponds is used by those who defecate to clean themselves before coming into the akhara proper. These swampy ponds serve as an important classificatory boundary, for they mark off the clean from the unclean in terms both of a personal physical condition and geographical space.

Inside the ring of pond water, up on a bluff, is a grove of trees which shade a small dharmashala (pilgrim rest-house), a large marble Hanuman temple, a new cement temple dedicated to Shiva, numerous small shrines honouring saints and lesser local godlings, the tin-roofed pit, exercise area, and large cement platform used for resting, dressing, and discussion. The focal point of the akhara is a deep well from which only the presiding guru is allowed to draw water. This well water is said to be very powerful. Its draws its strength from the geomancy of the area, particularly the unique soil, the specific configuration of trees, and its proximity to the Ganga. No one may use this water for bathing.

It is only for drinking, and one must drink it in litre draughts rather than by the glass. (This is said to be part of the prescription even for those who drink the water as a tonic rather than as a cure.) I was asked numerous times how I felt after drinking the water: "Has it settled your stomach?" "Do you feel different?" "Isn't it fresh and cooling?" In effect, ingestion of the well water, which is the nexus of the akhara, is an internalisation of the essence of the akhara, a kind of geomantic sacrament. In this respect it provides a harmonic symmetry to the defecation in the sandy field. It further puts one in touch with the ineffable aura of the akhara space. Evacuation on the periphery of the space is balanced and reflected-in inversion-by internalisation at its hub. The body of the wrestler, or of any other akhara visitor, mirrors through its action the spatial layout of the akhara.

Next to the drinking well at Bari Gaivi is a large sunken tank from which water is drawn to dampen the ground and settle the compound dust. There is also a separate well used exclusively for washing clothes and bathing. This system of hydraulic classification—swampy water to clean one's anus, water to dampen the ground, water to wash one's self and one's clothes, and water to drink-serves to structure akhara space and one's movement through this space.

After work many men come to the akhara from all over the city of Benaras simply to defecate, drink some water, bathe, change clothes, and talk with friends. In this social context of camaraderie, the atmosphere and mood of the akhara space is everything, for it charges these "simple pleasures" with therapeutic significance. The mood and aesthetic appeal of the akhara environment is captured in the term anand (satisfaction) which is used to summarise the feeling that one comes to the akhara to experience (cf. Kumar 1986, 1988).

Parallel to the picturesque aesthetic of the akhara is its sanctity and purity. The akhara is not only clean and pure in a physical sense, but it is also a holy place. The soil of the akhara is most pure, as it represents the essence of Mother Earth. Water is naturally pure in Hindu cosmology, but the water of an akhara well is considered purer than most. Similarly, pipal, banyan, and nim trees have general religious and ritual importance (R. Dixit 1967; R. Sharma n.d.), but those on akhara grounds are charged with extra significance.

Every akhara has at least one shrine dedicated to Lord Hanuman. This shrine is the focus of akhara religious activity. The image of Hanuman is cleaned at least twice a week and is anointed with sindur (vermilion paste). His "clothes" are cleaned regularly, offerings are made to him twice a week, he is prayed to every morning when his blessing is invoked, and he is saluted whenever someone enters or leaves the akhara. Most akharas have numerous shrines and temples dedicated to a host of gods, goddesses, godlings, and saints. Lingams are often found either in shrines by themselves, at the base of trees, or in conjunction with small images of Hanuman.

Many akharas also have a shrine dedicated to the founding guru. For instance, the images of Munni Pahalwan in Delhi and Sant Ram in Benaras are life-size figures accorded a central position in their respective akhara pantheons (see plate 13). The founders of many akharas are reputed to have been superhuman, saintly men who possessed great spiritual and physical strength by virtue of their strict adherence to a wrestling regimen of diet, exercise, and religious faith.

Akhara temples and shrines are serviced by informal functionaries who serve as semi resident priests. Even predicated with the qualifiers "informal" and "semi resident" the term priest denotes a much too well-defined and structured role for what is, in fact, a purely ad-hoc situation. A few examples will illustrate the point.

On Tuesdays and Saturdays, the two days sacred to Hanuman, two men come to the Akhara Ram Singh temple and offer Prasad of crystallized sugar and soaked chana to the image of the Lord. This Prasad is distributed among the wrestlers (who often demand a second handful) and the two men then return to their respective jobs, one as cloth merchant and the other as coal trader. The two men are "religiously disposed" to the extent that they spend a great deal of their time reading scriptures and listening to the teachings of itinerant sannyasis who hold forth in a nearby public park. That they service the akhara temple is, however, purely coincidental and is neither mandated nor expected.

Baba Bhole Das, a sannyasi, has taken up residence and responsibility for the two large and elabourately decorated images of Lord Hanuman at Gaya Seth Akhara. He goes about his task of washing and bathing the images while chanting softly to himself. Devotees who are not wrestlers come and sing with Babaji on occasion, but for the most part he goes about his business with little regard for the wrestling routine that structures akhara life. Because Babaji is a mendicant it is his prerogative to service the akhara temple, but it is also his prerogative to go on indefinite pilgrimage or to simply move on to some other place.

Sonu Maharaj of Ram Kund Akhara is a dry-goods merchant. At sixty-two he has shifted his orientation away from his small business and toward devotion and a routine of contemplative prayer. He comes to the akhara every morning with a bundle of jasmine and marigold flowers and lights a lamp and stick of incense in front of the figures of Hanuman, Shiva and Parvati, Ganesh, and Surnath. Having blessed and garlanded each image he bows to the rock-bench, which symbolises the founding guru. He then digs the pit and calls on some of the younger members to wrestle with him. Sonu affects the long hair of a mendicant, and his social orientation is clearly otherworldly.

There are many other examples of men who have taken it on themselves to serve as the guardians of akhara shrines. Many of these men, like the wrestlers themselves, have oriented their lives away from everyday concerns of wealth and property and towards spiritual contemplation. Baba Shyam Lal of Bara Ganesh donates his annual earnings as a metal merchant to the poor. Such men bring a sense of religious purpose to the akharas they serve.

To some extent it may be said that akhara temple functionaries shoulder the burden of religious duty for all akhara members. This is particularly the case at Dharmsangh, Aghornath Takiya, Bari Gaivi, and other akharas affiliated with large institutionalised religious centres. Despite the religiosity of these akharas the role of temple "priest" is surprisingly marginal to the wrestling activities.

When I spoke to the mahant (abbot, head priest) of the Aghornath Takiya complex it was apparent that he did not pay much attention to what went on in the akhara itself. He was actively involved in philosophical contemplation and metaphysical research and came into contact with the members of the akhara only when arti puja was performed every evening at eight. Beyond this he was not interested in the regimen the wrestlers followed.

An akhara as a whole may be considered to be a religious environment where exercise and wrestling are acts of devotion to a way of life. This is not meant in some abstract sense, for a literal parallel is drawn between the rote recitation of prayer and the repetitive exercise routines performed every morning by wrestlers. Both require the same mindset and concentration. The very act of wrestling is charged with religious significance. As the institutionalised icons of formal religion, temples and shrines on akhara grounds serve to enhance a general feeling of commitment to an idealised way of life. All wrestlers are responsible for the akhara's environment of religiosity, and they affect this as much through exercise as through washing the temple steps or lighting a votive lamp in the niche of a shrine.

An akhara pantheon is eclectic and extensive, and there is a regular regime of obeisance and ritualised prayer. However, there is not a rich or textured mystical appreciation for "things religious." Hanuman, for instance, is a real part of the akhara complex, and as such his role is set and established. He marks certain attitudes and reaffirms precedents. For all his importance, however, he does not evoke an attitude of mystery or esoteric and problematic questions of theological faith. In a religious sense, Hanuman is a practical and pragmatic figure. Wrestlers do not discuss in any great detail or trouble themselves unduly over Hanuman's metaphysical significance. What is important about him is self-evident and is regarded by wrestlers as comfortably mundane. When I asked about the significance of sindur, for instance, I was told that it was put on Hanuman in the same way that wrestlers put on oil: as an invigorating tonic and a mark of beauty. Similarly, prayers, offerings, and salutes to Hanuman are all interpreted in a generic sense as various forms of showing respect. Such acts are neither complex nor esoteric. As such they provide a deeply felt multidimensional psychological rootedness. A wrestler's general attitude is antimystical, where devotion is a holistic, pragmatic, and unambiguous way of life.

The religious life of the akhara complex is an important part of wrestling culture; yet prayer, obeisance, and other ritual events, while emotive, are not ecstatic. Nor are acts of propitiation, in and of themselves, charged with complex significance. However much temples, shrines, lamps, garlands, and incense create an atmosphere of sanctity, these things do not indicate that formal religion subsumes akhara life. It does not define the boundaries of wrestling life, but it does, as will be shown, provide a strong baseline for the construction of personal identity. While pervasive, religion is supplementary, and so one is more often than not religious as a wrestler rather than a wrestler who happens to be religious.

## Daily Routine

The details of daily routine vary somewhat from one akhara to another. Nevertheless, it is possible to discern some general patterns. Though not followed to the letter, important rules define wrestling as a comprehensive discipline. A wrestler's quotidian schedule is not strictly or dogmatically defined. Rules read more like a lexicon than a litany in the sense that what is ordered and given structure is not an outline per se but a scheme of elabouration. One is not solely enjoined to do something; how it is to be done, why it is efficacious, and where it fits, etiologically, in the larger scheme of things is equally important.

A wrestler is enjoined to wake at three in the morning, when the air is pure and cool. After drinking a glass of water with lime juice, he is to go out into a forest area or scrub jungle and relieve himself. As Ratan Patodi writes, although a wrestler is not a doctor, he should inspect his feces in order to evaluate his health. If it "is coiled like a snake about to strike" then his digestion is in good order. However, if it is loose, then he should consult his guru about a dietary change (1973a: 24-25). Daily and regular evacuation of the bowels is also prescribed by Mujumdar (1950), for "if the bowels are not clean, blood becomes impure and easily leads to disease" (ibid: 675).

Following evacuation, and before the sun rises, a wrestler should brush his teeth. This must be done before dawn because the warmth of the sun turns the food particles in the mouth into poison which can cause illness and indigestion. Moreover, the strong ultraviolet light of the sun can cause a wrestler's vision to blur while he squats down to brush his teeth. Generally speaking, the cleaner one's teeth, the sharper one's vision. Patodi further details rules for dental hygiene:

One should only brush for five or six minutes otherwise the gums will be severely damaged. God has placed two glands beneath the tongue which produce saliva and aid considerably in mastication and digestion. Excessive brushing can cause a reduction in the amount of saliva produced, and this will adversely affect digestion. One can use either babul or nim twigs for brushing, but one should not always use nim. It is astringent and can burn one's mouth. The toasted skin of almonds is also a good tooth powder. I have seen that some people use burnt tobacco and snuff but these tend to tarnish the natural brightness of one's teeth. It should also be remembered that after brushing one side of the mouth, one should rinse before brushing the other side. This prevents the germs of decay on one side from spreading to the teeth on the other side (ibid: 25-26).

Of course, these prescriptions are not exclusively devised for wrestlers. Much of what wrestlers do as concerns personal hygiene and diet derives from Ayurvedic principals and other traditions of health and healing. Here, however, I am only concerned with the mechanical aesthetic of the acts that structure a wrestler's day, and not with the "natural economy" of health per se. For a wrestler, brushing is an important part of an integrated daily regime. Mujumdar is no less specific than Patodi in prescribing a regime of dental hygiene for wrestlers. The following passage illustrates the fine detail and mechanical exactness of what is a very small part of a larger intricate system.

The toothbrush (Dantakashtha) should be made of a fresh twig of a tree or a bush grown on a commendable tract and it should be straight, not worm-eaten, devoid of any knots, or utmost with one knot only and should be the width of twelve fingers in length and like the small finger in girth. The potency and strength of the twig [toothbrush] should be determined by or varying according to the season of the year and the preponderance of any particular Dosha in the physical temperament of its user. The twig of a plant possessed of any of the four tastes-sweet, bitter, astringent, and pungent-should be the only kind collected and used. Nim is the best of all bitter trees, Khadira of the astringent ones, Madhuk of the sweet, and Karanja of the pungent ones. The teeth should be daily cleaned with [a compound consisting of] honey, powdered tri-katu, tri-varga, tejovati, Saindhava and oil. Each tooth should be separately cleansed with the cleansing paste applied on [the top of the twig bitten into the form of] a soft brush and care should be taken not to hurt the gums anyways during rubbing....

The use of a thin, smooth and flexible foil of gold, silver or wood, ten fingers in length is commended for the purpose of cleansing the tongue by scraping. This gives relief and removes bad taste, foetor, swelling, and numbness of the mouth (1950: 675).

A regular feature of the morning activities at Akhara Ram Singh would be for a junior wrestler to climb up the large nim tree and carefully select a number of twigs for the senior wrestlers to use. Senior wrestlers who no longer engage in wrestling practice would come to the akhara and brush their teeth with careful, if somewhat distracted, precision as they watched the younger wards grapple.

After a wrestler has brushed his teeth, he must bathe before entering the akhara. As one person put it, "One can and should bathe at any time of day, but the morning bath is the most purifying." Not only does the morning bath make a person pure enough to enter the akhara precinct, but it also "removes somnolence, body heat and fatigue. It allays thirst and checks itching and perspiration, brings on a fresh relish for food, removes all bodily impurities, clears the sense organs, gladdens the mind, purifies the blood, increases the appetising power, destroys drowsiness and sinful thoughts, and increases semen. The sight of a man is invigorated by applying cold water to the head at the time of bathing, while the pouring of warm water on the head tends to injure the eyesight" (ibid: 679). Bathing in cold water invigorates the body in winter and cools it in the summer. One should not bathe in very cold water when the air temperature is cold, or hot water when it is hot. This upsets the balance of the bodily humours. After bathing a wrestler should rub his body lightly with oil before starting his morning regime of physical exercise and practice.

Bathing, of course, has important ritual implications as well. The akhara compound is pure, and one must wash away the impurities accrued to the body through secular everyday life-sleeping, eating, urinating, and defecating—before entering the precinct. When visiting akharas I was often asked whether or not I had bathed. An answer in the affirmative ensured admittance. In the wrestler's mind there is only a very vague line, if any, between the health and ritual dimension of the morning bath. Religious qualities are somatically coded, and if one is impure, one is also unhealthy.

Physical training is the focal point of a wrestler's daily routine and will be considered in detail in a later chapter. In outline, however, a wrestler starts his regime by running a few kilometres. He then digs the pit and wrestles with a number of partners. The routine concludes with a series of gymnastic and aerobic exercises. The whole schedule takes some two and a half hours.

After exercising, a wrestler rubs his body with the earth of the akhara to dry his perspiration. This prevents his body from cooling too rapidly, and thus guards against illness. While resting, he is rubbed down. As the earth dries on his skin it is scraped off by other wrestlers. By the time the earth is scraped, the body is cool enough for the wrestler to bathe.

It is vitally important that a person not bathe while still hot, for this will inevitably enrage the body and cause serious illness. A wrestler must urinate before bathing in order to relieve the body's inner heat. I was often caught out on this fine point of keeping fit as wrestlers at Akhara Ram Singh kept a more watchful eye on my movements than I was apt to do myself. On a few occasions I witnessed other wrestlers who, on the verge of bathing, suddenly realised that they had not yet urinated. They would quickly retire to a nearby wall, set things right, and thereby ensure better health.

The whole body is anointed with mustard oil after bathing. This gives the skin a glossy radiance and a soft, uniform texture. It prevents it from drying out and scaling. It also combines with the natural odors of the body to produce a pleasant, clean fragrance. The application of oil to the body is an important part of massage, an integral part of the exercise regime, and will be given due consideration in a later chapter. Some of the efficacious qualities of oil should be mentioned here, however, since anointing the body—as distinct from a full massage—is an important part of the daily routine.

Anointing the head with oil is a good cure for the affections of the head. It makes the hair grow luxuriantly and imparts thickness, softness, and a dark gloss to them. It soothes and invigorates the head and sense organs and removes the wrinkles of the face. Combing the hair improves its growth, removes dandruff and dirt and destroys the parasites of the scalp. Pouring oil [Karna-purana] into the cavities of the ears is highly efficacious in pains of the jaw, and acts as a good cure for headache and earache. Anointing the feet with oil, etc. brings on sleep. It is refreshing and invigorating to the body and sight, removes all drowsiness and sense of fatigue and softens the skin of the soles of the feet. Anointing the body imparts a glossy softness to the skin, guards against the aggravation of the Vayu [wind] and the kapha [phlegm], improves the colour and strength and gives a tone to the root-principles [dhatus] of the body. The use of oil at a bath causes the oil to penetrate into the system through the mouths of the arteries, veins of the body, as [sic] also the roots of the hair, and thus soothes and invigorates the body with its own essence (ibid: 676).

Wrestlers are enjoined to shave and cut their nails regularly. As Mujumdar notes, this leads to the "expiation of one's sins, makes a man cheerful, and tends to appease his fate, increase his energy and impart a lightness to his frame" (ibid: 678). Clearly here there is a dramatic intersection of somatic practices, personality traits, auspiciousness, and karmic balance. In Benaras the English term "personality" was often used to denote such an intersection of physical health, beauty, and reputable character. Having bathed, wrestlers offer prayers to Lord Hanuman. After dressing they show their respect to the guru by touching his feet. Asking his blessing, they leave the akhara.

A person must not eat or drink for two full hours after exercising. A wrestler's diet is an integral part of his regime. From roughly nine 'o'clock, when the morning practice session ends, until four 'o'clock, when the evening exercise routine begins, a wrestler must rest, eat, and sleep. Although this is a "passive" part of the wrestler's regime, it is important for his recuperation and physical development.

As everyone is quick to point out, to relax all day long is an unrealistic prescription given modern priorities and work schedules. It is nevertheless an ideal that is taken very seriously. After morning practice most wrestlers go to work or to school. Many complain that there is not enough time for proper training and that they are too tired to study or work. Anand, a wrestler at Akhara Ram Singh, bicycles almost fifteen miles a day to attend the morning practice session. He then goes directly to school and then back to his village south of the city, where he must help out on the family farm. I would often be walking through downtown Benaras and be greeted by a wrestler working in his father's sweet shop, selling general merchandise, stacking gunnysack material, weighing coal, or checking goods at the railway station. Even national-level champion wrestlers hold jobs: Naresh Kumar is head clerk at the Delhi railway office (Asiaweek 1989); Chandagi Ram, the national champion of the late 1960s and early 1970s, is well known as "master ji" because of his training as a schoolteacher (Link 1969: 35; S. Sharma 1985). Regardless of the incompatibility of a wrestling lifestyle with the requirements and duties of working life, most who come to the akharas have adapted to accommodate the rigours of work with a modified daily schedule of exercise, diet, and sleep.

Many wrestlers now argue that formal education and wrestling are somewhat compatible (Areya 1978). While the wrestler rests his body he can develop his intellect; but this is something of a forced rationalisation based on an artificial dichotomy of mind and body. Even when not achieved, the ideal of a purely akhara-oriented schedule sets the tone for a wrestler's perception of his day. As such, it structures his attitude if not his time.

Having eaten, rested, defecated, and bathed, wrestlers return to the akhara at about four in the afternoon. Although the pit is dug for exercise, no wrestling is practiced in the afternoon. The workout consists of a number of exercises and lasts about three hours. After a second bath the wrestler leaves the akhara. Before going to sleep at sunset he eats and rests some more. Although sleeping is a period of inactivity, it is an important part of the wrestler's day. As Atreya writes in an article entitled "The Place of Sleep and Rest in the Wrestling Regimen," sleep is just as important as food, air, and water (1978: 19). Sleep is particularly important because it gives strained muscles and tendons a chance to recuperate. Sleep transforms the fatigue of exertion into the vigor of stamina. It also promotes digestion and thus helps a person put on weight and gain strength. Going to sleep at a regular time and getting enough sleep establishes a psychosomatic rhythm which produces a proper chemical and mineral balance in the body.

In turn, this conditions the various body mechanisms responsible for producing semen. A lack of sleep produces illness, emaciation, weakness, impotence, and the risk of premature death. In general, wrestlers sleep better than other people because they exert themselves more. Wrestlers get more rest in a shorter period of time because their sleep is deeper and less agitated with dreams and restlessness. The exact amount of sleep one needs is something one's guru must determine, but the following points apply:

A fundamental principle of wrestling is to go to sleep at sunset and wake three hours before dawn. One must sleep with an open window near one's head and never sleep with your head covered. Never sleep in the dew or on the damp ground. Sleeping on a comfortable cot or bed produces an efficacious rest and promotes endurance. When fatigue and flatulence are expunged, then semen is produced. Sleeping on an uncomfortable bed produces bad effects. This point needs to be emphasised. One should turn over repeatedly while sleeping and never sleep flat on one's back. Also, the body will suffer if one goes to sleep on an empty stomach (ibid: 23-24).

Although a wrestler's bed should be comfortable, it should be hard rather than soft; a board is better than a rope cot. "Sleep is the natural dharma of the body," writes Atreya (ibid: 20), and so, for the wrestler and for all who aspire to health and long life, it is crucial that they not merely sleep, but sleep properly. When wrestlers talk of trips they have taken to tournaments away from home they often comment on the nature and quality of the accomodation provided. The senior wrestlers of Akhara Bara Ganesh told me many times how they hosted wrestlers from the Punjab and made them very comfortable in a guest house/exercise room constructed so that, among other things, it affords a healthy place to sleep. At a tournament in Gaziabad I was told by some of my Benaras acquaintances that they had performed badly on account of having had to sleep on the floor in a stuffy, crowded room. In my very first encounter with a wrestler he showed me his sleeping accommodations and described the comfort and qualities of bed, mattress, and pillow as an indication of how complete and well appointed were the facilities at his disposal.

The daily life of a wrestler is a regime of integrated health and fitness drawn out, on, through, and in his body. In this regard the guru is both taskmaster and sculptor. As I was told by many wrestlers, a person must not so much as urinate or drink without first asking his guru's permission. A disciple's role is not to think, but to be molded and shaped, to allow himself to be cut in the pattern of perfection. Subscription to this kind of discipline requires extreme self-sacrifice-as a common aphorism has it, a willingness to "chew iron chana" or to "drink a bitter cup." Total commitment to the espoused ideals is rarely if ever realised. Nevertheless, there is a strong feeling of obligation and responsibility to live by the spirit if not the letter of one's guru's prescripts.

I have described in some detail the routine of a wrestler's daily life. Considerable license is given for idiosyncratic interpretation, and rationalisations abound for "imperfect" conduct. Some wrestlers advocate massage before practice as well as after. Others disagree on whether or not to bathe in well water during the winter. Although most agree that it is proper to get up at three in the morning, the more usual practice is to wake at four-thirty or five. Similarly, most wrestlers wait only half an hour rather than the prescribed two hours after practice before drinking water or eating food. Very few go to bed at sunset. In spite of the inexact nature and outright contradiction of some alternative practices, most wrestlers agree with the basic tenets outlined above.

If there is disagreement on the sequence of a particular part of the regime, more importance is placed on the rigor of whatever one chooses to do rather than on protocol. One can do virtually anything—within the tacitly agreed-on range of interpretations that make sense—as long as it is logically rationalised and is not just a random whim. Moreover, an idiosyncratic interpretation is more likely to be regarded as generally valid if it is articulated in great detail. For instance, diet is often a topic on which there is a degree of disagreement. Some wrestlers advocate a vegetarian diet, while others do not. The minority of Hindu wrestlers who eat meat are likely to give fairly detailed reasons for why their body in particular either requires the beneficial properties which meat provides or is relatively immune to the adverse effects meat has on the body. I am almost certain that no one would explain eating meat purely in terms of taste. When a wrestler from the warm dry plains visited in the cool damp hills he explained his request for chicken in terms of the warming effect it would have on his body.

A wrestler's routine follows the pattern of a logical sequence of events built one upon the other. Sleep complements diet and exercise; bathing, dental hygiene, defecation, and sleep are all directly linked to health and strength. Themes of physical purity, strength, semen production, and aesthetic beauty run through and give continuity and texture to the day's events. As such, the regime of day-to-day life does not read so much like a catalogue with separately articulated parts in cumulative sequence as it does a recipe where each step is important and unique in its own right and the sum is a complement of interdependent parts. For this reason the spirit of the "law" is more significant than a literal interpretation. It is not so important to figure out exactly what is best in any particular situation. What is important is that the whole routine be rhythmically structured and consistent with reference to itself. Lived properly, the whole day produces a whole, healthy, and harmonically balanced body.

A wrestler's daily routine extends the world of wrestling out of the strictly defined precinct of exercise and competition. It makes the practice of wrestling a significant factor in both the domestic sphere of family life and the world of work and labour. Concepts of health and strength are necessarily projected into the home, the field, the shop, the office. Although the akhara provides a pivotal point around which the wrestler's day is organised, a wrestler must also work and raise a family. It is therefore important briefly to consider the social composition of the Benaras wrestling community.

## Akhara Membership

Akhara membership is nearly impossible to determine in any objective empirical sense. Most akhara elders with whom I spoke claimed that their "irregular membership"—those who come when they have time but do not follow a strict regime of exercise-numbered in the hundreds. Some elders generalised to the point of saying that everyone in their proximal neighbourhood was in theory an akhara member. Moreover, a number of people claimed membership in one akhara or another on the basis of very casual and circuitous association: friends of friends, neighbours, or hyperextended kinship.

The larger akharas—Ram Singh, Bara Ganesh, Swaminath, and Gaya Seth—estimate that their regular membership is between sixty and seventy. However, on any one day there are between twenty-five and thirty wrestlers who attend morning practice (see plate 12). At the smaller akharas-Ram Kund, Ishvarigangi, Ram Sevak, Sant Ram, and Ragunath Maharaj—regular membership is between forty and fifty, with fifteen to twenty wrestlers attending on any one day. My use of the term "member" refers to anyone who comes to an akhara regularly, however "regularly" may be defined. It is a purposefully vague formulation and is in keeping with the attitude of most wrestlers. An example will help illustrate this point.

The akhara with which I affiliated is formally known by the title Antrashtriya, Sarwajanik Akhara Ram Singh (The International, Public Akhara Ram Singh) which appears in bold blue letters on the pavilion's entablature. One year when the akhara was repainted there was serious disagreement as to whether the word "public" (sarwajanik) ought to be part of the official name. Most members say that an akhara is eminently public and that this should be made explicit. Many members are proud of the fact that anyone can come to their akhara. Exercise, they argue, is something that ought not to be restricted through exclusive membership. However, even those who aspire to such high ideals of egalitarian inclusiveness recognise that in some Hindu akharas Muslims and untouchables are either overtly excluded or covertly discriminated against.

One can say that the problematic meaning of the term "public" is derived from the juxtaposition of a general ethic of equality set over and against social exclusiveness and caste chauvinism. The reason a number of akhara members were against including the word "public" in the title was that it would reify a comfortably ambiguous situation. Those in favour wanted to preempt that ambiguity by formalising an ideal of total inclusiveness. In the end the word "public" was painted on the entablature, which played no small role in the trials and tribulations of a not-quite-postpositivist ethnographer's search for demographic statistics. "Just how many wards do you have, Guru ji?" I asked. And he replied, "Who knows, my son, it is a public place."

Although membership is free and easy, an initiation ceremony formally inducts a novice wrestler into an akhara. The ritual of initiation varies from one akhara to another but is generally as follows. After attending an akhara for some time the guru will tell a wrestler that it is time for his initiation. On the appointed day the young wrestler brings with him a new langot, a sapha (head cloth/turban), Prasad (usually in the form of laddus made of besan [chickpea flour] and sugar), paraffin or oil, cotton to make a wick for the prayer lamp, and a garland of flowers to place around the image of Hanuman. After practice the sapha and langot are offered to the guru along with cash. The sum is usually eleven rupees but any multiple of ten plus one is acceptable. The guru then takes the garland and lights the lamp after placing the Prasad in front of the figure of Hanuman.

The initiate is asked to honour Lord Hanuman and to swear allegiance to the akhara and the founding guru. The Prasad is then taken and distributed among the other members of the akhara. The conclusion and most important part of the ceremony is when five laddus are taken and buried in the four corners and centre of the pit. There is no drama associated with this rite. The whole event is rather low-key and does not seem to mark a dramatic change of status. The initiate still comes to the akhara as before and there are no privileges attached to initiated membership. Indeed, the distinction between one who has and one who has not been initiated is rarely made. Initiation does establish a bond between guru and chela. Although a guru will instruct an uninitiated member, it is said that a person can only really understand what a guru is telling him after having been initiated. Initiation is not a marker of membership in any empirical sense, but it effects a bond of respect and obligation between teacher and disciple.

## Akhara Demographics

A survey of eight akharas supports the general observation that there is little variation in the demographic profile of Benaras akharas. There does not seem to be any variation in the caste, class, or status makeup of different akharas.

Every akhara I visited had a majority of Yadavs as regular members. Yadavs are a low-caste (technically Sudra) group with considerable political, economic, and demographic strength in the Benaras area. Their social mobility and group identity is linked to a longstanding traditional association with the military (Rao 1964) and with wrestling. Although many Yadavs are lawyers, doctors, businessmen, teachers, and writers, many follow their traditional caste vocation of herding and dairy farming. Of the 118 wrestlers interviewed, thirty-five reported that they were involved in some form of dairying or milk business. While most dairy farmers are Yadavs, not all Yadavs who wrestle are dairy farmers. I would estimate that some 50 per cent of all wrestlers in Benaras are Yadavs. Thakurs, including Bhumihar Rais, comprise the second-largest caste group involved in wrestling, roughly 20 per cent. Brahmans make up about 15 per cent of the wrestling population, with the remaining 15 per cent coming from a wide range of caste groups including Dhobis, Chandals, Chamars, Nais, and others.

The clear majority of dairy farmers is explained not only by caste identity. Dairy farmers have direct access to two of the most important and otherwise expensive ingredients in a wrestler's diet: milk and ghi. In fact, the association between wrestling and dairy farming in Benaras is so great that men who deal in milk or milk products are called pahalwan irrespective of whether or not they take part in the regimen of practice and exercise.

In general, many wrestlers are in business for themselves or in government service. Apart from seven weavers, very few wrestlers with whom I spoke were employed as factory workers or simple wage labourers. This may be a function of sample error; however, it is important to note that the nature of work in a factory or commercial handicraft industry would mitigate against a rigorous and exacting extracurricular "leisure" activity such as wrestling. Workers who are paid a low daily or weekly wage may well frequent akharas in order to bathe and relax, but in my casual as well as programmatic surveys of akhara life I encountered relatively few "serious wrestlers" who would fall in this class bracket. Similarly, although most wrestlers come from a comparatively low economic class bracket, irregularly employed wage labourers-rickshaw pullers, street hawkers, and others whose income is low-tend not to be involved in wrestling. A few brief portraits help fill out the occupational profile of the wrestling community:

- Kanta Pahalwan is a railway porter who works at the Dehra Dun station. His family is from a village in northwestern Bihar to which he returns every year to help with the harvest and planting. Although porters have a fairly secure position with the railway and are government-licensed, there are few perquisites. Income is low. Kanta shares room and board with other porters and sends money back to his family in Bihar.

- Sita Ram Yadav came to Benaras as a young boy and found work with a well-known and respected wrestling patron, Ram Narian Sarien, who owns an umbrella shop in the city. Ram Narian Sarien supported Sita Ram Yadav and saw to his training as a young wrestler. After considerable success as a wrestler Sita Ram was given a job with the Benaras Diesel Locomotive Works, where he works as an office clerk.
- Dr. Shanti Prakash Atreya, one-time state wrestling champion of Uttar Pradesh, earned his M.A. and Ph.D. from Benaras Hindu University, where he has taught both yoga and philosophy. Atreya is currently affiliated as a teacher with a school in Saharanpur. He also runs an institute for the study of yoga and psychology at Kuthal Gate in Dehra Dun District. His family lives in Bandarjuddha, a large, wealthy village near Deoband in Uttar Pradesh.
- Nathu Lal Yadav, the guru of Karanghanta Akhara, is a well-known purveyor of pan. In his small shop, an extension of a shrine dedicated to Lord Shiva, there is room for one person only to sit. By his own admission Nathu Lal is more concerned with philosophical questions than he is with making money. As he points out, he enjoys what he does and it is enough to support him and his immediate family.
- Ram ji, a member of Jhalani Akhara, comes from a very well-to-do Yadav family who own a number of hotels, sweet shops, and other business interests in Benaras. Ram ji works under his brother as the junior manager of one of the family hotels in Chaitganj.
- Kaniya, a B.A. candidate at Benaras Hindu University, works at his father's small tea and sweet shop. He regrets not having been able to take his degree sooner,

but as the eldest son he is responsible for the day-to-day management of the family business.

Although wrestlers come from different economic backgrounds, wealth and social status are not very important factors in daily interaction. In terms of the wrestling ethic, wealth is simply irrelevant. Money enables one to have a better diet—an important consideration in its own right—but in and of itself money is not valued. This is not to say that poor wrestlers would not rather be rich or wish a better life for themselves and their families. Given the opportunity they would certainly seek to improve their lot. However, as an ethical life path wrestling takes precedence over material concerns of class and occupation.

## Age and Education

Of 123 wrestlers interviewed from eight akharas, fifteen were under age fifteen, fifty-five were between the ages of fifteen and twenty-three, twenty-eight were between the ages of twenty-three and thirty-five, and twenty-five were over thirty-five years old. This indicates not only the obvious-that most wrestlers are teenagers or young men in their early twenties—but also that men in their mid-to late twenties and early thirties are not very involved in akhara activities. Once men marry and take on the responsibility of raising a family they tend to come to the akhara less frequently. When they have established an occupation of some sort and have children of their own, these men return to the akhara as senior members. On account of this there is a sharp generational break in the membership of most akharas. Senior members are to junior members as fathers are to sons or uncles to nephews. Respect, however, is tempered with a good deal of joking and informality. True respect is reserved for the guru.

It is also important to note that wrestlers who are between twenty-three and thirty-five years old are usually the ones who have made a name for themselves. Though numerically in the minority, as individuals they represent an ideal and have great prestige. These members are regarded as quintessential wrestlers and virtually define the quality of the akhara by their presence. Shamu Pahalwan of Akhara Ram Singh is one such wrestler, and Ashok Kumar, who has taken part in national and international competitions, is another. Krishna Kumar Singh of Bara Ganesh has won national recognition as a wrestler for the northern railway team, and Ram ji, of Jhalani Akhara, has won titles in Delhi and Uttar Pradesh state tournaments.

Educational experience corresponds to the generational split in akhara membership. Older members are not educated to the same level as younger members. Of those over thirty-five, only two had the equivalent of a high-school degree. Most were educated up to a sixth-grade level. All were literate but four had gone to school for less than two years.

In sharp contrast are the data on the educational background of the ninety-nine wrestlers interviewed who were under the age of thirty-five: as of 1987, two had M.A. degrees, fourteen had B.A. degrees, thirty had the equivalent of a high-school diploma, and one had left school in tenth grade, thirteen in the ninth, eighteen in the eighth, four in the seventh, and nineteen in the fifth. Even though these data are biased by the fact that Benaras is a cultural and intellectual centre, the fact remains that a significant percentage of young wrestlers are well educated compared to their senior fellows.

Having said this, it must be pointed out that education, like wealth, is not a very significant factor in the scheme of akhara activities. Education is valuable in its own right but does not figure in the wrestling rubric as a particularly important virtue. Learning and wisdom are of great importance in the construction of a wrestler's identity, but education is not regarded as the source of these skills. Where it is seen as valuable is as a prerequisite for modern life and as a vehicle for gaining employment, but this is more by default than by design. As it is institutionalised in modern India, formal education is regarded by cynical wrestlers as a somewhat benign manifestation of modern moral decay. It does not inspire; it creates an irreverent attitude and a general lack of respect. The value of education is not in its innate virtue but in its practical utility. For instance, while generally decrying modern materialist pre-occupations with status and upward mobility, one wrestler spent a hot summer day networking so that his nephew and niece would gain admission into a well-regarded elementary school.

By way of contrast, Atma Ram's father places no stock in a formal education. Instead he sent his son to the akhara, saying that there he will learn all that he needs to know. Atma Ram is illiterate, but at age twenty-two he is known in Benaras as a good wrestler. Friends have been networking to get him employment with the railway.

Anand Rai's father, a schoolteacher in Kotdwar and well-to-do land owner in Benaras district, appreciates the value of a good education but recognises the virtue of akhara training. Anand bicycles the fifteen kilometers to Akhara Ram Singh every morning and then goes from the akhara to school. When Anand was about twenty-three, after three failed attempts, he finally passed his matriculation exams and his father invited members of the akhara and village neighbours to a banquet celebration. At the banquet Anand was admonished to keep up with his physical training and to develop himself as a good wrestler.

The following amalgam describes the typical Benaras wrestler with the least synoptic violence. He is a boy in his late teens who is nearing the end of his intermediate education. Some members of his family live in Benaras city proper while others live in a village not too far away. In the city he lives in a small, modestly appointed cement building. One or two of this typical wrestler's elder brothers used to wrestle and he had an uncle who, despite hardship, "was the champion of his village district." One of his older brothers runs a dairy enterprise and has rented space on the outskirts of the city where twelve or thirteen buffalos are tethered. The other brother works in a modest sweet shop located off a main street. The typical wrestler hopes to join the army, the police, or the railway, but his father in the village needs help managing the family's land holdings, and so the wrestler is forced to curb his ambition in the interest of more immediate demands.

It must be emphasised, however, that within the framework of a wrestling way of life, family wealth and status are not important considerations. As a wrestler Atma, who can neither read nor write, is on the same footing as Babul, who has a B.A. from Benaras Hindu University. Similarly, Ashok, whose family owns only a few buffalos and a small tea shop, is a better wrestler than is Ram ji, who comes from one of the wealthiest families in Benaras.

The claim that education and wealth are unimportant factors in the akhara would be false and acrimonious but for the fact that wrestling is not just an extracurricular leisure activity. It is, rather, a holistic integrated way of life. As a person, a wrestler must of necessity live in a world of social and economic obligation where status, class rank, and educational training play a strong hand. As a wrestler, however, a person must bracket himself out of the obligations and expectations which ensue from his involvement in this larger, divisive world.

## Akharas and Bodybuilding Clubs

Wrestling akharas stand in sharp contrast to bodybuilding clubs in Benaras. Bodybuilding clubs are a fairly recent phenomenon in India, dating perhaps to the early part of the twentieth century, when Ram Murti Naidu, among others, established institutes for physical training and exercise. In Benaras today bodybuilding is modelled on a Western aesthetic and on Western notions of strength and fitness. Wrestlers and bodybuilders sharply juxtapose their respective activities. Each defines himself against the negative backdrop of the other, self-definition through a "we-are-not-like-them" formulation. As with any such formulation there are enough parallels between the two activities to generate a dialectic rather than to create a situation of total rejection and disregard. In the interest of summarising what an akhara is in terms of aesthetic appeal, health nexus, and demographic composition, it is useful to reflect the akhara, as a whole, against its more modern analog.

The Mazdoor Health Improvement Association, established in 1931 to foster ideals of physical fitness and national self-determination among mazdurs (wage labourers), is located down a small gali in Madanpura. The association is almost entirely Muslim, and most of the members come from the immediate neighbourhood of Al 'lu ka Masjid. Many current members work in the area as weavers, traders, transporters, or tailors of silk and other fabrics. The gali is narrow, dark, and, as with other such galis in Benaras, littered with refuse and piles of rubble. Open doors look in on huge looms sunk into the floors of family houses, where young children sit and weave the silk saris for which Benaras is famous.

The gym is open only at night. At about 6:00 P.M. the first member to arrive picks up the key from Masoom's pan shop just across the road from the gali entrance. A sign above the gym door announces the name of the organisation in English and in Urdu and Devanagari script.

The gym is a small room, six meters square, crowded with dumbbells, weightlifting bars, weights of all sizes and shapes, a set of parallel bars, and a chin-up bar hung on old rusted chains suspended from a sagging central beam. In one corner is a broken pulley and bicycle-chain contraption used to lift a stack of iron-plate weights. Next to the parallel bars is an improvised bench-press board, and in front of that, set into the hard-packed earth floor, a set of wooden stumps on which to do push-ups. Pegs are set into the lime-washed bricks on each wall. Members hold on to these and stand on polished wooden boards while doing squats and deep knee bends. The boards keep the floor dry, for otherwise sweat would quickly turn the earth to slippery mud.

The central column, decorated with mirrors, supports a ceiling sagged under the weight of three upper floors. Other mirrors decorate three of the walls. Between the mirrors and the iron-barred windows which look out narrowly onto a small dusty garden, old black and white portraits of local champions palely reflect the technicolor aura of pin-ups from American bodybuilding magazines.

A raised area two and a half meters square is set apart in the small room and on it are four large chairs and a carpet. A small ceiling fan turns above this area, cooling the club manager and others who come to watch the regular members exercise. Between two of the chairs and one wall is a two by one-half metre area used for changing. Clothes are hung on pegs above the chairs and the parallel bars. On the wall above the platform are old photos of the founding association. A few plaques, commemorating long since forgotten functions, recall a time when the club had a larger membership. A penned poster, set on a shallow ledge above a covered bucket of tap water, states the club rules in Urdu script.

If there is one word which characterises the Mazdoor Health Improvement Association, it is compact; there is a certain aesthetic appeal to the close-fitting, womblike character of the place. Contrary to what one might expect, the air in the gym is a quite pleasant combination of musty earth, mustard oil and sweat. Exercise is done with mechanical efficiency. A person doing push-ups makes way for a person doing squats who is just beyond the arch of another person swinging on the parallel bars. No more than thirteen people can exercise in the gym at any one time, and even with nine people working out, movement must be choreographed for efficiency and safety.

The contrast with wrestling akharas is obvious. While both are clearly bounded arenas, the bodybuilding club is closed and confined while the akhara is open. Earth, water, wind, and trees have no place in the confines of the closed, covered, mechanised space of the gym.

If there is a dramatic difference in the relative aesthetic appeal of clubs and akharas, there is an even more significant difference concerning management and organisation. Wrestling akharas are the essence of informality. There are few if any set duties, offices, or responsibilities. The guru is nominally in charge of all akhara facilities and activities, but in fact an ad-hoc committee of elder members often serves as a decision-making body. The English term "committee" is used by akhara members to refer to any group of two or more who come to a decision on any subject; for example, taking up a collection for a new bucket and rope for the akhara well, buying fresh lime-wash for repainting the akhara buildings, negotiating for a truckload of earth for the pit, or persuading someone to paint new designs on the akhara walls. In any akhara, as in many other social contexts, there are those who take charge of situations and are able to motivate people and implement their own ideas. There are also inevitable conflicts of interest and points of view. But there is no codified structure to this kind of management and organisation.

In the akhara there is an informal pecking order which ensures that things get done. At the top of the pecking order is the guru and his cohort of senior members: a very loosely defined group at best. If the guru makes a demand of some sort it is acted on immediately and without comment. The guru's age cohort, known as dadas, can order anyone who is a junior member to do such things as fetch incense for the morning pit benediction, get mustard oil from a nearby shop, pick up flower garlands, run various errands anywhere in town, draw water for a bath, deliver a message, sweep fallen leaves from the akhara compound, throw water on the earth to settle the dust, climb up a tree to break off a toothbrush, put equipment away, wash clothes, or chase a stray dog out of the pit.

Among the junior members beneath the dada cohort, seniority and age structure the pecking order. Older members may pass on responsibility to anyone younger and less aggressive than themselves. The ethic of respect for one's elders is used as a moral lever. There is merit in being of service. However, the pecking order is characterised as much by acrimony as by smooth efficiency, as one dada discovered when he spent a whole morning cursing the laziness and disrespect of the younger generation while fishing with a large hook for a bucket lost at the bottom of the well.

While the pecking order is hierarchically multitiered in theory, in fact it is always the youngest members with whom the buck stops. During my stay at the akhara young Kailash was always going off to get something for someone, Airi was always called upon to perform his expert massage, and Govind was chasing stray dogs and cows; unless someone younger has come along, Rajindar may still be drawing water from the well. In any case, water gets drawn and the grounds are kept clean, but often to the tune of half-meant threats, disgruntled retorts, and a great deal of joking.

The akhara is characterised by a lack of bureaucracy and by ad-hoc management. By way of contrast, the following is an index of the offices of the Benaras School of Physical Culture, a bodybuilding club in Jangambari: Chief Patron, Mr. Dalip Kumar (IAS), district officer and president of the association for the advancement of physical education; Patron, Mr. N. G. Bhattacharya, regional sports officer and secretary of the association for the advancement of physical education; Physical Director, Dr. Uma Shankar Rai Chaudhuri; President, Mr. Raj Kumar; Vice President, Mr. Ajay Sharma. The list continues with such titles as chief officer, deputy officer, secretary, chief in charge of the club, and treasurer. In addition to these permanent officers, a chief advisor was appointed to organise the club's annual bodybuilding competition. In this capacity he was supported by seven deputy advisors, an organiser, deputy organiser, organising committee, committee in charge of the competition, and a committee in charge of prizes.

Where akharas are ad-hoc, clubs seem to be obsessive about a strict division of administrative labour. I have no idea how responsibility was distributed through the administrative hierarchy of the Jangambari club, or how decisions were made at any one level. A similar hierarchy of management appears on the letterhead of the Bhelupura Vyayamshala, another bodybuilding club, which also sponsors an annual competition.

The Bhelupura Vyayamshala also illustrates another striking contrast between akharas and clubs. Stepping into many bodybuilding clubs, the first thing that strikes the eye is a prominently posted list of rules and regulations. At Bhelupura Vyayamshala the rules are as follows:

1. Non-members are not allowed in without permission.
2. Members may not bring friends with them into the club.
3. Every member must pay a 2 rupee membership fee by the fifteenth of each month.
4. The gym will be open from 5-8 am and from 5-11 pm.
5. The gym will be closed every Sunday.
6. No one is allowed to enter the "exercise temple" wearing their shoes.
7. No smoking or chewing tobacco in the gym.
8. No spitting anywhere in the compound.

9. Everyone must be careful and watch out that others are exercising safely.
10. If someone breaks any piece of equipment he is responsible for its replacement.
11. Members should park their bicycles where they won't get in the way.

Similar rules are found posted in other bodybuilding clubs, but I have never seen a posted list of regulations at any akhara where wrestling is practised. Wrestling akharas are governed more by established precedent and the model of the guru than by objective rules as such. Wrestlers would agree with the injunction against tobacco, but their abstinence derives from moral conviction rather than a concern for regulations per se.

While bodybuilding clubs follow the Western calendar and take Sunday off, akharas break their weekly routine on Wednesday. Unlike the clubs, akharas are not closed on their "day off." Wednesday is a day for massage in the akhara and is thus integral to the weekly regime. In the akhara, spitting, flatulence, and nose blowing are restricted to the border area of the compound where they do not threaten the purity of the sacred space. In the club, spitting is more an issue of generic hygiene than of moral, somatic health. In the akhara purity rather than civic-mindedness is as much if not more of an issue. In the club, spitting must be stipulated against, while in the akhara the same restraint is inspired by ideological conviction and is therefore a point of common sense.

Membership is another crucial point of difference between the club and the akhara. Every exercise club I visited charged a monthly membership fee. On the other hand, akhara members consider fees to be anathema. None of the akharas I visited charged fees of any kind. Moreover, clubs often keep careful record of who has and has not paid, thus sharply defining membership. Akhara membership, as we have seen, is eminently flexible and variable. Whereas clubs are exclusive and private, wrestlers see the akhara as an inclusive, public arena.

Because of membership dues, bodybuilding clubs are able to finance building repairs, equipment improvement, and fairly lavish annual events. There are other expenses as well. The Mazdoor Health Improvement Association must pay rent on its small room and also cover the cost of electricity. In contrast to club dues, akharas draw all of their resources from chanda, public donations collected from members, neighbourhood residents, and local businesses. Taking up chanda is an ad-hoc activity. If a new rope is needed, a few of the akhara dadas get together and share the expense. Expenses are minimal. I have never known of a wrestling akhara on which rent was paid. Electricity is rarely needed, but for the occasional installation of a light or fan it is most often donated by a wealthy member. When there is a large expense, such as the annual Nag Panchami festival or construction of a new building, the chanda is more formal and structured.

However, the money collected is almost always designated for a specific project. Contributing to a chanda is one way in which the larger akhara neighbourhood can participate in wrestling activities. A person who contributes two thousand rupees towards a new akhara pit achieves status in proportion to his contribution. For their part, the akhara members receive public acclaim and prestige in proportion to the total amount collected. While chanda is a common way for many groups-temple associations, neighbourhood committees, and union fundraisers—to raise money, it is characteristic of the akhara system of organisation rather than of the bodybuilding club.

Monthly dues, though nominal, restrict membership. A few clubs, such as the well-furnished Health Improvement Association, charge a very exclusive one hundred rupees per month. Some clubs have a wealthier clientele than others. This is not the pattern in akharas, where the economic and social profile of the wrestling community is fairly eclectic. Rich and poor wrestlers meet on common ground. Although I have not collected a great deal of information on body building club membership, my general impression is that specific body-building clubs restrict membership to particular groups. As noted, a large number of Muslims have become avid bodybuilders. Muslims aside, body-building seems to be popular among many of the more "Westernised" urban youth. The aesthetic of the bodybuilder's sleek physique is in keeping with other Western images of fast motorcycles, high-tech sound systems, digital watches, and so forth.

Some exercise clubs, like the Mazdoor Health Improvement Association, were established to target a particular class of people such as the urban labour force. The Benaras School of Physical Culture was established in 1943 for the benefit of "lower class children." My impression is that many body-building clubs were established by paternalistic upper-class patrons who felt some kind of commitment to better the health of India's masses. In other words, initial impetus and funding for groups like the Mazdoor Health Improvement Association, Benaras School of Physical Culture, and Bhelupura Vyayamshala seems to have come from wealthy doctors, bankers, and industrialists. I was shown around one of these clubs by a young, wealthy accountant who said that his family had a long-standing role in maintaining exercise facilities for the poorer, disadvantaged youth of the city. By contrast, one does not find any kind of exclusive recruitment strategy or class-based paternalism in the akhara. No particular group is targeted. Akhara members make a general appeal for everyone to join an akhara, but this is inclusive rather than exclusive and is, as we shall see, part of a broader nationalistic rhetoric.

A final point of contrast between the akhara and the club concerns the place of formal religion in the organisational scheme of daily activities. Temples give akharas an atmosphere of religiosity, and every wrestler is enjoined to take Hanuman into his heart. In contrast, body building clubs are for the most part secular institutions.

Small Hanuman shrines are found at Bhelupura Vyayamshala, the Benaras School of Physical Culture, and, as the name might imply, Hanuman Vyayamshala. In every instance these shrines are small and marginal. The members are more concerned with the "cut" of their muscles and the trimness of their waists than they are with contemplating Hanuman's service to Ram. Besides, Hanuman's physique is not that of a bodybuilder, except as portrayed in some modern calendar art, but that of a wrestler. Bodybuilders defer to

Hanuman, but they draw their strength almost exclusively from "pumping iron" and not from the devotional exercise of a daily regimen.

Wrestlers in Benaras point towards bodybuilders and criticise their "balloonlike bodies," which have form but no substance. They smirk at narrow waists that would snap in two at the slightest touch, and grimace at protruding tendons wrapped tight by the work of an iron machine. One wrestler laughed at the picture of a body builder, saying that he looked like separate pieces of meat slapped together in a random manner. Another, echoing a similar aesthetic critique, said that bodybuilders look as though they come in parts, each a gross protrusion disembodied from its larger corporeal context. While the body-builder is seen as bits and pieces of random flesh, the wrestler's body is a smooth, integrated whole; as they say, ek rang ka sharir, a body of one colour and uniform texture.

Wrestlers regard body building clubs as mere pale reflections of the akhara. For their part some club members see akharas as simply anachronistic institutions following the dictates of outmoded tradition. (In general exercise-club members are far more tolerant of akharas than the other way around.)

I have made a rather sharp distinction between the akhara and the body building club. In doing so some points of overlap between the two styles of physical culture have been deemphasised. But this, too, is in keeping with the perspective of both wrestlers and bodybuilders. Somewhat like closely allied and therefore antagonistic academic disciplines, both groups prefer to define their respective paths clearly and sharply rather than blur together formal and superficial similarities. Whether motivated by strong conviction or fear that the edifice of difference will crumble once assailed, the wrestler and the body builder choose to narrow their respective visions while at the same time magnifying the significance of their singular predilections. Each defines itself against a negative backdrop of the other. In the case of wrestlers, this delineation serves to make the akhara more distinct and therefore more clearly defined as the locus of a specific way of life.

# 4

# The Stages of Life Systems in Hindu Religion

There are four stages of life, *viz.* Brahmachari (student), Grihasta (Householder) Vanaprasta (forest dweller or Hermit in semi retirement) Sannyasi (the renounced one in full retirement) and the Dharma of each is different. The four stages may be said to represent periods of Preparation, Production, Service and Retirement.

> *"People do not have to be taught to want to be happy, to want to be secure or to want the respect and admiration of their friends and associates—though often they need instruction 'how' to secure these things. Deeper Hindu thinking suggests, however, that there is also a natural progression of these values so that one should grow toward more fundamental interests. This movement toward more enduring and satisfying values has been institutionalised in the understanding of the four stages of life known as 'Ashramas".*

## Brahmacharya (Celibate)

Brahmacharya means Student, usually between 12 and 24 years of age.The first stage is Brahmacharya. The duty of a student is to study. On initiation into Brahmacharya by means of the Upanayana rites, he becomes a 'Dvija' (a twice born). 'Upanayana' means 'bringing near'-the disciple is brought near the Guru for receiving the initiation of mantras. For the Brahmachari, celibacy is his forte, discipline is his norm, devotion to his Guru is his duty and concentration in studies is his vocation.

In "Gurukula Vasam"(or staying with the preceptor) he learns the nuances and intricate renderings and interpretations of Vedas, Upanishads and Sastras though by means of rote so that when he comes of age the significance of what he learnt would be realised by him in real life situations, which he would be facing in his next Ashrama.

Thus, it is a period of probation, a period of training, in a practical manner without prejudice to the injunctions of Sastras he had so studiously learnt as a Brahmachari. Only when someone consoles we feel relief; only the 'Guru Upadesa' can change our mental attitude. The first lesson of the student is the performance of 'Sandhya Vandanam' at morn, noon and evening, Ablutions, recitation of Gayatri, breath control, sipping and sprinkling of water, pouring libations of water to the Sun-God, etc. were enjoined on the twice-born and they could never be missed.

## Grihastaashrama

Grihasta means House-holder usually between 24 and 48 years of age. The next stage is of the householder. After the 'Gurukula Vasa' he graduates himself into the mundane world, taking a wife to assist him in his performance of Dharmic duties. All Sastras proclaim the importance of the Grihastaasrama as the fulcrum of all other Ashramas. People in the other three Ashramas heavily lean on the Grihasta for support and sustenance required to carry out their respective duties. The Grihasta earns his livelihood by whatever a vocation befitting his being a member of his group, raising children, supporting his own family, kith and kin besides the persons performing their duties in the other three Ashramas.

The life of a Grihasta is therefore, considered a 'Jivayagna'—a lifelong saga of self sacrifice for the benefit of others in society. Marriage is not meant as a means to satisfy carnal craving. It is regarded as a means to spiritual glory, a sin qua non for the development of lineage—a necessary link between the dead past and an unborn future that must come alive to be undertaken as a part of spiritual duty with devotion (Shraddha) to perpetuate the family tradition.

According to Bhagavata Purana, a Griha (house) is not a person for one who has controlled his senses, delights in spirit and is eager for knowledge.

Partners who enter in wedlock are not 'paragons of virtue' as they appear in the first flush of enthusiasm. None is perfect and to seek for perfection in the partner is like seeking a mirage in the desert. Perfect relationship is created by conscious effort and not discovered all of a sudden. The incompatibilities have to be resolved by a continual mutual adjustment and reconciliation by a willing attitude of 'give and take'.

Marriage is marriage and is not a mere love affair which is but an infatuation. Love affair is a relationship just for the pleasure of the person involved and it has no consideration of the families of the persons. When the pleasure wears out, the affair is gone. But, marriage is a life commitment.If you make a sacrifice, you are not sacrificing to that person. It is a sacrifice to a permanent relationship. Love bears all, endures all. If the relationship has pains, remember that life is a mixture of joys and sorrows.

The practice in India that a husband and wife could continue to remain as husband and wife till death and also celebrate the Golden jubilee of their wedding at the 60th age of the husband is still very common. Those that end in divorce or separation are misfits for the marriage life who have no understanding of the marriage and its divinity. They fail in 'making it work' and deserve the real pain, indeed the devastating trauma attaching thereto. The duties of the Grihasta include the performance of 'Panchmahayagna' (five great sacrifices) laid down in Manu Dharma Sastra.

***Deva Yagna:*** (Deity worship) The daily worship and puja to Ganapathi,Kula devata and Ishta devata. Visiting kula devata temple often or atleast once in a year.

***Brahma Yagna:*** (Seer worship) Each day the householder expresses his debt to the the human kind by doing some services to the society. Performing ones own profession/vocation with the standards of ethics itself is a service to the society. Brahma Yagna also includes Guru worship and studying, teaching, repeating and meditating upon the Vedic scriptures.(Vedic rituals)

***Pitru Yagna:*** (Ancestor Worship) Respecting the ancestors, parents of the self and spouse and getting their blessings by making salutations to them by leaning towards their foot. Parentless children should perform Annual Shraddas (Thithi) and observe fasting during new moon days and beginning of months, offer rice balls (pindas) to crows or in holy river.Those persons who do not know the thithi of their parents death should perform thithi on the new moon day of the month "Thai" which usally comes between the second week of January and the second week of February. The thithi given or the fasting observed on thai amavasya constitute a remembrance of ancestors back to the 7th generation.

***Bhuta Yagna:*** Worship of living beings by scattering grains, offering food at the threshold for animals, birds, insects, etc. Loving and watering plants also do constitute bhuta yagna.

*Nara Yagna or Purusha Yagna or Manushya Yagna* (Guest worship) Obligation to love and honour ties of fellowship with humanity by showing hospitality to fellow humans, friends, relatives or even strangers and beggars.

It is to be noted here that a person performing his Panchmahayagna everyday without fail will not be disturbed by kali purusha.

Marriage is an integral part of a Grihasta for it is said that no ritual is efficacious without the presence of the wife, the Sahadharmini.

The wife always accompanies the husband in discharging his duties. Marriage is no doubt, primarily for begetting children but it was also required for the proper performance of worship.

Marriage is not only a contract between individuals but a contract between families.

The difference in the family values as between those obtaining in India and in the West would reveal how different are the expectations about marriage in these two cultures.

The first three nights after marriage, the couple are expected to remain continent to impress that marriage is not a license for sexual pleasures but a holy and irrevocable contract not only between the man and wife but also casts the burden of ensuring it to be so, till the very last, on the community comprising of the families of both sides.

The husband is expected to first satisfy the wife's soul and the wife satisfies the husband with her body and gets his soul.

On Abortion, the Sastras are very clearly against it. The foetus is considered to be a living person with consciousness who is required to be protected and reared with care and affection.

Rigveda even goes to the extent of pleading for mercy on behalf of the foetus.

Atharvaveda characterises the killer of a foetus as brunagni, one of the most heinous sins.

Kaushitaki Upanishad equates it to the killing of one's parents.

Gauthama Dharma Sastra advises such persons as having lost their caste status-considered in those days as equal to capital punishment.

Susrutha Samhita the medical treatise, however, permits abortion on purely medical grounds Mudhagarbha which explains the steps to be taken to save both mother and child in case of emergency and advises that if the foetus is alive, every attempt should be made to remove it from the mother's womb alive. If dead, it may be removed in the normal course. Surgical removal (Caesarian) should not be resorted to if it is likely to harm the mother and / or the child. In extreme cases, it permits inducing miscarriage of the foetus if that were the only means to prevent the loss of the mother. Children were loved to the point of becoming spoilt darlings.

## Vanaprasta Ashrama (The Anchorite)

Vanaprasta is the third stage of Elder Advisor usually between 48 and 72 years of age. A stage comes when business, family, secular life like the beauties and hopes of youth have exhausted themselves and need to be left behind. The person retires usually from worldly attachments to lead a life of contemplation and meditation alone or with his wife.

What life holds beyond middle age depends in the end not on fancy and imagination but on the realities of the values of life we regard as inviolable. Vanaprasta may be termed as the beginning of a person's real 'adult education' to evaluate his performance thus for as Grihasta and reorder his life in such a way as to discover who he is and what life is all about.

"The time had come for him to probe 'the secret of 'I' with which he has been on such intimate terms all these years yet which remains a stranger, full of inexplicable quirks, baffling surds, irrational impulses."

It is curious to find that many do not wish to venture into this but would like to remain in Grihastashrama even by remarrying if the first spouse predeceases the man.

A playboy of 25 may impress but how could one pose perpetually as the 'prince charming' at 50, 60 or 70 years of age? Look at those who try hard to do this. However hard they might try, they not only fail to receive recognition but also incur the derision of people whom they seek to impress.

***Sannyasa Ashrama (The Renounced):*** Sannyasi is the fourth stage of an Ascetic-Solitaire-usually beyond 72 years of age. This means 'Samyak Nyasa'—'Total detachment' from worldly pleasures including the bare necessities to subsist. This is the last 'Ashrama'. He does not aspire to be recognised as somebody who matters—he wish of the Sannyasi is just to be a 'persona non grata'—one who exists almost without giving any thought to his being-with no desire for name or fame or recognition.

> *"He no more cares whether his body falls or remains than does a cow what becomes a garland that someone has hung around her neck—for the faculties of his mind are now at rest in the holy power, the essence of bliss."*
>
> *"Business, family, secular life, the beauties and hopes of youth and the success of maturity have now been left behind, Eternity alone remains. And, so it is to that—*

*and, not to the tasks and worries of their life, already gone which came and passed like a dream-that the mind is turned."*

*"The Sannyasi has his spiritual eye on goods that men can't give and cares little for anything that men can take away. Therefore, he is beyond the possibility of either seduction or threat."*

***Sannyasa is of Four Kinds:*** 'Vidvat'-born out of real wisdom and is spontaneous 'Vividisha' springing from a yearning for self-realisation through study of the Scriptures and practicing the rigours prescribed Aatura upon one's deathbed when there is no hope in living further, and Markata-embracing Sannyasa as an escape from great misery, disappointment or misfortune that one is not able to face in worldly activities.

No one is encouraged to become a 'Sannyasi' unless one has gone through one's natural impulses through the three previous Ashramas. He who runs away from marriage (Grihastaashrama) is no better than a coward deserting the battle field.

The student's attention is directed inward, preparing for life ahead. In Grihasta and Vanaprasta attention is directed outward-Grihasta supporting the entire society, Vanasprasta sharing his experiences for the good of others. The Sannyasi is again inner directed. Having contributed to society and having received from society what he needed, he prepares himself for the final release. Sannyasa means renunciation not of life alone but of Kama, Artha and even worldly Dharmas. Sannyasa may be deemed a second phase of Brahmacharya.

The first was a preparation for life; the second a preparation for death. While Brahmacharya and Grihasta show the 'Pravritti Marga (towards the world), Vanaprasta and Sannyasa indicate the 'Nivritti Marga' (away from the world) through introspection and renunciation.

Thus, while 'Varna' is determined by past 'Karma', Ashrama is determined by the stage of maturity displayed by individuals in viewing the goals of life.

"Varnas stress human nature; Ashramas stress human nurture".

And, Lord Krishna advises "One's own duty, though done imperfectly is preferable to the duty of another even if well performed. Even death in doing one's own duty is blissful; doing another's duty is frightful".

So, everyone is advised to do his / her 'Dharma' according to one's Varna and Ashrama—and not to venture doing those outside one's own. Every person has his Svabhava (natural being) fitting him for his Svadharma (natural function). We cannot change either our natural being or our natural function because nature cannot be forced into a change by our whims and fancies.

A Sadhu was rescuing a scorpion that had fallen into a pond. Every time he lifted it out of water, it stung him but he would not give up until it was saved. One of his disciples asked why he was persistent in saving the scorpion that stung him. The Sadhu replied: "The `Dharma' or nature of scorpion is to sting; the nature or Dharma of a Sadhu is to rescue a being from distress—and in this case sure death by drowning. So long as the scorpion does not give up its Dharma why should I give up mine and give up saving it?" The `Dharma' of fire is to burn, of water is to be cool, of wind is to blow. So, the Dharma of man is to be humane. This story emphasises how one should go on doing one's duty even if obstacles, impediments and difficulties intervene in discharging it.

The Dharma of a student is to study. If the student—neglects his studies he neglects his svadharma; if fire does not burn, it is not fire; When heated by fire (by external influence) water loses its nature (Svadharma) of being cool. When Svadharma is not practiced, there ensues an imbalance in the environment. This understanding and adherence to Svadharma is what distinguishes human beings from other beings.

## Purusharthas

Purusha means human being and artha means object or objective. Purusharthas means objectives of man. According to Hindu way of life, a man should strive to achieve four chief objectives (Purusharthas) in his life. They are:

1. dharma (righteousness),

2. artha (material wealth),
3. kama (desire) and
4. moksha (salvation).

Every individual in a society is expected to achieve these four objectives and seek fulfillment in his life before departing from here. The concept of Purusharthas clearly establishes the fact that Hinduism does not advocate a life of self negation and hardship, but a life of balance, achievement and fulfillment.

***Dharma:*** Dharma is a very complicated word, for which there is no equivalent word in any other language, including English. Dharma actually means that which upholds this entire creation. It is a Divine law that is inherent and invisible, but responsible for all existence. Dharma exists in all planes, in all aspects and at all levels of creation. In the context of human life, dharma consists of all that an individual undertakes in harmony with Divine expectations and his own inner spiritual aspirations, actions that would ensure order and harmony with in himself and in the environment in which he lives. Since this world is deluded, a human being may not know what is right and what is wrong or what is dharma and what is adharma. Hence he should rely upon the scriptures and adhere to the injunctions contained there in. In short, dharma for a human being means developing divine virtues and performing actions that are in harmony with the divine laws.

Dharma is considered to be the first cardinal aim because it is at the root of everything and upholds everything. For example see what happens when a person amasses wealth without observing dharma or indulges in sexual passion against the social norms or established moral values. Any action performed without observing dharma is bound to bring misery and suffering and delay ones salvation. Hinduism therefore considers it rightly as the first cardinal aim of life.

In ancient India dharmasastras (law books) provided guidance to people in their day to day lives and helped them to adhere to dharma. These law books were written for a particular time frame and are no more relevant to the modern world. The best way to know what is dharma and what is adharma, is to follow the religious scriptures such as the

Bhagavad Gita and the Upanishads or any other scripture that contains the words of God.

***Artha:*** Artha means wealth. Hinduism recognises the importance of material wealth for the overall happiness and well being of an individual. A house holder requires wealth, because he has to perform many duties to uphold dharma and ensure the welfare and progress of his family and society. A person may have the intention to uphold the dharma, but if he has no money he would not be able to perform his duties and fulfil his dharma.

Hinduism therefore rightly places material wealth as the second most important objective in human life. Lord Vishnu is the best example for any householder who wants to lead a life of luxury and still be on the side of God doing his duties. As the preserver of the universe, Lord Vishnu lives in Vaikunth amid pomp and glory, with the goddess of wealth herself by his side and yet helps the poor and the needy, protects the weak, upholds the dharma and sometimes leaving everything aside rushes to the earth as an incarnation to uphold dharma.

Hinduism advocates austerity, simplicity and detachment, but does not glorify poverty. Hinduism also emphasises the need to observe dharma while amassing the wealth. Poverty has become a grotesque reality in present day Hindu society. Hindus have become so poverty conscious that if a saint or a sage leads a comfortable life, they scoff at him, saying that he is not a true yogi. They have to remind themselves of the simple fact that none of the Hindu gods and goddesses are really poor.

Hinduism believes that both spiritualism and materialism are important for the salvation of human beings. It is unfortunate that Hinduism came to be associated more with spiritualism, probably because of the influence of Buddhism, where as in truth Hinduism does not exclude either of them. As Swami Vivekananda rightly said religion is not for the empty stomachs. Religion is not for those whose main concern from morning till evening is how to make both ends meet. Poverty crushes the spirit of man and renders him an easy prey to wicked forces.

In ancient India Artha Sastras (scriptures on wealth) provided necessary guidance to people on the finer aspects of managing their wealth. Kautilya's Artha Sastra, which is probably a compilation of many independent works, gives us a glimpse of how money matters were handled in ancient India.

***Kama:*** Kama in a wider sense means desire and in a narrow sense, sexual desire. Hinduism prescribes fulfilment of sexual passions for the householders and abstinence from it for the students and ascetics who are engaged in the study of the scriptures and in the pursuit of Brahman.

The Bhagavad Gita informs us that desire is an aspect of delusion and one has to be wary of its various movements and manifestations. The best way to deal with desires is to develop detachment and perform desireless actions without seeking the fruit of ones actions and making an offering of all the actions to God. This way our actions would not bind us to the cycle of births and deaths.

Hinduism permits sexual freedom so long as it is not in conflict with the first aim, *i.e.* dharma. Hindu scriptures emphasise that the purpose of sex is procreation and perpetuation of family and society, while the purpose of dharma is to ensure order in the institution of family and society. A householder has the permission to indulge in sex, but also has the responsibility to pursue it in accordance with the laws of dharma. Marriage is a recognised social institution and marriage with wife for the purpose of producing children is legitimate and in line with the aims of dharma.

One of the important sects of Hinduism is Tantricism. It recognises the importance of sexual freedom in the liberation of soul. The Tantrics accept sex as an important means to experience the blissful nature of God and the best way to experience God in physical form. They also refer to the concept of Purusharthas to justify their doctrines. They believe that sexual energy is divine energy and it can be transformed into spiritual energy through controlled expression of sex.

Just as the Dharmasastras were written for the sake of dharma, and Arthasastras for artha, Kamasastras were composed in ancient India for providing guidance in matters of sex. We have lost many of them because of the extreme secrecy and social disapproval associated with the subject.

***Moksha:*** If dharma guides the life of a human being from below acting as the earth, showing him the way from above like a star studded mysterious sky is Moksha. Dharma constitutes the legs of a Purusha that walk upon the earth; both artha and kama constitute his two limbs active in the middle region; while Moksha constitutes the head that rests in the heaven.

Human life is very precious because of all the beings in all the worlds, only human beings have the best opportunity to realise the Higher self. It is also precious because it is attained after many hundreds and thousands of lives. Rightly, salvation should be its ultimate aim.

Moksha actually means absence of moha or delusion. Delusion is caused by the inter play of the triple gunas. When a person overcomes these gunas, he attains liberation. The gunas can be overcome by detachment, self control, surrender to god and offering ones actions to God.

If dharma is the centre of the wheel of human life, artha and kama are the two spokes and Moksha is its circumference. If dharma is at the centre of human life, beyond Moksha there is no human life, but only a life divine.

The four Purusharthas are also like the four wheels of a chariot called human life. They collectively uphold it and lead it. Each influences the movement of the other three, and in the absence of any one of them, the chariot comes to a halt.

The Four Yogas as Spiritual Discipline to follow the Dharma

*Karman.yevaadhikaaras the' maa phalesuu kadaachana |*
*Maa karma-phala-hethur bhoor maa the sangosthv-akarmani ||* *-II-47 || Chapter II-47*

*Thou hast a right to action or work alone, and never to its fruits;*
*let not the fruit of work be thy motive, let not thy attachment to inaction.*

*yoga-sthah: kuru karmaani sangam thyakthvaa dhananjaya |*

*siddhy-asiddhyoh: samo bhootvaa samathvam yoga uchyate' | |* *-II-48 | | Chapter II-48*

*Do thy work being steadfast in devotion and abandoning attachment, O Arjuna !*

*and being equal in success and failure. This evenness of mind is called Yoga*

*doore'na hy avaram karma buddh'i-yogaadh dh'ananjaya |*

*buddh'au saranam annnviccha kr.panaah phala-hethavah: | |* *-II-49 | | Chapter II-49*

*Bhagavad Gita*

'O' Arjuna mere action performed with attachment is inferior to action performed with mind poised in evenness. Seek shelter in this state of unperturbed evenness in a desireless mind. Those who work for selfish gains are indeed pitiable.

***The Spiritual Discipline and Teachings Applied for the Practice:*** The Philosophical teachings of Hinduism, like any scientific theory, are of no use to the common man unless it is applied for their daily practice. It has survived the test of time for many thousand years and still remains popular due to the sound principles on which its practice is based. It gives different rules of ethics and conducts for various categories of people. The Dharma Sastras and Smritis teach us of normal conduct in performing our work. Dharma, Artha, Kama and Moksha are the four Purusharthas that govern out activity. Dharma is the proper rules of one's duty, which literally means "that which holds" the universe and its beings. They are classified as Samanya Dharma or the general and universal rules and Visesha Dharma or specific personal rules for each individual. They give peace, joy, strength and tranquillity. Artha and Kama are the materialistic desire and passion, that also govern our actions. Unless one seeks the material benefits and pleasures within the scope of Dharma, it will cause grief with greed and lust. Moksha is the relief from pain and suffering and ultimate liberation that is the main reason for all our actions.

***The Four Yogas as Spiritual Discipline :*** As rituals became popular and were being considered as the sole path for the eternal bliss, the soundness of its philosophy and ethics of practice were reestablished by the sages. The four Yogas give us the spiritual discipline of our conduct. Karma Yoga is the correct path of performing work without greed or desire and the action performed without looking for the fruits of benefit or loss. Raja Yoga is the discipline of control of our body and mind. It teaches concentration, meditation, breathing and physical exercise and a state of equanimity of the mind as a natural reaction to all activities. Bhakti Yoga is the spiritual discipline of absolute devotion and love of God. It teaches prayers and surrender to God at all times. It teaches to see and feel God in all people and all actions. Jnana Yoga is the path of obtaining Spiritual knowledge through action, study, meditation and devotion.

***Three Gunas :*** Vedas describe three personality traits, Sathvika, Rajasika and Tamasika. Sathvika Gunas are present in the pious person who follows all teachings of the faith and Dharma. Compassion to all animals, Ahimsa and vegetarianism are advocated as Sathva Guna. The Rajasika Gunas are present in people who enjoyed some amount of worldly pleasures directed by desire and ego, which are Artha and Kama. Tamasika persons have no knowledge of the proper Dharma or they do not care for them. They are driven solely by Artha and Kama which are passion, greed and lust.

These Gunas are present in all but one is dominant. The Yogas advocate the ways to follow the superior Sathva Guna and the ways to suppress the undesirable Artha and Kama without the proper Dharma. Performance of proper Dharma and all the Karma leads to a sense of peace and equanimity of mind and eternal bliss. The individual makeup of a person, his Guna and effects of his Karma determines the rebirth and ultimate liberation. Performance of one's duty without devotion to God is dry and empty. Performance of such duty should be without any attachment to its fruit but as a devotion to God. Hinduism gave us the four Vedas, the three Agamas, the six Dharsanas and the four Yogas.

*Bhakti Yoga, the attainment of Divinity through worship.*

*Guru Brahmah Gurur Vishnuhuhu Guru Devoo Maheswaraha*

*Guru Sakshath Para Brahma Tasmai Sree Gurave' Namaha*

*Guru is Lord Brahma, Lord Vishnu and Lord Maheswara,*

*Guru is nothing but the Supreme Brahman devoid of attributes.*

*That is the reason why we bow to the Guru.*

*Bhakti Yoga, the methods of worship.*

### *Various forms of Devotion and Sanskara*

Hindu Religious Faith and practice are based on its strong philosophy and the ancient tradition. Most of the followers know about the Vedas and the Vedantha philosophy. Every one understands that there is one God who is worshipped in many forms. Most of them are familiar with the Advaita theory and Vedanta philosophy of oneness of the Divine and the human soul. However, the practice is much more closer to the Dvaita and Visista-advaita theories for the worship of the Divine. The paths of Karma yoga, Raja yoga, Bhakti yoga and Gnana yoga are taught as the spiritual disciplines for the practice. Some feel that Gnana or the path of wisdom is the ultimate while others consider that after performing duties without attachment as in Karma yoga, practicing meditation and controlling thoughts as in Raja yoga and gaining knowledge of Gnana path one will reach the state of ultimate surrender of Bhakti yoga.

Among all the paths of Hinduism, the most common and popular ones have been the ritualistic [Sanskara] path and the Devotional [Bhakti] paths of worship. The ritualistic path involves the practice of sanskaara which are performing the regular rituals for the formless Supreme Divine as prescribed in the Karma kanda and Upasana kanda portions of the Vedas. They are performed every day and for various events in one's life. These are practised and performed mostly by persons knowledgeablc in the Vedas and the Hindu philosophy and those initiated to the practice of these rituals.

The Bhakti pathway is much easier to follow for everyone. It teaches a method of love and attachment towards a supreme God through one of His manifestations as in the Agamas and Puranas with devotional prayers and worship to various forms of Deities through poojas and bhajans. This form of Bhakti develops into various levels and degrees as an inner attitude of an attachment and feeling of love towards God, from a blind faith and devotion to God in one form to total surrender to the Supreme.

***Bhakti Yoga-the Devotional Pathway:*** Para-Bhakti is the form of devotion with contemplation on the formless and unmanifested Brahmam. It is the highest form of Bhakti suitable only for few learned people, the Jnana Yogis, who have the true knowledge of God.

Apara-Bhakti or Gauni-Bhakti is the primal level of love and devotion to a manifested Iswara and prayers to one of His forms accepted as Ishta-Devatha or a personal God. There are many levels or grades in this, the most important being Bhaya-Bhakti, Anyaya-Bhakti and Ekantha-Bhakti.

Bhaya-Bhakti is the very external form of worship of a Deity as God. It is the adoration paid to a form of God outside ourselves. It is the most basic form of a faith, based on the unenlightened or Tamasika feeling that God is external to us and dwells in a particular locality like the prayer room or Temple. The pilgrimages, worship of several images of God, symbols and sacred books are examples of this. Most popular religions do not rise above this level.

Anyaya-Bhakti [meaning "not another"] is the exclusive and passionate, or the Rajasika, form of worship of one's Ishta-Devatha in the heart. It is an intense form of monotheism and gives a healthy direction to the spirit of devotion. But, it shall not give rise to bigotry and cruelty towards those who have different concept of God and different methods of approach. Among Hindus, it is well recognised that the gods whom others worship are only different forms of his own Ishta-devatha.

Ekantha-Bhakti is the purest and Sattvika form of devotion. Here, the devotee loves God for His own sake and not for His gifts. He learns to crave for his personal God alone, in prosperity as well as in adversity. He sees the presence of God, as his Ishta-devata, in all places, at all times.

*Bhavas as an expression of Devotion and Love*

1. Santha Bhava: [means calmness of mind] The mind of the devotee is filled with divine knowledge and is emotionless, always undisturbed, peaceful and tranquil. Only Yogis and Jñanis, like Bhishma, who are highly developed and have had direct experience of God will be able to practice Santha Bhava.
2. Dasya Bhava: The devotee considers himself as inferior to God. He takes God to be his Master and looks upon himself as just a humble servant. He considers it is his duty to worship and to love God. Hanuman is an example of Dasya Bhakti.
3. Sakhya Bhava: The devotee considers God to be a dear friend, the sole supreme companion, and as his equal in relation, with pure friendship not degenerating into familiarity. Arjuna is an example of Sakhya Bhaktha.
4. Vatsalya Bhava: The devotee considers God as his Child and the themselves as the mother giving and also getting the unconditional love of the Child. Mother Yashoda had Vatsalya Bhakti towards Child Krishna as her own child.
5. Kantha Bhava: This is the expression of devotion with a feeling like the one a wife gets and gives towards her husband, as in the case of devotion of Sita or Rukmini towards Sri Rama and Sri Krishna, called Kantha Bhava.
6. Madhurya Bhava: This is the highest expression of Divine love. Here, the devotee takes the lord to be his beloved, with deep love, devotion and surrenders himself. When Gopikas like Radha develops Bhakti towards Sri Krishna, it is the romantic love and surrender of the self to the lover, without any sensuality but with pure devotion and surrender, called Madhurya Bhava.

***Fundamental Disciplines needed for Bhakti Yoga***

1. *Abhyasa:* Practice of constantly and continuously remembering God with a steady mind.
2. *Viveka:* Discrimination, the ability to choose between right and wrong.
3. *Vimoka:* Intense longing for God, rejecting everything that hinders our progress.
4. *Sathyam:* Truthfulness, to be always observed as a basic rule of spiritual ethics. We have to live a life of truth, think truth alone, speak truth and listen carefully to their own inner voice called conscience.
5. *Arjavam:* This is straightforwardness or honesty.
6. *Kriya:* Doing good to all beings, as the devotee will God in all forms.
7. *Kalyana:* This is wishing well of others with a loving heart, praying to the Lord for the well being of others, for the peace and welfare of the world.
8. *Dhaya:* Compassion, as God is love, mercy and compassion personified. As we seek to realise Him, we, too, must develop the same qualities.
9. *Ahimsa:* The practice of non-violence, non-injury to all creatures, by way of action, thought or word.
10. *Dhaana:* Abundant and spontaneous charity with a pure heart, for relieving the suffering of the distressed is a potent means of growing spiritually.
11. *Anavasada:* To be cheerful and hopeful is an essential quality of a devotee. One must always have faith and hope.

*manmana bhava madh-bhakto madh-yaaji man namaskuru |*
*mam-e'Vaishyasi sathyam the' prathijane' priyo'sime' | |*

*Bhagavad Gita Chapter XVIII-65*

With your mind engrossed in Me, become My devotee, worship Me and salute Me.

I promise you that you will come to Me alone, as you are so dear to Me.

*Etham Vibhoothim Yogam Cha; Mama Yo Ve'tthi Thatthvathah: |*
*So'vikalpena Yogena Yujyate'; Nathra Samsayah | |*
*Bhagavad Gita Chapter X-7.*

He who knows about this manifestation of My divine majesties and my power unites with Me in steady and unfaltering communion. About this there is no doubt.

*Cycles of time as recorded in the Vedas and Upanishads*

*Here are cycles of time as recorded in the Vedas and Upanishads.*

Small Yuga: 2,000 years. The axis of the earth spends 2,000 years in an astrological sign and the moves on to the next sign, going backwards through the signs of the zodiac. Since we are finishing the Pisceaen cycle, we are ready to enter the Aquarian cycle for the next 2,000 years. We commonly refer to entering Aquârius as the "dawning of the age of Aquarius."

Complete Cycle of Small Yugas: 24,000 years. This is the amount of time needed for the earth to spend 2,000 years in each sign of the zodiac.

***The Great Cycle:*** In addition to the earth's axis moving in an arc as it travels through the signs of the zodiac, there is another cycle. This is a cycle which involves the revolution of the entire solar system around the Central Sun of the Galaxy. The orbit is elliptical rather than circular. To make the elliptical movement of the solar system around a great central point more understandable, the analogy of "seasons" is used. This is a useful analogy because changes in overall states of consciousness are represented as "seasons" through which the solar system passes on its journey.

When consciousness is in a high state, it is summer. At this time, 90 per cent of the inhabitants of the earth are enlightened. This is called Satya Yuga, or the Age of Truth. When Fall or Spring are in full swing, the numbers of enlightened beings drops to less than 10 per cent. When Winter comes, far less than 1 per cent of the people on earth are enlightened. However, there arc trade offs.

First, it is easier to make progress in the "'winter of consciousness." The analogy is often used that if one tries to row one's boat in air, very little progress will be achieved. But when the oars are placed in water, much more rapid progress can be made. This is because compared to air, the resistance of water is much higher enabling the work of the oars to bear fruit. It is the resistance itself which provides a route to rapid progress. Similarly, in spiritual winter our efforts to achieve spiritual growth produce much faster results than they would in any other age of consciousness because of the great general resistance to things spiritual.

There is no disagreement among all the sages, pandits, gurus and swamis that Kali Yuga, the present spiritual winter, affords an opportunity for more rapid spiritual progress than any other age. Further, the medium for rapid growth is almost universally prescribed by these same classes of spiritual teachers as divine sound through the medium of mantra. Here are the various seasons and ages of the universe as measured in human years.

Winter (Kali Yuga): 432,000 years

The year 2001 is 5,093 years from the beginning of Kali Yuga of the long cycle. For the short cycle, winter is ending with the entrance of the planetary axis into Aquarius, which begins the season of Spring for the shorter, 24,000 year cycle.

*Spring: (Treta Yuga) 1,296,000 years*

*Summer (Ṣatya or Krita Yuga) 1,728,000 years*

*Autumn (Dwapara Yuga) 864,000 years*

*Total Time for One Cycle or Manvantara: 4,320,000,000 years*

*This is called "A Day of Brahma" and is followed by a night of equal length.*

*One complete day and night of Brahma: 8,640,000,000 years*

*360 of these days is called "One Year of Brahma": 3,110,400,000,000 years*

*100 of these years constitute the life of Brahma called a Maha Kalpa: 311,040,000,000,000 years*

At the end of a "Maha Kalpa" or cycle of creation, Shiva manifests his destructive influence and the universe is dissolved. The ancient texts call this the cosmic dissolution. All the levels of the manifest universe disappear. After a great cosmic rest cycle, another creative cycle begins as a new Brahma emerges out of the navel of Narayana and the universe is created anew.

Another item of importance is that one who has achieved the highest level of conscious realisation is said to realise and become one with Brahman. At this point, all individuality as we know it disappears. The individual Jiva, Soul or Atman retums to its source from which it will not return of its own volition. However, for reasons known only to itself, certain souls may return for reasons understood only by Narayana.

## Samskara

The ultimate goal of every Hindu is to attain Moksha. This can only come through atma-vidya, which is knowing one's self, through thought and introspection. To attain this, the scriptures give some guidelines. The first step is to master eight characteristics. These called atmagunas are:

1. Compassion (daya)
2. Forgiveness or patience (kshanti)
3. Absence of jealousy (anasuya)
4. Cleanliness (sauchyam)
5. Not feeling mental strain or doing work with effortless ease (anayasa)
6. Auspiciousness (mangala)
7. Non-miserliness (akarpanya)
8. Non-grasping or non-desiring nature (asprha).

Toward cultivation of these characteristics, the Vedas also give guidelines as to the rituals to be performed over one's lifetime. Sixteen such rituals are collectively called Shodasha Samskara. Samskara denotes purification ritual. Starting from the time when the child is in the womb, these sixteen rituals end in the final journey of the body into the afterlife. They can be divided into those performed during five different stages of life, *i.e.* prenatal, childhood, student, adult life and old age or wisdom years. Forty rituals are discussed but sixteen are still in practice.

1. *Garbhadana Samskara:* Performed by a married couple when conceiving a child. This important samskara raises the act of conception to a sacred occasion, and is powerfully purifying and uplifting for the unborn child.
2. *Pumsavana Samskara:* Usually performed between the second and fourth month of pregnancy. Its purpose is, first, to promote the birth of a male child (for perpetuation of the family line and tradition); second, to insure the good health of the fetus and the proper formation of its organs, regardless of gender.
3. *Simantonoyana Samskara:* In the fourth or fifth month of pregnancy, the mind of the fetus begins to develop. This is when simantonoyana samskara is performed. Its purpose is to protect the fetus—especially its newly forming mind—from all negative influences, and also to stimulate the development of the unborn child's intellect.
4. *Jatakarma Samskara :* It is the ritual performed at the birth of a child. It awakens the child's intellect, gives it strength and promotes long life for the child.
5. *Namakarana Samskara:* On the 11th day after the child's birth, namakarana samskara is performed. In this ceremony, the child receives its name.
6. *Nishkramana Samskara:* The baby's first outing into the world, beyond the confines of the home, is the occasion of nishkramana samskara.
7. *Annaprashana Samskara:* The first feeding of solid food to the baby, usually in the sixth month after birth, is the occasion of Annaprashana samskara.
8. *Karnavedha Samskara:* Usually performed in the sixth or seventh month after birth, consists of the piercing of the baby's ear lobes, so earrings may be worn.
9. *Chudakarana Samskara:* At the end of the first year, or during the third year, the child's hair is shaved—

all but a tuft on the top of the head. This ritual shaving of hair, performed with ceremony, prayers and Vedic chanting is for both boys and girls.

10. *Vidyarambha Samskara:* This samskara begins a student's primary education by ceremonially introducing the child to the alphabet.
11. *Upanayana Samskara:* Initiates the formal study of the Vedas. It is one of the most important and esteemed of the samskaras. Upon performance of upanayana, a boy traditionally moves from home to live in the ashram of the Guru.
12. *Samavartana Samskara:* With samavartana samskara the disciple graduates from his Vedic studies and returns from the house of his Guru. Thereafter, the disciple will marry and raise a family, and so enter the stage of householder, grihasthaashrama.
13. *Vivaha Samskara:* The traditional Hindu wedding ceremony. It is considered by many to be the most important of all the samskaras.
14. *Panchamahayajna Samskara:* A married couple performs these five great sacrifices daily. In this samskara, one honours, in turn, the rishis (ancient seers of Truth), the gods, the ancestors, humankind and all created beings.
15. *Vanaprastha Samskara:* According to the Vedic tradition, vanaprastha is the third stage of life, following brahmacharya (Vedic student/disciple) and grihastha (householder). Here, a man leaves behind his life in the world and retires to the forest (with or without his wife), to live an ascetic life devoted to study of the scriptures and to meditation.
16. *Antyeshti Samskara:* The final sacrament, the funeral rites.

***Initiation or Upanayana:*** The initiation ceremony called the Upanayana or the second birth is a very ancient practice. The boy who undergoes the ceremony is said to be twice born or Dvija. He is also now considered an Aryan. The ritual consists of wearing a sacred thread called Yajnopavita with the utterance of the sacred mantra, which goes as follows:

*"Om yajnopaveetam paramam pavitram prajapateryat sahajam purastaat.*

*Aayushyamagryam pratimuncha shubhram yajnopaveetam balamastu tejah."*

*"The sacred thread is great and pure.*

*It came to existence along with the birth of Brahma.*

*It is as old as He is.*

*May it, which is blessed by celestials, give us long life, strength and radiance."*

The sacred thread is hung over the left shoulder and under the right arm. The cord is not to be removed once placed unless it is defiled by death or birth in the family. The cord was made of three threads, each of nine twisted strands made of cotton, hemp or wool, for Brahman, Kshatriya and Vaishya classes respectively. At this ceremony the boy (called Vatu) is taught the sacred Gayatri Mantra, whispered in his ear by his father and Guru (called Brahmopadesha). Only the higher classes can recite this mantra. It is as follows:

*"Om Bhuh, Om Bhuvah, Om Suvah, Om Maha, Om Janah, Om Tapah, Om Satyam,*

*Om, Tat Savitur vareniam, Bhargo devasya dhimahi, Dhiyo yonah prachodayat."*

*"Om Earth, Om Sky, Om Heaven, Om Middle Region, Om Place of Births,*

*Om Mansion of the Blessed, Om Abode of Truth,*

*Let us think of the lovely splendor of God Savitur (Sun) that he may inspire our minds."*

The Gayatri Mantra can also be translated as "That Eternal God or Creator, Independent Reality, the Worshipful, One who has no Beginning, Light of Wisdom and Truth. That Lord who manifests through the Sun (Savitur), propitiated by the highest Gods; One who bestows wisdom, bliss and everlasting life; we meditate on that Light. May that Light of God illuminate our intellect." A long time ago, most Kshatriyas and Vaishyas ceased to perform the initiation ceremony in its full form. The term 'twice born (dvija)' came to be applied more and more to the Brahman class.

***Panch Mahayajna:*** Performance of numerous religious duties consists of proper following of one's Dharma. These are the bounden or obligatory karma of a Hindu. There are five great sacrifices (Pancha-mahayajna). These are to be performed thrice daily at sunrise, noon and sunset. They consist of:

- Brahmayajna, the worship of the Brahman the World Spirit, by reciting the Vedas:
- Pitryayajna, the worship of the ancestors, by libations of water and periodical Shraddha
- Devayajna, the worship of the gods, by pouring ghee on the sacred fire.
- Bhutayajna, the worship of all living things, by scattering grains and food for the animals and spirits.
- Purusayajna, the worship of men, by showing hospitality.

Kama was a legitimate branch of human activity and physical love was not disparaged. Though the term generally means desire, the word has definite sexual connotation. The Hindu literature, both religious and secular, is full of sexual allusions and symbolisms. The temple carvings of the Middle Ages are full of couples in full embrace and sexual positions. Vatsyayana's Kamasutra is the most famous text dedicated to Kama. It is a remarkable work giving detailed instructions of erotic technique and aphrodisiac recipes and charms. There is emphasis on mutual gratification and foreplay. There are at least sixteen types of kisses detailed! In the historical perspective it gives a great insight into the life of Hindu upper class of the times.

It is important to remember the difference between similar sounding words. 'Brahman' is the Universal World Soul mentioned in the Vedas. 'Brahmanas' are the appendices to Upanishad where the sacrificial rituals are carefully delineated. 'Brahman' or 'Brahmana' is the priest class of Hindus, which is one of the four castes.

# 5

# The Sixteen Hindu Samskaras (Sacraments)

Man Making is a science. Like a gardener, parents & teachers work on a person so that the best can flower out from him or her. The whole thrust is to help bring about greater awareness & love in the mind, and canalise the interest & energies into positive fields. The whole 'work' is on the mind alone, and is comparable to the work of a genetic engineer. The only difference is that while a genetic engineer plays & transforms with the basic structure, a teacher works to manifest the basic inherent beauty, freedom & potential which facilitates to carve out a dynamic, creative, intelligent & magnanimous personality.

Interest is a very subjective thing, and has to come out from within. It can never be imposed. Interests are created by impressions & knowledge. That is what ad agencies too do. They create impressions, and this 'works' on the mind of the person to bring about the interest in him in the desired field. Once the interest has been manifested we can just sit back and see the person work for his or her field of interest in a dynamic way. While the experts of the advertisement world are generally seen to use this 'knowledge of impressing minds' for their selfish & commercial ends, the Vedic Masters used this knowledge to help bring out a positive & dynamic personality. While the former conditions the mind to the extent that the very thinking process of their target crowd is conditioned in their favour, but the Rishis saw to it that the very power to think & question daringly, independently & creatively grew.

Thus we have all our scriptures in the form of question & answers.

These deliberate & positive impressions which help create a deep & lasting impressions on the mind of a person—so as to generate interest in him about the Truth & Dharma, help bring out a positive personality and free the mind of its negativities are called 'Samskaras'. No one while living in the world remains free of the conditionings of his or her environs & teachings, so the question is not whether we can stop all conditionings but to see to it that a person is looked after like a plant and help his or her potentials bloom. To a question whether Samskaras are deliberate positive conditionings, well the answer is that, the objective of the entire exercise is to help a person awake to a state which is free from all conditionings, so while impressions are certainly put effectively & deliberately yet they are the very antithesis of what is implied by the word conditionings. This is one of the finest & blessed science, and has been perfected here as an art form too.

Samskaras are the turning points of life and need to be celebrated. Celebrations are very important ingredients of Samskaras. They directly or indirectly involve our respected elders, scholars, near & dear ones. Everyone gets together to convey their best wishes & blessings to the person concerned and thus there is social & religious sanction for the act & ceremony. Samskaras are great, time-tested tools in our traditional systems which help carve out a great personality. Apart from scriptural validation, history also proves to us the great effectiveness of these methods. When Vedic Masters had their way, India was on top of the world. The people of the far off land prayed that they will one day see this great land of plenty, prosperity & righteousness.

In this section we shall present an introduction to these famous sixteen Samskaras of Hindus which cover the entire life span of a person and take him to the door steps to Truth.

1. *Garbhadan:* The first coming together of the husband & wife for bringing about conception.
2. *Pumsvan:* Ceremony performed when the first signs of

conception are seen, and is to be performed when someone desires a male child.

3. *Seemantonayan:* A ceremony of parting of the hairs of the expectant mother to keep her spirits high & positive. Special music is arranged for her.
4. *Jatakarma:* After the birth of the child, the child is given a secret name, he is given taste of honey & ghee, mother starts the first breast-feeding after chanting of a mantra.
5. *Nama-karana:* In this ceremony the child is given a formal name. Performed on the 11th day.
6. *Nishkramana:* In this the formal darshan of sun & moon is done for the child.
7. *Annaprashana:* This ceremony is performed, when the child is given solid food (anna) for the first time.
8. *Chudakarana:* Cuda means the 'lock or tuft of hair' kept after the remaining part is shaved off.
9. *Karna-vedha:* Done in 7th or 8th month. Piercing of the ears.
10. *Upanayan and Vedarambha:* The thread ceremony. The child is thereafter authorized to perform all rituals. Studies of Vedas begins with the Guru.
11. *Keshanta:* Hairs are cut, guru dakshina is given
12. *Samavartan:* Returning to the house
13. *Vivaha:* Marriage ceremony
14. *Vanprastha:* As old age approaches, the person retires for a life of tapas & studies.
15. *Sanyas:* Before leaving the body a Hinddu sheds all sense of responsibility & relationships to awake & revel in the timeless truth.
16. *Antyeshthi:* The last rites done after the death.

***Objects of Samskara***

Samskaras (Sacraments) are rituals and sacrifices. By virtue of thoir performances the life of the performer receives a higher sanctity. Samskaras cover the entire life of a Hindu from the moment he is conceived in the mother's womb till his death-inclusive of his funeral ceremonies and thereafter, for the smooth passage of his soul to another world.

Just as gold and diamonds that are dug out from the ore need refining and polishing in order to shine in all their splendour, man too needs these Samskaras or purificatory ceremonies in order to shine in his best form physically, psychically and spiritually.

There are several objects of the Samskaras, as can be seen from the Mantras and symbolism used in the ceremonies. These can be broadly divided into two categories; to invoke beneficence from the kindly gods and to keep away or remove hostile or evil powers that beset human life at various stages.

Samskaras aim in the first instance at material gain to the individual. During some ceremonies prayers are offered to gods for health, wealth, children, intellect etc., which contribute to domestic and social felicity. Samskaras mirror self-expression of joys and sorrows, hopes and ambitions, which man exhibits in a dignified way when he celebrates these functions with feasts, presents, decoration, music and also in funeral ceremonies in an appropriate mood.

Samskaras also create an awareness of the attainment of social status and privileges for the individual. The boy who is given the sacred thread acquires the right to study the Vedas; the married man gains the title to perform the Dharmas mentioned in the Vedas.

Samskaras bring about cultural gains. The ancient lawgivers underscored the introduction of higher religion and sanctity in the lives of those who undergo Samskaras. Some impurity is inherently attached to the prenatal stage of birth and Manu and Yajnavalkya see in the Samskara ceremonies, the removal of those impurities, so that man's body is made fit to become a temple for God to reside. Samskaras are moulders of character.

Sage Angiras poetically refers to the development of personality that the Samskaras endow on its adherents: "Just as a picture is painted with various colours, so the character of the individual is formed by the proper performance of the

Samskaras." Sage Gautama said that Samskaras along with the eight Atmagunas take one to Brahman (Supreme Self) or Moksha.

In short, the whole gamut of Samskaras is designed to channel the entire energies of man towards the creation of a perfect secular as well as spiritual life in himself in a manner that is not only ingenious but essentially practical, dignified and compulsory in the interest of all-round human welfare.

To quote Max Muller, the emphasis placed upon these ceremonies by the ancients disclose "the deep-rooted tendency in the heart of man to bring the chief events of human life into contact with a higher power, and to give to our joys and sufferings a deeper significance and a religious sanctification.

***History and Sources***

The earliest suggestion of Samskaras are found in the Rig-Veda. Hymns now used in the rituals of marriage, conception and funeral are to be found there, besides others that are generally recited during all rituals. In the Yajurv Veda we have references to the tonsure ceremony. This is common to the Shrauta or Yaga ceremonies.

The Atharva Veda is a rich source of Mantras relating to several of the Samskaras like marriage, funeral, initiation for Vedic studies etc.

Coming down to the Brahmana period, Gopatha Brahmana contains references to Upanayana or the thread-ceremony. The word Brahmacharya is to be found in Sathapatha Brahmana.

Taittiriya Aranyaka contains Mantras for cremation.

Chandogya Upanishad relates how a Brahmacharin is admitted to the Gurukula (boarding school).

Mention of Gayatri Mantra is made in Brahadaranyaka and other Upanishads. Taittiriya Upanishad contains the famous convocation address. This Upanishad also contains Mantras used for begetting a learned son and also relating to funeral ceremonies.

It is reasonable to conclude that Samskaras were developed, amplified, codified and given an institutional bias in later years with the development of civilization, catering to the needs of the time for giving stability to the community.

***Sources***

The rituals constituting the Brahmanas received systematic treatment in what are called Kalpa-Sutras. These are exegetical texts of the Vedas. The need for them arose because short manuals were required by the priests as an aid for their daily performance. Among these texts, those that deal with Vedic sacrifices are called Srauta-Sutras and those that deal with domestic rituals are called Grihya-Sutras which, though not valuable as pieces of literature, are yet valuable as "Folk-lore" journals of ancient India. They portray an accurate picture of the social lie, popular customs and usage of ancient India.

Some important Grihya Sutras are listed below: 1.Apastamba 2. Aswalayana 3.Baudhayana 4.Bharadwaja 5.Gobhila 6. Hiranyakesia 7.Jaimineeya 8.Khadira 9.Manava 10.Paraskara 11.Sankhayana 12.Varaha Grihya Sutras.

There is another class of texts called Dharma Sutras that are an extension of the Grihya Sutras. These texts deal mainly with secular and religious laws relating to the Ashramas. These are again supplemented by what are called Parisishtas or addenda. The Commentaries of which 25 are known; Prayogas, of which 24 are known. There are also a dozen Karikas or specialised treatises on individual Samskaras.

In addition to these are Apta-vakyas or the words of the saints and the wise who observe and follow Sanatan Dharma (Vedic religion). They have the sanctity of Smritis in cases of doubt. These, then, are the real sources of information about the Samskaras. It can easily be seen from the number of works on the subject, how important the ancients considered the Samskaras.

## Sixteen Main Sacraments

### *Pre-Natal Samskaras*

1. *Garbhadhana:* We can call it the conception ceremony. There are certain Do's and Don'ts during the 'Ritu'

period of the woman, which are of great psychological significance. The propitious day and time are fixed astrologically for Garbhadhana and the ritual follows a set pattern. The Mantras uttered in this Samskaras are essentially prayers offered to God to help the bride conceive a good son. The Mantras make use of occasional metaphors of joint action. They can be freely translated thus:

"May we produce strong and long-lived sons as fire is produced by friction; may he be well behaved. I am part of God and I shall produce good sons to liberate my ancestors. May we beget shining, wealthy children. May we donate liberally to the needy and attain moksha. May God make you fit for conception. Let the evil spirit flee from you. Let your child be free from defects like lameness, deafness etc. Be you like the divine Kamadhenu etc."

Procreation is a compulsory duty enjoined on the Hindu to repay his ancestral debt, except when either or both the partners are functionally unfit.

2. *Punsavanam:* This ceremony is performed in the second, third and the fourth month of pregnancy. The meaning and object of this ceremony is to "quicken a male child" in the woman. The Punsavana is performed on a day of male Nakshatra. During this ritual, a few drops of the juice of the Banyan stem are put into the right nostril of the pregnant lady to inhale it, with a prayer for the birth of a son or a worthy child. According to Susruta, the great Ayurvedic writer, the juice of the Banyan tree has all the properties of relieving trouble during pregnancy.

Sanctified thread is tied to the left wrist of the lady by way of protection. The mantras, freely rendered, pray: ""May God Isana fulfil our wishes; Dhata bless the world with children and wealth. May He bless this household too with children. May the immortals live in this house. May Agni bless me with sons. May Indra bless me with children. May I have handsome children."

[Note: The following explanations are from the writings of Swami Dayananda Saraswati (The founder of The Arya Samaj). The translation is by Acharya Vaidyanath Shastri].

Placing his hand on the womb of his pregnant wife the husband should pronounce the following Mantra from the Yajurveda, the meaning of which is given below:

"O soul in the womb! May you have the swiftness of nice-winged swift bird, may there arise in your head the trio of action, contemplation and learning. Gayatri be your eye. Brihat and Rathantara like your sides. Rigveda your soul, metres your limbs. The hymns of Yajuh are your name. The Vamadevya is your body. The deeds worth doing and shunning are your hind part. The yajnas are like your hooves, the feet. You are a noble soul, the master of noble qualities. Acquire knowledge and attain to happiness in life and beyond."

After this the pregnant lady should live in a disciplined way and lead a life with proper (restricted) diet and confined movements. She should eat a small quantity of the cocculus cordiclius (giloy) Brahmi herb, and dry ginger (Soonth) with milk. She should avoid too much sleep, avoid too much talking, avoid saltish food preparations, avoid sour, pungent, bitter things and avoid purgatives like Termunallia Chebula (Haritaki). She should avoid anger, aversion, greed etc. and should always keep her mind joyful and happy. She should lead a life of good conduct.

3. *Simantonnayana:* The third in the series of prenatal Samskaras, this is performed during the period between the fifth and the eighth months of pregnancy. The specific materials used during this Samskara, that are for the lady only, are, the quill of a porcupine, an ear of ripe paddy and some Udumbara leaves. The deity invoked is Rika, the presiding deity of the full-moon. Their implications are: that the pregnancy should be fruitful; the child should be endowed with sharp and penetrating intellect (like the sharp quill of the porcupine). The child should be beautiful like the full-moon. The gist of the Mantra is: "I beseech the goddess

Raka. May she make this ceremony blameless. May my son be endowed with sharp intellect."

Music, especially on the veena, is indicated to be played on this occasion. This increases the mother's suckling power besides conferring other psychological benefits. Ladies are asked to sing: "Be a mother of heroic sons" thus creating a heroic atmosphere. The mother fasts and keeps silent after the ceremony till night time when the stars become visible. At the close of the ceremony she touches a male calf, symbolising a son.

"I, the husband, call my wife who is as beautiful as the full moon in the night and is possessed of good words of praise for me, I call her to participate in all the functions of the prayers. Let her, the lady of good fortunes, listen to my words and understand them with her spirit. May she perform the functions of progeny in such a good way as she sews the clothes etc. with the needle that does not pierce the fingers when sewing. May she give me a brave son. Whatever is uttered herein is true. The oblation offered is meant for Raka and it is not me."

"O full-moon like beautiful lady, and who is munificent nature, come to me with heart full of joy, and with wealth of praiseworthy advice regarding various physical and spiritual wealth. O lucky one, come to me giving a thousand kinds of fortunes. Whatever is uttered herein is true. The oblation offered is meant for Raka and it is not for me."

"My husband who is potentially vigorous has established the embryo of life in me, who is desirous of a son or vigorous child. May husband be free from all evils and accompany me with noble son."

***Post-Natal Samskaras***

4. *Jatakarma:* The persons concerned sprinkle water on the woman that is giving birth to a child.

This is the authority from Paraskar Grihya Sutra and thus the same has been written in the Ashvalayana, Gobhiliya and Shaunakiya Grihya Sutra.

At the time when delivery is going to take place, the sprinkling of water on the body of the pregnant woman should be done with the Mantras from the Yajurveda and from other sources. The ceremony proper should be performed (unless prevented by death in close family circles) before the umbilical cord of the child is severed. The father looks at the face of the newly born infant and this at once redeems his debt to his ancestors. Thereafter he must immediately bathe in cold water with his clothes on. Actually, he must jump into a river or a lake so as to cause the splashing waters to rise in the air as high as a palm tree. He is then enjoined to perform dana, dharma etc. (charity and other good deeds) as the merits earned by him at that time are of immense benefit.

The father then touches the tongue of the infant with a drop of honey touched by a gold ring, uttering Mantras. This action endows the child with Medha or intelligence. Susruta praises honey's properties in this respect.

A name is also given to the child, in secret, lest his enemies should practice black magic on the child with that name. Then the father utters a prayer for long life in the ear of the infant. Other Brahmins (priests) too bless the child with long life by breathing the breath of life upon the infant. The father prays to Mother Earth "May we live a hundred years." By another hymn that says: "Be a stone; be an axe (unto enemies); be the imperishable gold." The father prays that the child be endowed with strength, valour and fame.

After severing the umbilical cord, the child is handed over to the mother to suckle when the husband prays to the water-god to protect the mother too.

[Note: The following abridged explanations (greatly abridged extracts selected at random) are from the writings of Swami Dayananda Saraswati (The founder of The Arya Samaj). The translation is by Acharya Vaidyanath Shastri].

After offering oblations with Mantras the husband should sing Vamadevayagana given at the end of Samanyaprakarana. There after the father of the child should write AUM syllable on the tongue of the child with the pre-prepared golden bar dipped in ghee (clarified butter) and honey mixed properly. Doing so he should whisper 'VEDOASITI' (your confidential name is Veda) in the right ear of the child and then, with the bar of the gold make the child lick a little of the mixed ghee and honey with the following Mantras:

"O child, for you I give this ghee and honey has been produced by God who is the producer of all the wealth of the world. May you be preserved and be protected by learned men and your parents. May you attain long life and live in this world for hundred autumns."

"I establish in you the idea of God who is the giver of life. I establish in you, O child, the idea of God who is all beatitude. I establish in you, O child, the idea of God who is the source of all movements. I establish in you the idea of God who is the life of all, all beatitude and the source of all movements."

"May we attain Divinity, who is thc Master of all the assembled masses of the world, who is wondrous and eternal, who is desired and attainable by individual souls and also the wisdom of discrimination."

After giving ghee and honey six times to the child to lick with these above listed Mantras, rice and barley in a very meager quantity should be cleaned and crushed and mixed with water. The liquid thus prepared be strained through a piece of cloth and be kept in a pot. The father of the child or a person concerned place a drop of this liquid in the mouth of the child using the thumb and the last finger taken together, pronouncing the following Mantra:

"This is ghee. This is grain or cereal. This is for life and this is immortality or the nectar of eatables."

[Note: This is the opinion of only Gobhiliya Grihya-Sutra and not of any other authorities]

Thereafter the father of the child should whisper in the right ear of the child the following Mantras:

"O child, may God, the creator of all bless you with firm wisdom. May Saraswati (the goddess of learning), the all knowing goddess bless you with firm wisdom. May the sun and the moon, stationed in space, be the source of firm wisdom for you."

"The fire is the source of life, it gains this power from the wood-fuel. May you attain long life, O child, with that life giving fire."

"Soma, the moon is the source of life. Knowledge and wisdom is the source of life. It gains this power with the Brahmanas, the knower of the Vedas. The enlightened persons are the source of long life. They gain this power through immortality. He seers (Rishis), possessing penetrative genius, are the source of life. They gain this power by austerity and discipline. The parents, grand-parents etc. are the source of life.. They gain this power from grains, cereals and other foods. The Yajna is the source of life. It gains this power through qualified ways of performance. The ocean is the source of life. It gains this power from the rivers. With that life of moon, with that life of knowledge and wisdom, with that life of the learned persons, with that life of the seers, with that life of parents and grand-parents, with that life of yajna, with that life of ocean, O child, may you attain long life, knowledge and wisdom."

These Mantras should again be recites in the left ear of the child. Thereafter, the father of the child, placing his hand very gently upon the shoulders of the child, should recite more Mantras. Of these one only is reproduced below:

"O child, may you become firm and strong like a rock. May you become like an axe to destroy injustice, may you become as bright as gold with knowledge and action. O child, you are my soul and spirit. May you not be subjected to an immature death. May you live a hundred autumns."

A month before the expected date of delivery, a maternity room (Sutikagriha) is selected on an auspicious day. The room should be in the south-west corner of the house; the ground should be even. The would-be mother enters the room a couple of days before the expected date, after worshipping the elders, family deities and accompanied by auspicious sounds like ringing of bells or music and also accompanied by experienced and pleasant mothers.

They cheer and otherwise prepare the lady for safe delivery by means of approved diet, ointments etc. The room is made comparatively dark, because it is said, the sunlight will be too bright for the new-born babe and for ensuring for it a black retina. When the time arrives, the would be mother is made to lie on her back. Mantras are chanted outside to ward off evil spirits. An elderly person at home unties several knots of a rope suggesting the loosening of muscles tying the child in the womb. The Turyanti leaves are placed near the lady to ward off evil forces and also to expedite delivery. If the delivery is difficult, the verse from the Atharva Veda meant for it, is chanted. On safe delivery a small fire called Sutika-fire is lighted in the room to purify and protect the child and its mother. Mustard seeds and grains are thrown into the fire to counteract evil forces and evil eyes.

5. *Namakarana Samskara (Naming the child):* This is a simple ceremony in which the child is given a name. According to Asvalayana, the names of boys should have an even number of syllables. A two-syllable name will bring material prosperity and fame and a four syllable name will bring religious fame.

The names of girls should have an odd number of syllables and end in "I" or "aa". They should be easy to pronounce, pleasing to the ear and auspicious. They should not suggest awkward suggestions. By traditions, names are chosen after the Nakshatras of birth (letters are allocated to the signs of the zodiac). Some people name their children after the ancestors.

The practice of naming children after favourite deities began from the Puranic times. The rise of the Bhakti (devotion) movement made this practice generally popular. By naming children after gods, we are deemed to gain several opportunities for uttering God's name whenever we call the child.

The Namakarana Samskar is performed, normally on the tenth or twelfth day after birth. If there are inconveniences then it is taken to the end of the first year.

After preliminaries, the parents give the offerings to gods and feel the breath of the child symbolising the awakening of its consciousness and utters in its ear three times: "Your name is .....". The Brahmins and elders are asked to follow, calling the child by that name and blessing it.

[Note: The following abridged explanations are from the writings of Swami Dayananda Saraswati (The founder of The Arya Samaj). The translation is by Acharya Vaidyanath Shastri].

The parents, Acharya (teacher) etc. give name to the child. It is written in the Gobhiliya 2/8/8-18 and the Shaunaka Grihya Sutra that a meritoriously attractive and pleasant name should be given to the child.

The name should be given to the child on the 11th day leaving 10 days from the day of birth of the child or on 101st day or on the very day of the birth of the child in the beginning of the second year.

On the day fixed for giving name to the child, the Yajaman (the father of the child) and the priests of the yajna invite the guests present and commence the ceremony.

After reciting prayers as prescribed in 8 Mantras from Samanya Prakarana, Svastivachana, Shantikarana, and the complete procedure of Samanya Prakarana, four oblations of Aghavarajyabhagahuti; four Vyahriti oblations; eight oblations with eight Mantras beginning with 'Tvanno Agne' from the Samanya prakarana, should be offered.

Thereafter, the mother of the child, bathing the child with clean water, dressing the child with nice clean clothes, coming near the Yajnakunda (sacred fire), passing behind the father of the child, stands on the right side of him (child's father) keeping the head of the child in the north direction. She then places the child into the hands of the child's father and she herself returns from the back side of her husband (the child's father). She should take her seat in the north side keeping her face in the east.

The father of the child, keeping the child's head in the north direction and feet in south direction, should give the child to his wife (the mother of the child). They then follow the procedure that has been mainly prescribed for Namakarana Samskara. A Yajna is performed. Filling the spoon with ghee, the Yajaman (father of the child) should offer one oblation (into the sacred fire) pronouncing this Mantra: "Om Prajapataye Swaha".

Thereafter, four oblations – one oblation with each of the Tithi, Nakshatra, Tithi Devata and Nakshatra-Devta should be offered. These Tithis and Nakshatras are the lunar dates and the stars under which the birth of the child took place.

Thereafter, one oblation with the "Svishtakrit Mantra" from the Samanya Prakarana and four Vyahriti oblations from Samanya prakarana, and thus totaling five oblations in all should be offered.

Then the mother taking the child in her lap sits on a nice seat and the father of the child feels the breaths being exhaled from the nostrils of the child. He then utters a few mantras.

### *Forbidden or Prohibited Names*

The following female names should be avoided.

Names after a constellation such as Rohini, Revati etc. should be avoided.

Names of trees and plants such as Champa, Tulasi etc.

Names of rivers such as Ganga, Yamuna, Saraswati etc.

Names formed on the basis of lowering merit like Chandali

Names of mountains like Vindhyachal, Himalaya,

Names of birds like Kokila, Hansa etc.

Names of snakes such as Sarpini, Nagin, etc.

Names suggestive of menial servants or other orderlies like Dasi, kinkakari etc.

Names that create an awe or fear like Bheema, Bhayankari, Chandika etc.

The above types of names are prohibited names for female children.

The scriptural authority for the above prohibitions is taken from Manu Smriti 3/9. Which reads as follows:

"Let him not marry a maiden named after a constellation, a tree, or a river, nor one bearing the name of a low caste, or of a mountain, nor one named after a bird, a snake, or a slave, nor one whose name inspires terror."

Distinguishing factors merit attention when giving names. For example take the names –Dev or Jaydev. In the case of the child possessing a promising tendency of becoming Brahmana, or the parents desiring to make their child a Brahmana should give him the name such as Devsharma. Similarly, in the case of Kshatriya, Vaisya and Sudra, the names be respectively given to children as Devavarma, Devgupta, and Devdas etc..

If the child is female, the name should be of one or three or five letters like Shree, Hrihi, Yashoda, Sukhada, Saubhagyaprada etc.

6. *Niskramana Samskara*

[Note: The following abridged explanations are from the writings of Swami Dayananda Saraswati (The founder of The Arya Samaj). The translation is by Acharya Vaidyanath Shastri].

The infant is taken out of the house into the climate of fresh air and sunshine.

From the Gobhil Grihyasutra 2.8.1:

"Chaturthemaasi Nishkramanika. Suryamudikshayati Tatchakshuriti.

Also

"Jananaadyastriteeyo jyoutsnastasya Triteeyaayaam."

The time of Niskramana. Two dates are mentioned.

The first date is the third lunar date of the third full-moon fortnight from the birth date of the child.

The second date is the birth Tithi (date) of the child in the fourth month from the date of birth.

***The Procedure:*** In the morning, after sunrise, the infant is bathed and dressed. The mother of the child brings the child in Yajnashala (place of Sacred Fire Ceremony), approaching from the right side of her husband faces her husband and gives the child into the hands of her husband, keeping the head of the child in the north direction and the child's face and chest facing upwards. The mother then walks clockwise from behind her husband and takes her seat on the left side of her husband keeping her face eastward.

The same ceremony and the same Mantras are used as for Jatakarma Samskaras.

Thereafter the father of the child gives the child to the mother, keeping the child's head in the north direction and the feet in the south direction. Keeping silence, the husband touches the head of his wife. The child is then taken out in the sun with the following Mantra from the Yajurveda. This Mantra is recited on behalf of the infant child.

"Om Tatchakshurdevahitam Purustaatshukramuccharat. Pashyema Sharadah Shatam Jeevema Sharadah Shatam Shrunuyaam Shradah Shatam Pra Bravaam Sharadha Shatamadeenaahaa syaama Sharadah Shatam Bhooyashcha Sharadah Shataat."

O Benefactor of devotees! I concentrate on Thy pure energy. Grant me perfect health. May my eyes, ears, tongue and the other organs function in a strong and healthy way for a hundred years. May I not become helpless and dependent during this time. Grant me a hundred years of joyous life free from disease.

After exposing the child to the sun and fresh air, the child is brought back into the Yajnashala where people bless the child with the following sentence:

"Tvam Jeeva Sharadah Shatam Vardhamaanah."

May you be endowed with health and strength and live a life of hundred years.

### *Exposing the Child to the Moonlit Night*

In the night, the mother brings the child approaching the husband from the right side, facing the husband gives the child to her husband, keeping the child's head in the north direction. The mother then walks clockwise walking behind her husband stands on his left side facing the moon. With a little water in her right hand palm a prayer is offered with the following Mantra.

*"Om Yadadashchandramasi Krishnam Prithivyaa Hridayam Shritam*

*Tadaham Vidvaagvam Statpashyanmaaham Pautramagham Rudam."*

The water in the hand is then sprinkled to the ground. The mother then walks anticlockwise from behind her husband and facing him takes the child. Then again walking clockwise from behind her husband stands to the left of her husband keeping the child's head in the north direction and feet in the south direction. This time the father of the child takes a little water in his right hand palm and recites the same Mantra..Then he sprinkles the water to the ground.

Thereafter both husband and wife, in a happy frame of mind, take the child back into the house.

7. *Annaprashana Smaskara:* This is the ceremony for the first feeding of cooked rice. The object of this ceremony is to pray to the gods with Vedic Mantras to bless the child with good digestive powers, good thoughts and talents. It is performed when the child is six months old which is the weaning time. Susruta commends this weaning time as best for both the mother and the child.

Offerings are made to the goddess of speech and vigour. Prayers are offered so that the child's senses have their full gratification and live a happy and contented life. The father feeds a little of the sweet food anointed with gold to the child with Mantras that say he feeds the child with food that may ensure a healthy life to the child and prevent ill-health.

Apart from the efficacy or otherwise of this ceremony, its observance creates in all concerned an awareness of the cumulative needs of the child at that age in a scientific and tender manner. Its systematic observance therefore ensures the results expected especially when fortified by Mantras.

[Note: The following abridged explanations are from the writings of Swami Dayananda Saraswati (The founder of The Arya Samaj). The translation is by Acharya Vaidyanath Shastri].

The first feeding of cereal to the child.

When the child is six months old.

The authority for Annaprashana Samskar derives from Ashvalayans Grihyasutra (1.16.1,4,5). Also the authority of Paraskar Grihya Sutra.

The Annaprashana ceremony should be performed at the time when the child gains strength to digest cereal and preparations made from cereals. The first feeding of cereal commences with this ceremony. He who desires his child to be brilliant and famous should feed cooked rice mixed with ghee (clarified butter) or the rice mixed with honey, curd and ghee. The samskar ceremony for the first feeding commences with prayer, followed by Svastivachana, Shanitkarana and complete Samanya Prakarana. It is indicated that this ceremony should be performed (when the child is six months old) on the day on which the child was born.

The rice should be prepared thus: Rice is washed, cleaned, cooked nicely and ghee in proper quantity is mixed in the rice when it is in the cooking process. When this rice has been cooked properly and has become cold, then it should be placed in Homasthali or the tray of Homa. From this Homashali the rice is then given in small containers to the Yajman, to Purohita and Ritvij (Priests), accompanied with chanting of Mantras.

The Yajmana (father of the child) then performs Agnyadhan and Samidadhana. Offers four oblations of Aghavarajya-bhagahuti and four oblations of Vyahriti. Thereafter the oblation of the cooked rice that was given to the Yajman and to the priests, should be offered with one Mantras from the Rig Veda and one Mantra from the Yajur Veda.

Thereafter the Yajmana mixes small quantity of curd, honey and ghee. Adds this to the rice that remained after the oblations. This should be fed to the child in minute quantity according to the desire of the child with the following Mantra from the Yajurveda:

*"Om Annapateannasya No Dehyanamivasya Shushminah /*

*Pra Pra Dataaram Taarisha Oorjvam No Dhehi Dwipade Chatushpade*

*"O Lord of plenty (of food)! Vouchsafe us a share of food that invigorates us, and brings no sickness. O Lord, thou art our leader. Grant us nourishment (maintenance) both for bipeds and for quadrupeds."*

Thereafter the child is blessed by the mother and father of the child and also by the priests, the elders and the guests. The child is blessed with the sentence:

*"Twam Annapatihi Annavo Vardhamano Bhooyaaha" meaning*

"O child, May you be endowed by God's grace with Anna (grains or food). May you grow in strength and may you live a long life."

8. *Chudakarma:* This ceremony of the first tonsure is to be performed in the third year of the male child.. Also it initiates the maintenance of a 'Sikha' (tuft of hair on the head) as a religious necessity after that age. According to Susruta, a tuft of hair on the head protects a vital part on the head.

Susruta and Charaka confirm that removing the hair, excess nails etc., contribute to strength, vigour, longevity, purity and beauty of the individual. An auspicious day is selected for the ceremony. A porcupine quill, Darbha grass, and a dummy razor are the specific materials used by the father for symbolically cutting the child's hair first. The gist of the Mantra used in this particular ceremony is:

"May the child live long beyond a hundred years. May his eye sight remain unimpaired. May he become prosperous and wealthy so that he can feed (and cater to the needs of others) liberally. May his digestion be perfect. Let him become a Varchasvi (prominent)."

[Note: The following abridged explanations are from the writings of Swami Dayananda Saraswati (The founder of The Arya Samaj). The translation is by Acharya Vaidyanath Shastri].

From Ashvalayana Grihyasutra:

*"Triteeye Varshe Chaulam. Uttaratoagne Vreervihiyavamaashatilaanaam prithakpoorna Sharaavaani Nidadhaati."*

*From Paraskara Grihyasutra:*

*"Samvatsavarikasya Choodaakaranam."*

*Gobhiliya Grihyasutra 2.8.10.6 is also of the same opinion.*

This ceremony should be performed in the third year or in the 1st year from the date of the child's birth. The dates for this ceremony should be chosen during the northern solstice and during the bright fortnight of the moon's phase.

***The Procedure:*** A hairdresser (Barber) is invited to this ceremony. Four earthenware pots are brought to the Yajnashala (place of sacred fire Ceremony). They contain rice, barley, Mung and in the fourth Sesumum (Til). These four pots are placed in the north side of the Yajnavedi (Havan Kund).

A Havan Ceremony is performed.

Thereafter, addressing the hairdresser, the following Mantra from the Atharvaveda is recited.

"Om Aayamagantsavita kshurenoshnena vaaya Udakenehi.

Aadityaa Rudraa Vasava Undantu Sa Chetasah Somasya . Ragno Vapata Prachetasah."

This barber, who is competent and swift has come with his razor (or a pair of scissors). Using lukewarm water, may the learned man (barber) known as Rudra and Vasu make the hair wet with utmost care and (thereafter) cut the hair like the king of Soma (as the Soma herbs are cut with care).

The father of the child mixes hot and cold water reciting the following Mantra.

*"Om Ushnena Vaaya Udakenehi."*

Let the hot water be mixed with cold water.

Thereafter, applying to the hair a mixture of the lukewarm water and a little butter or curd to moisten the hair of the child. The following mantra is recited.

*From Atharvaveda:*

*"Om Aditihi Shashru Vapatvaapa Undantu Varchasaa*

*Chikitsu Prajapati Deerghaayutvaaya Chakshase."*

Let this unbreakable razor (or scissors) cut the locks (hair on the head), let the waters with their moistening (softening) power soften the hair of the child, May the Lord of creatures (God) remove disease from this child. May this child attain to long life. May this child acquire knowledge.

*From Paraksara Grihyasutra:*

*"Om Savitra Prasoota Daivyaa Aapa*
*Undantu Te Tanu Deerghayutvaaya Varchase."*

O Child! Let the mighty celestial waters produced by the sun drench your head. May you attain a long life. May you acquire knowledge.

The father takes a comb in his hand and using the comb, gathers some hair from the right side of the child's head. Taking three blades of the Darbha (kusa) grass, while touching the hair with the grass and slightly pressing the hair against the grass, the following Mantra is recited.

*From Gobhiliya Grihyasutra, 219.14*

*"Om Oshadhe Traayasvainam."*

*Let the herb protect this child.*

Then holding the razor in a hand the father recites the following Mantra

*From Gobhiliya Grihyasutra, 219.13-1.6.4*
*"Vishnorda Ashtroasi "*

This instrument (razor) is the means in the performance of this Yajna (Samskara) of Chudakarma.

*From the Yajurveda:*

*"Om Shivo Namaasi Svadhitiste Pitaa Namaste (Astu)*
*Ma Ma Hrimsihi."*

This instrument (razor) is for auspiciousness. It is made of steel (metal) that is as strong as Vajra (a weapon). Let this razor be fit for cutting the hair. Let it not cause any pain whatsoever.

*From the Yajurveda:*

*"Om Svadhite Mai Nam hrimsihi"*

*Let not this steel razor inflict any harm to this child.*
*From Yajurveda:*

*"Om Nivarttayaam Yaayusheannaadyaaya Prananaaya*
*Raayasposhaaya Soooprajaastvaaya Suviryaaya."*

O Child! I perform this tuft-ceremony so that you can

attain to long life, constructive power, strength and wealth, good progeny and vigour.

The father of the child then holds the child's locks in a loop made from the Kusa grass and applies the first cut with the following Mantra.

*From the Atharvaveda:* The meaning of the Mantra is:

"O priest and all the learned guests! This competent barber shaves this child by the same razor (or scissors) that he uses to shave the head of our glorious King and the heads of noble men (men of merit). May this child be prosperous, wealthy and have good progeny."

All the hair cut by the razor or scissors, together with Kusa grass and the leaves of Mimosa (Shami) should be placed in an earthenware container. All lose hair pieces on the floor should be carefully picked up and placed in this container.

(The detailed procedure entails the father cutting a little of the hair first from the right side of the child's head. Appropriate Mantras being recited. Then the same sequence is followed for the left side of the head. The third time from the back of the head The fourth time again the father cuts a little hair from the back of the hair.)

Thereafter the father of the child blesses the child (with Mantra) by placing his right hand on the head of the child.

Then with the following Mantra, the father gives the razor (and scissors) to the barber.

*From Ashvalayana Grihyasutra, 1.17.15*

"Om Yatkshurena Marchayata Supeshasaa Vaptaa Vapasi Keshaan Shundhi Shiro Maasyayuhu Pra Moshihi."

O Barber! You are the cutter of the hair. Cut and shave the head of the child with that swift soft razor. Do not decrease (cut or shorten) the child's life.

The father then tells the barber to sharpen his razor on his sharpening stone. The father then requests the barber to gently drench the child's head with lukewarm water and that he should shave attentively with smooth hand, avoiding any cut from the razor. With these words he leads the barber to the north of the Yajna-Kunda. He sits with the child facing eastward. The barber shaves the child's head.

A little tuft of hair may be left on the head. It is considered more proper to shave all the hair in the first year. A little tuft of hair should be left on the head when Chudakarma Samskara is performed in the third year.

The barber is given the four earthenware containers filled with cereal grains together with clothes, money etc. The barber carries the cut hair together with the Darbha grass, Shami leaves etc. to some remote place *e.g.*, river side or in the woods; there to bury these in the ground. A member of the family or a friend can accompany the barber.

The father then rubs a little butter or curd on the head of the child. The child is then bathed. When the child is dressed, the father sits with the child facing eastward and chants Mahadeva Gana. The guests, before leaving, bless the child saying:

"Om Tvam Jeeva Sharadah Shatam Vardhamaanah."

O Child! May you live a hundred autumns growing in strength and vigour.

9. *Karnavedha:* Piercing the ears in the third or fifth year

*From Katyayana Griyhasutra 1.2*

"Karnavedho Varshe Triteeye Panchame Vaa."

The piercing of the child's ear should be done in the third or the fifth year (from the date of birth.)

An experienced physician who is a specialist and who has studied the treatise of Charaka and of Sushruta is invited to this ceremony.

In the morning, after bathing and getting the child dressed with clothes and ornaments, the mother brings the child to the Yajnashala. A Havan ceremony (Sacred Fire Ceremony) is performed with Mantras from the Samanya Prakarana.

The physician then should pierce the right ear first with the following Mantra:

*From the Yajurveda: 25.21*

"Om Bhadram Karnebhihi Srunuyaama Devaa Bhadram Pashyemaakshabhiryajatraa Sthirairangai Stushtumam Sastanoobhirvyashemahi Devahitam Yadaayuhu."

O sociable learned persons, may we with our ears listen to what is good, and with our eyes see what is good. With limbs and bodies firm may we, extolling God lead a life conducive to the good of the sages.

He physician should pierce the left ear with the following Mantra:

*From the Yajurveda 29.40.*

"Vakshyanti Veda ganeeganti Karnam Priyam Sakhaayam Parishasvajaanaa Yoshevaa Shing Kte Vitataadhi Dhanvatrjyaa eeyam samane paarayanti."

This bow string strained on the bow whispers like a woman, and protects us in the combat, as a wife fain to speak, offering advice, embraces her affectionate, praiseworthy husband.

The physician then inserts thin wire like objects in the freshly pierced ears to prevent the holes from closing up. The physician then applies healing ointments to the ears.

10. A. Upanayana and B. Vedarambha

Sacred Thread and Commencing the Study of the Vedas

### *Investiture of Sacred Thread (Janoi)*

The thread giving ceremony is performed in the eighth, eleventh and twelfth years of the male child calculated from the date of conception, for the first three Varnas (Brahman eighth year, Kshatriya eleventh year and Vaisya twelfth year) respectively. Etymologically, the word Upanayana means taking the child to the teacher or to Gayatri Mantra, according to some.

This ceremony gives the child a second birth (Dwija), as it were, where the Guru (teacher) becomes his father and Gayatri becomes his mother. The investiture with the Sacred thread entitles the child to study the Vedas and participate in Vedic functions. In essence, the child commences his journey on the road to spiritual life. This is contrasted with a life of eating, sleeping and procreating, which kinds of life animals also live. The Gurukula (Boarding school) type of education seeks to mould the child for an ideal life.

Gayatri is the most powerful of the Mantras. Initiation into it is described as 'Brahmopadesa'. It leads to the realisation of Brahman (the Supreme Reality). Along with this Mantra the Guru imparts his Shakti (power) too to the child; hence the Guru and the disciple are insulated by means of silken clothes at the time of the initiation.

The materials used in this ceremony are full of mystical significance. The Yajnopavita or the holy Thread consists of three folds, symbolising the three Gunas – Sattwa, Rajas and Tamas. It reminds one of the threefold debt one owes to one's manes (ancestors), Rishis (Seers who realised spiritual wisdom), and gods. The three threads also reminds one of the three letters of Pranava-AUM – as also Brahma, Vishnu and Shiva (Creator, Sustainer and Destroyer).

While investing it, the Acharya (the principal teacher) asks for strength, illumination and long life for the boy. The deerskin attached to the thread signifies spiritual and intellectual preeminence. The Kaupina or undercloth is the garment of immortality. The girdle (Mekhala) shows that the three Vedas (Rigveda, Samaveda and Yajurveda) encircle the boy. Mekhala is "the daughter of Faith and sister of Rishis," protecting his purity and warding off evil.

The staff (stick) of palasa wood given to the boy to hold makes him a guardian of the Vedas, and gives him long life, lustre and holiness.

Before initiating the boy into the Gayatri Mantra, the Guru (the spiritual father) pours water in the joined palms of the boy. This is to symbolise purifying him before receiving the Mantra.

The boy is asked to see the Sun. He is asked to learn from the Sun unswerving duty and discipline. The boy offers prayers to the Sun for attainment of virtues.

By mounting a stone the boy is asked to develop firmness of resolve and steadfastness in his duties and studies, and develop physical strength and excellent health.

During the performance of the Samskara of Upanayana, certain Vratas or vows are undertaken. These are the vows 1. To uphold vows 2. To attain prominence in the world 3. To engage in creative activities 4. To perform charity 5. To please the gods 6. To please fellow-men 7. To protect subjects or dependants 8. To procreate when married 9. To keep equipoise 10. To serve the elders etc.

The invocation of the three entities Pranava, Medha and Sraddha – God, Intelligence and Faith – in this function is the coping stone of the edifice of Brahmacharya or bachelorhood, whose daily chore is regulated by good habits, collectively going by the name Ahnika (Sandhya, Samidadhana Havan etc.). One cannot conceive of a more thoughtful scheme of timetable calculated for the development of character in the young.

[Note: The following abridged explanations are from the writings of Swami Dayananda Saraswati (The founder of The Arya Samaj). The translation is by Acharya Vaidyanath Shastri].

*From Ashvalayana Grihyasutra 1-19-1-6.*

"Ashtame Varshe Brahmanamupanayet (1). Garbhaashtame va (2). Ekaadashe Kshatriyam (3). Dvaadashe Vaishyam (4). Aashodashaad Braahmanasyaanateetah Kaala (5). Shraadhhaavimshaatkshatriyasya, Aachaturvishaaddvaisyasya, Ata urdhvam Patitasavitrikaa Bhvanti." (6)

The Brahman, the child of the Brahman, or the child promising to be a Brahman, should be invested with the sacred Thread in the eighth year from the date of birth or from the date of conception. The Kshatriya, the child of Kshatriya, or the child promising to be Kshatriya, should be invested with the Sacred Thread in the eleventh year from the date of birth or from the date of conception. Vaisya, the child of Vaisya or the child promising to be Vaisya, should be invested with the Sacred Thread in the twelfth year from the date of his birth or from the date of conception. Positively the children of Brahmana, Kshatriya and Vaisya should respectively be invested with the Sacred Thread before the years 16$^{th}$, 22$^{nd}$ and 24$^{th}$ of their age. If they are not invested with the Sacred

Thread during these years, then they are regarded or treated as having fallen from their duties.

Similar sayings are found in the Paraskara Grihyasutra etc.

*From Manusmriti:*

"The time for the Savitri (Gayatri) initiation of a Brahmana does not pass until the completion of the sixteenth year (after conception), of a Kshatriya until the completion of the twenty-second year, and of a vaisya until the completion of the twenty-fourth." 2.38.

"After those periods, men of these three castes who have not received the sacrament at the proper time, become Vratyas (outcastes), excluded from the Savitri initiation and despised by the Aryans." 2.39.

"With such men, if they have not been purified according to the rule, let no Brahmana ever, even in times of distress, form a connection either through the Veda or by marriage." 2.40.

The time for the Yajnopavita Samskar.

*From Shatpath Brahmana, 2.13.5.*

"Vasante Braahmanamupanayet. Grishne Raajanyam. Sharadi Vaishyam. Sarvakaalameke."

The child of Brahmana in the spring season. The child of Kshatriya in the summer season and the child of Vaisya in autumn be respectively be invested with Sacred Thread. Or the investiture of Sacred Thread can be performed in all seasons. (Morning time is the best period for the performance of this ceremony.)

***Limited Fasting***

"Payovrato Braahmano Yavaagoovrato

Raajanya Aamikshaavrato Vaishya."

For three days (or for at least one day) prior to the day of the ceremony, the child should drink only milk (once a day or more than once a day). The child of a Kshatriya should eat only barley gruel (Yavaag), prepared from crushed barley, boiled in water with sugar to taste. The child of Vaisya should complete his fast by eating only Aamikshaa. This is sometimes called Shrikhanda or Sikhanda. This is prepared from cottage cheese four parts, milk one part, sugar to taste and saffron (Keshar). This preparation is strained through a piece of cloth. The children of the three Varnas, as describes above, should eat only those foods prescribed for them respectively when they feel hungry and should not eat or drink any thing else.

***The Procedure:*** The utensils to be used in the Yajna etc. should be collected and appropriately sorted and cleansed a day before the ceremony. On the day of the ceremony, everything that is needed for the Yajna as mentioned in the Samanya Prakarana should be arranged by the Yajna Kunda.

The boy to be invested with the Sacred Thread should have his head shaved, bathed and should dress appropriately. Either the father of the child or the Acharya, having fed the child with sweets, eatables etc. leads him to his seat to the west of the Yajnavedi (Havan Kunda), keeping his face eastward. The father of the child and the priests of the Yajna as mentioned in the Samanya Prakarana, should take their seats in the prescribed manner perform Aachaman (sipping of water) and Angasparsha (touching various limbs with water). (Om Amrito Pastaramasi Swaha etc. and Om Vangme Asyestu etc.)

Thereafter, the Acharya conducting the ceremony should make the child pronounce the following sentence from the child's own mouth.

"May I observe the discipline of celibacy and thus may I be a celibate."

The Acharya then pronounces the following Mantra and gives to the child a garment and a Upavastra to wear.

From Paraskara Grihyasutra, 2.2.7.

"Om yenendraaya brihaspatirvaasah Paryadadhaadamritam.

Ten Tvaa Paridadhaamyaayushe Deerghaayutvaaya Balaaya Varchase."

O Child! I give this garment to you to wear for your long life, strength and vigour. This is in accordance with the tradition whereby the Acharya gives a strong and durable garment to his disciple.

Thereafter the child holds the Sacred Thread in his hand and sits in front of the Acharya. The Acharya invests the child with the Sacred Thread with the following Mantra and places (makes the child wear) the Sacred Thread on the left shoulder and slung across under the right armpit.

"Yagnopavitam Param Pavitram Prajaapatayeryatsahajam Purastaat.

Aayushyamagr Yam Pratimuncha Shubhram Yajnopavitam Balamastu Tejah.

*Yajnopaveetamasi Yagnasya Tvayajyapayaveetenopanaahayàami."*

This Yajnopavita (Sacred Thread) is very sacrosanct. Prajapati Himself has sanctioned this Sacred Thread. I invest you with this white Yajnopavita (Sacred Thread). This is the main (most important) article for you. May it bring you strength and vigour.

This sacred Thread is really a Sacred Thread.

I tie you with this for the purpose of performing Yajna.

The Acharya then performs the Yajna (Havan) ceremony with the child seated on the right side of the Acharya. Some of the oblations (ahutis) are to be offered by the child.

Some of the Mantras used during this ceremony:

*"Om Agne Vratapate Vratam Charishyami Tatte Prabraveemi Tatchhakeyam.*

*Tenrdhyaasimidamahamarnritaat Satyam Upaimi Svaaha. Idamagnaye Idanna Mama.*

*Om Vayo Vratapate Svaaha. Idam Vaayave Idanna Mama.*

*Om Surya Vratapate Svaaha. Idam Suryaaya Idanna Mama.*

*Om Chandra Vratapate Svaaha. Idam Chandraaya Idanna Mama.*

*Om Vrataanaam Vratapate Svaaha. Idamindraaya Vratapataye Idanna Mama."*

O Self-refulgent God! Thou art the master of vows. I declare before Thee, I shall observe the vows and disciplines of celibacy. May I be enabled to observe this vow. May I prosper with this vow and attain the highest truth. Whatever has been uttered herein is true. The oblation offered is meant for Agni and it is not for me.

(Oblations are offered to all moving god Vayu, All effulgent Surya, all blissful Chandra, the lord of all vows and laws Indra).

The Acharya then sits to the north of the Yajna Kunda keeping his face eastward. The child sits in front of the Acharya keeping his face westward. Looking at the child, the Acharya should recite the following Mantra. The meaning of the Mantra:

O Self-refulgent God! We have received excellent cooperation from this child. Kindly lead us to the company of good men and good teachers. Together with this youth, may we follow the path of knowledge with ease. May this child do whatever is auspicious for him and for all.

Addressing the Acharya, the child says :

O Acharya! I have resolved to observe the disciplines of continence. Kindly admit me and invest me with the Sacred Thread.

The Acharya says:

What is your name?

The child states his name.

The Acharya makes the child hold water in his right hand palm. The Acharya recites Mantras.

The waters are the source of happiness. May the waters be helpful to us in attaining grains and may they help us to retain good eye sight.

Let the pleasant essence of waters be useful to us, like the mothers who, for the well-being of their children, give them their breasts to suckle..

Let the waters enable us to grow cereals and herbaceous plants. Let these be used for the welfare of our progeny.

The Acharya then takes water in his right hand palm and empties this water in the right hand palm of the child, mixing the two waters. This is done while the Acharya chants Mantra.

For our maintenance we accept whatever good food has been provided by God, who is the mighty power and Creator of the world. We also accept the strength and might of all-powerful God who maintains and preserves the existence of all the objects of creation.

The Acharya, chanting Mantra, then makes the child empty the water from his palm into a container.

O Child! I admit you in this life so that you can attain power and prosperity bestowed by God, who is the Creator of the world. I hold your hand in my own with the firmness and strength of the vital breaths called Prana and Apana and with the firmness and strength of Pushan, the all preserving vitality of the body.

The Acharya takes water in his right hand palm and empties it into the child's right hand palm. Holding the child's hand the Acharya chants Mantra.

O Child! Your hand has been grasped by Savitar, the mighty teacher who is the preserver of all knowledge.

The child then empties the water from his palm into the container.

For the third time, the same procedure is followed, the Acharya giving water into the palm of the child.

O Child! Again, the Self-refulgent God is your Acharya. (God is your real teacher).

Thereafter, the Acharya takes the child outside and while standing and facing the sun shows the sun to the child with chanting of Mantras.

O Creator and Lord of the world! This child is the Brahmacharin (student observing celibacy) of Thine. Please protect and preserve him. May he perform his duties well.

The Acharya returns to the Yajna Mandap with the child; both seating to the north of the Yajnakund. The child sits facing the Acharya. The Acharya pronounces the following two Mantras.

"Om Yuvaa suvaasaahaa Pariveeta Aagaatsa oo Shreyan Bhavati Jaayamanah"

This child (pronounce the name of the child), possessing strong physique, dressed in nice garments, wearing the sacred Thread, and who seated before me, has taken the second birth. May he (successfully study) the Vedas and acquire respect."

"Om Suryaasyaavritamanvaavarttasva Asou."

O Child, You circumambulate yore Acharya who is the sun (source) of knowledge. (As the sun is the source of life so the Acharya is the source of knowledge.)

The child circumambulates the Acharya.

The Acharya then places his right hand upon the right shoulder of the child, covering his hand with a piece of cloth. A Mantra is chanted about the vital airs.

Then the Acharya touches the child's belly, heart, again the right shoulder with various Mantras.

O Child, I appoint you (to study and) attain the knowledge of God and follow God's commands.

The Acharya touches the child's left shoulder, breast, saying Mantras.

Let the learned men of firm intentions and swift intellects, attaining the highest feats of knowledge through their minds and spirits, elevate this student to high status of genius and character.

O disciple! Make one (fine tune) your mind and heart with my mind always, and becoming fully attentive grasp my words with affection and understand the meaning of these words. May God, who is the Master of Vèdic speech, unite you with me in thought and action according to your vow from this very day.

And the child replies in the affirmative.

Then the Acharya asks the student: "What is your name?"

The Student says : "Sir, my name is ..........."

Acharya: "Whose Brahmachari are you?"

Student: "Yours, Sir."

The Acharya pronounces the following Mantra.

"Indrasya Brahmah Achaaryyasya, Agnihi Achaaryastvaahamaachaaryastava Asou."

O Child! You are the Brahmachari of Almighty God. The Self-refulgent God is your Acharya. I am your Acharya as God's representative.

*Further Mantras:*

O Child! You are the Brahmachari of Prajapati. You are the Brahmachari of Prana, God who is the all pervading Soul. Prajapati invests you with the Sacred Thread for your happiness. I also urge you to follow the command of Prajapati.

O Child! I urge you to attain the knowledge of Prajapati who is the Lord of all creatures. I urge you to attain the knowledge of the might sun. I urge you to attain the knowledge of liquids and herbs, of the earth and the heavenly regions, of all the physical and spiritual forces. May you be successful in maintaining peace and tranquility among all beings.

Upon the completion of the Upanayana ceremony, if time permits, the Vedarambha (commencing the study of the Vedas) ceremony should preferably take place on the very same day. Otherwise, the Vedarambha ceremony can take place on another day.

The mother, the father, the Acharya and other guests then bless the child together with the following words.

"Om tvam jeeva Sharadah Shatam Vardhamaanah.

Aayushmaan Tejasvee varchasvee Bhooyaaha."

O Child! May you grow in strength and vigour and live a hundred autumns. May you become long lived, brilliant and radiant.

10 B. *Vedarambha:* To observe the disciplines and to commence and undertake the studies of the Vedas and their branches (systems and limbs known as 'Sangopanga') – is called Vedarambha.

***The Procedure:*** In the morning, the student, after bathing and wearing clean clothes, sits to the west of the Yajnavedi (Havankund), keeping his face eastward. The Acharya begins the ceremony with Achaman Mantra (sipping of water) and Angasparsha Mantra (touching various organs with water) followed by Ishwar Upasana (prayer), Svatsivachan, Santikarana.

The Havan ceremony (Sacred fire ceremony) is then commenced. The student participates in the Yajna and offers ahutis (oblations). During the Havan ceremony, before the Purnahuti, Vishesh Mantras (Mantras used for Vedarambha) are used.

Some of these Mantras are described below.

O famous Acharya! Please make me earn fame in the field of education. O Acharya! Enable me to attain to your status of learning and prominence and a preserver of knowledge, Yajanas etc.

The student then standing on the south side of the Yajnakunda and keeping his face northward, takes a samidha (small wooden stick), dips it in ghee, and offers it in the middle of the fire as oblation with the following Mantra.

I am offering this ahuti (oblation) to add to the burning flame of the Yajna that is mighty in nature and present in all the created beings and objects of the world. As this fire blazes forth with the samidha (wood-fuel), so may I shine with wisdom, knowledge of the Vedas and of Brahman (God) and may I be endowed with vigour, long life, progeny and wealth. Grant long life to my Acharya and to his sons. May I be enriched with high intellectual power. May I not be arrogant to anyone. Grant me prominence, vigour, divine merits and food and grains.

Two further oblations are offered with samidha dipped in ghee.

The student now sits in the west side of the Vedi facing the east. Applying a little of the shesh water on the palms of his hands, holds them by the fire warming the hands. With each of the seven mantras, he should apply the water over his face and on the head.

1. This fire is the preserver of the body. May it preserve my body.
2. This fire is the giver of life. May it grant me long life.
3. This fire is the giver of brilliancy. May it grant me brilliancy.
4. Whatever gets exhausted in my body, let this fire replenish that.
5. May Savita grant me wisdom. May the goddess Saraswati grant me wisdom.
6. Let the teacher and preacher, wearing garlands, give us knowledge.

The student then touches various organs with various Mantras.

*"Om Vak Cha Ma Aapyaayataam." (touches the mouth)*

*"Om Praanascha Ma Aapyaayataam." (touches the nose)*

*"Om Chakshushcha Ma Aapyaayataam." (touches the eyes)*

*"Om Shrotrancha Ma Aapyaayataam." (touches the ears)*

*"Om Yasho Balancha Ma Aapyaayaataam." (Touches both arms)*

O Lord! May my organ of speech be sound and well developed. May my nose, eyes, ears be sound and well developed. May my arms, which are the source of fame and strength, be strong and develop properly.

The student then meditates (offers prayer) with the following Mantra.

May Agni, the Self-refulgent God give me wisdom, progeny and strength, May Indra, the almighty god, bestow upon me the favour of wisdom, progeny, and properly developed organs. May Surya, the all controlling god, grant me wisdom, progeny and brilliance. O effulgent and powerful Lord, grant me effulgence, power and prominence.

Now the student walks to the north side of the Yajnakunda. Facing the east, he kneels on his knees before the Acharya.

Balakoktihi: (The student says:)

"Aadhihi Bhuhu Savitri Bho Anubroohi."

O Acharya! Please instruct me 'The Gayatri Mantra', the subject matter of which is Savitar, the sun. Please teach me.

The Acharya then places a piece of cloth on his own shoulder and on the shoulder of the student, and holding both hands of the student in his hands, teaches the Gayatri Mantra to the student in three parts.

*First part:*

The Acharya makes the student pronounce the following, word by word.:

"Om Bhurbhuvah Svah Tatsaviturvarenyam."

*Second part:*

"Om Bhurbhuvah Svah Tatsaviturvarenyam Bargo Devasya Dhimahi."

*Third part:*

"Om Bhurbhuvah Svah Tatsaviturvarenyam

Bargo Devasya Dhimahi Dhiyo Yo Nah Prachodayaat."

The Acharya then explains in short the meaning of the Gayatri Mantra.

Thereafter the student affirms vows. (The same vows as for the Sacred Thread ceremony).

The student is given a girdle and a wooden staff (rod, well-made, smooth and free of any defect). For the Brahmana boy, the girdle be made of Darbha or Munja grass, for the Kshatriya boy, the girdle be made from Dhanusa grass and for the Vaisya boy, the girdle be made from Jute.

The Brahmana boy should be given a rod (stick) made of Palash or Bilva wood. The length of the rod to extend from the ground to top of the head.

The Kshatriya boy should be given a rod made from Vat or Khadir wood. The length of the rod from the ground till his eyebrow.

The Vaisya student should be given a rod made from Peepul or Gular wood. The length of the rod to reach from the ground till the tip of his nose.

In addition the student is given a deerskin to sit on, one pot or container to hold water, and two small pots or containers.

The student, holding the rod, says:

This staff (rod) that I hold, I accept it specially for the attainment of long life, knowledge of the Vedas, for (adherence to) disciplines and strength of continence.

***Father's Advice to His Son***

The father of the celibate student then gives general information regarding the life of a Brahmacharin (celibate student) and preaches the code of conduct. [Scriptural sources Gobhil Grihyasutra, Ashvalayans Grihyasutra, Paraskar Grihyasutra]

You realise that you are a Brahmachari (celibate) from today. You must always sip a little clean (pure) water and say your food prayer before taking meals.

Always keep away from evil acts and do all pious and righteous acts. You do not ever sleep in day time.

Remaining under the guidance and control of your Acharya, you will always with perseverance learn the Vedas with all their limbs and sub-limbs.

Always follow the rules of Dharma (righteousness) under your Acharya. You do not ever do anything of Adharma (unrighteous), even if such request be made by your Acharya even (to do anything of adharma).

You must abstain from anger. Always speak the truth (do not tell a lie.)

Always keep away from the eight kinds of acts of passion.

[Note: these eight acts of passion are: 1. To think of a woman. 2. To gossip about woman. 3. To touch a woman. 4. To play with a woman. 5. To gaze at a woman. 6. To embrace a woman. 7. To be alone with a woman. 8. To cohabit with a woman.]

Sleep only on the ground and not on beds with four legs.

Never be in the habit of Kaushilava (bad songs sung or

played on musical instruments, dances; abominable acts, use of perfumes etc.).

Always observe rules of moderation in bathing, eating, sleeping, and keeping awake. The same applies to greed, undue indulgence, fear and grief.

Always wake up and rise from bed during the early hours of Brahmamuhurta (between 4 and 6 in the morning). Perform your daily ablutions. You must take a bath everyday. Twice every day you must do acts of communion with God, pray, meditate and practice Yogic systems.

Do not eat meat. Do not eat dry, coarse cereals. Do not drink intoxicating drinks.

Do not ride on bullocks, horses, elephants, camels etc.

You are not to stay in any village (any place inhabited by people) except in Gurukula (Gurukula is a system of boarding school within the compounds of which stay only the teachers and the students).

As a Brahmachari you do not use shoes or umbrella.

Do not play with the organ of procreation (so as to prevent the discharge of semen). By conserving the semen in the body it transforms into Ojas, opening the full potential of your mind and intellect, becoming the source of attaining knowledge of the Vedas and all their branches. Do not massage your body with oil etc. Do jot use mustard-paste (cosmetics) for the beauty of the body.

Do not eat foods that are very sour like tamarind etc., very pungent like chilies etc., very astringent like haldi, very purgative like Jamalgota, very saltish foods, or very acidic foods.

Do your daily chores with care and regularity and be fully attentive to the task of learning (acquiring knowledge and wisdom).

You will always possess good character. You should never be extravagant in talk. Cultivate good behaviour and develop courtesies when meeting people, sitting in assemblies.

Keep yourself bound by the duties of wearing the girdle, keeping the wooden staff (stick) and the rules of mendicancy.

[Note: A Brahman's child, when asking for alms from a man should address him "Bhavaan Bhikshaam Dadaat." When asking for alms from a woman, he should address "Bhavati Bhikshaam Dadaatu." The Kshatriya student to men "Bhikshaam Bhavaan Dadaatu." To women "Bhikshaam Bhavati Dadaatu." Vaisya student should address men, "Bhikshaam dadaat Bhavaan" To woman, "Bhikshaan Dadaat Bhavati."]

Do not deviate from the daily performance of: your daily bath, daily prayer and meditation, Prostrate with reverence before your Acharya every morning and every evening.

These are the deeds of your daily performance. You should abstain from acts that have been prohibited.

The student then with folded hands bows (or prostrates before his father). The student addressing his father says:

"I shall certainly act according to your instructions and advice."

Thereafter the celibate student circumambulates the fire of the Yajnakunda and stands in the west of the Yajnavedi. He then asks for alms from his mother, father, brother, sister, maternal uncle, mother's' sister, uncle etc., who do not hesitate in giving alms. The student hands over all the alms to the Acharya. The Acharya takes some wheat cereals from the alms and gives to the student.

The Acharya then asks for some cooked rice for offering oblations. Mixing with a little ghee, three oblations are offered with the following Mantras.

*Having worshipped with truthful action and speech, God, who is wondrous, the lovely friend of the soul, May I acquire wisdom that discriminates between truth and untruth.* *-Yajurveda 32.13.*

"Tatsavituvarenyam Bhargo Devasya Dhimahi Dhiyo Yo Nah Prachodayaat" Svaha, Idam Savitar Idam Na Mama.

*"O creator of the universe! O All holy and worthy of adoration. May we contemplate Thy adorable Self. May*

*Thou guide our understanding." Whatever has been uttered herein is true. The oblation offered is meant for Savitar and it is not for me. -Yajurveda 22.9*

"Om Rishibhyah Svaaha. Idam Rishibhyah Idam Na Mama."

*We pay homage to Rishis (seers) who study the Vedas and understand their meanings. Whatever has been uttered herein is true. The oblation offered is for the Rishis and it is not for me.*
*-Ashvalayana Grihyasutra a 1.22.14*

Thereafter the Acharya offers a fourth ahuti with the Swishtakrit Homahuti Mantra "Om Yadasya Karmanah Tyariricham ......"

Thereafter the Havan ceremony is brought to conclusion with the rest of the Mantras and the Purnahuti.

The student seats facing the east, addresses the Acharya:

"Amuk (mention here the name of the family) Gotrotpanno Aham Bho Bhavantam Abhivaadaye"—Gobhil Grihyasutra 2/10/25

I, born in the genealogy of ...........(name of family) salute you (prostrate before you), O my teacher.

The student then prostrates before the acharya.

The Acharya says:

"Ayusmaan Vidyaavan Bhava Saumya."

(O my dear disciple!) May you be long lived and may you attain knowledge with wisdom.

After the Acharya has given his blessings to the Brahmachari, some of the food remaining from the Yajna (cooked rice, cereals, sweetmeats etc.) should be give to the Acharya, and to the student to eat.

Thereafter, all the guests are served meals prepared for this function.

Before leaving, people bless the student with the following sentence:

*"O Child! May you, by the grace of God, become learned, strong in body and soul, blessed with skills, vigour and*

*excellent health. After having attained knowledge of the Vedas and all their branches, may you come back from the Gurukula, with the desire of seeing us."*

### *The Qualified Student*

The Brahmachari (celibate student), shining with knowledge, becoming fully fledged, upon completion of his studies in the Gurukula, completing the state of Brahmacharya called Purvasamudra, enters immediately into the householder's life called Uttarsamudra (gets married). He encourages all people to achieve their goals. He exerts continuously to achieve the goal of life (Dharma, Artha, Kama and Moksha). He makes the world happy with his speech of righteousness and truth.

### *Only That is the King (qualities needed to lead a nation)*

Only that is the king who by observing austerities, strict disciplines of celibacy, has become a perfectly learned man (with knowledge and wisdom), perfectly educated (in arts and sciences) and who is a symbol of good conduct, who is self controlled and can rule the country in various ways (all the various departments of government).

### *Only that is the Acharya (qualities needed to become a teacher)*

In the same manner, only that is the Acharya who by observing austerities and strict disciplines of celibacy, leading a life of continence, has become a perfectly learned man (with knowledge and wisdom), perfectly educated (in arts and sciences) and who is a symbol of good conduct. Only such a person can desire to teach a celibate student. Only such a person can become the Acharya in the real sense.

### *Education for Girls*

As the boys, completing the life of perfect Brahmachari, attaining the complete knowledge of the Vedas and all their branches, knowledge of all the sciences, and in the full bloom of youth, are now fit to wed girls, so the girls, completing the courses of all sciences with perfect disciplines of continence, in the full bloom of their youth, should wed young men.

[Note: Women are barred from the study of the Vedas. Therefore, study of the sciences only is mentioned. Study of the Vedas is not mentioned here. The Laws of Manu, IX, 18 states: "For women no sacramental rite is performed with sacred texts, thus the law is settled; women who are destitute of strength and destitute of the knowledge of Vedic texts, are as impure as falsehood itself, that is a fixed rule."

11. *Samavartana:* Upon completion of studies, the teacher instructs the pupil (From Taittiriya Upanishad, 1.11)

Translations by Swami Nikhilananda, Sri Ramakrishna-Vivekananda Center, New York

Having taught the Vedas, the teacher thus instructs the pupil:

Speak the truth. Practise Dharma (religious duties; righteousness and ritualistic worship). Do not neglect the study of the Vedas. Having brought to the teacher the gift desired by him, (enter the householder's life and see that) the line of progeny is not cut off. Do not swerve from the truth. Do not swerve from Dharma. Do not neglect (personal) welfare. Do not neglect prosperity (refers to righteous actions by which wealth is earned). Do not neglect the study and teaching of Vedas.

Do not neglect your duties to the gods and the Manes. Treat your mother as god (Matru Devo Bhava). Treat your father as god (Pitru Devo Bhava). Treat your teacher as god (Aacharya Devo Bhava). Treat your guest as god (Atithi Devo Bhava). Whatever deeds are faultless, these are to be performed-not others. Whatever good works have been performed by us, those should be performed by you-not others.

Those Brahmins who are superior to us-you should comfort them by giving them seats. Whatever is to be given should be given with faith, not without faith-according to one's means, with modesty, with fear (of the scriptures or of sin), with sympathy.

Now, if there arises in your mind any doubt concerning conduct, you should conduct yourself in such matters as Brahmins would conduct themselves-Brahmins who are competent to judge, who (of their own accord) are devoted to good deeds, and are not urged to their performance by others, and who are not too severe, but are lovers of Dharma.

Now, with regard to persons spoken against, you should conduct yourself in such a way as Brahmins would conduct themselves-Brahmins who are competent to judge, who (of their own accord) are devoted to good deeds and that are not urged to their performance by others, and who are not too severe, but are lovers of Dharma.

This is the rule. This is the teaching. This is the secret wisdom of the Vedas. This is the command of God.

This you should observe. This alone should be observed.

### *Funeral-Antyeshti the Last Rites of the Dead*

The last rites of the dead body are called the Antyeshti Samskara. There is no other Samskara thereafter for this body. This Samskara is also called by the names of Naramedha, Purushmedha, Narayaga and Purusheayaga.

*From the Yajurveda 40.15 (also Isa Upanishad).*

"Vayurnilammamritamathedam Bhasmantam Shariram

Om Krto Smara. Klibe Smara. Kritghvam Smara."

O active soul, at the time of death, remember OM, remember God for thy vitality and thy eternity, remember thy deeds. Know that soul is immaterial and immortal but the body is finally reduced to ashes. (translation by Devi Chand)

***The Procedure:*** Source Ashwalayana Grihyasutras:

1. The dead, if male, should be given bath by men and if female, should be given bath by women. Sandal-wood paste should be applied to the body. The dead body should be dressed with new clothes.
2. Ghee (clarified butter) should be in equal proportion to the weight of the dead. Well-to-do people can use more ghee but in the case of poor people, the ghee should not be less than ½ mound in weight. The poor should be assisted by a moneyed man or by the head of the Panchayat (5 man village council), or contributions from

the people. Well-to-do people can add or mix with the ghee the following items.

Kesar, Saffron – One masha in each one Seer of Ghee

Kasturi, Musk – One Ratti in each one Seer of Ghee

Agar Acquilaria Malaccensis-One Seer in each one mound

Tagar Veleriana Walichli—One Seer in each one Maund

Sandal-wood powder-One Seer in each one mound

Camphor—As the circumstances permit

3. Well-to-do people should arrange for one maund Sandal-wood, twelve maunds of fuel wood and Samagri two times the weight of the dead body.
4. All these items should be brought to the cremation ground (crematorium).
5. If there is a permanent Kunda made in the cremation ground for the purpose of cremation, then it should be used. If not, then a new one should be made (dug out). The dimensions of the Kunda should be as follows:
    - I. Length of the Kunda should be equal to the length of a man standing with his hands stretched upwards.
    - II. The breadth (width) should be equal to the a person sleeping with his two hands stretched outwards (more than 1 ½ yards).
    - III. Depth should be chest high (taking into account average heights of men).
    - IV. The bottom should be one yard in breadth.
6. The Kunda should be made clean and if cow-dung is available, it should be purified by applying that.
7. Wood fuel should be arranged in the Kunda in the manner of how bricks are arranged when building a wall.
8. Ghee should be liquid (not solidified or frozen).
9. Four big size spoons should be firmly attached to the end of long sticks so that oblations can be offered into the blazing fire burning inside the Kunda. Four men at a time should offer ahutis (oblations). The size of

each spoon should be big enough to hold ghee that is not less than half chhatak and should not be so big that it holds more than one chhatak of ghee.

10. Cremation ground should be situated in the south (of village, town etc.).
11. The dead body should be laid on the fuel pyre arranged in the Kunda. The dead body should be totally covered with fuel-wood. The head of the dead should be in the north direction and the feet in the south.
12. The hair of the dead should be removed before giving bath to it.
13. First a diya (small lamp) should to be lit. Camphor (placed in the spoon) should be lit from the diya (lamp) and this should be used to set alight the pyre. Begin lighting the pyre from that end of the pyre where the head is and ending by the feet. Thus the whole pyre should be set ablaze.

Oblations should be offered in the blazing fire with the following Mantras.

"Om Agnaye Svaha/ This oblation is for Agni. Whatever is uttered herein is true.

*Om Somaaya Svaha / """"Soma.""""*

*Om Lokaaya Svaha / """"This world Loka)""""*

*Om Anumataye Svaha / """Earth"""*

*Om swargaaya Lokaaya Svaha / "the other world (heaven)"*

***Funeral Prayer***

"Om Suryam Chakshurgacchatu Vatimaatmaa Dyaam Cha Gachchha Prithivim Cha Dharmana/

Apo Va Gachchha Yadi Tatra Te Hitamoshadhishu Pratimtishtha Sharirai svaha."

O Jiva (Soul)! After thy death, (may all the components of thy body be merged into the five elements). May the power of thy sight be absorbed in the sun and thy breath be absorbed in the air (atmosphere). May thy other parts be absorbed in appropriate elements. And in accordance with the meritorious deeds thou hast performed here, may thy spirit dwell in the appropriate body.

***The Rigveda***

From the Yajurveda 40.15 (also Isa Upanishad).

"Vayurnilammamritamathedam Bhasmantam Shariram

Om Krto Smara. Klibe Smara. Kritghvam Smara."

(Translations by Pandit Nardev Vedalankar assisted by Mr.Sookraj Chotai, B.A., B.Ed.)

The spirit which is immortal is not made of the five elements and does not perish. This body will be reduced to ashes. Therefore, O mortal! (At the time of death) remember the almighty Om, remember God, and remember thy past deeds, as by so doing can one attain salvation.

*From the Atharvaveda:*

O effulgent God! Thou art the dispenser of justice. Thou recompense every one according to his or her deeds. Peace be to the spirit of this dead body in the westward direction. May there be peace to this spirit in the east, the north and the south and all the other directions. O Omniscient and all-illuminating God! Thou art the Creator, the Sustainer and the destroyer of this universe. May thou bestow a worthy abode to this soul.

*From the Rigveda:*

O Jiva! By thy austerity and enlightenment, and by they good deeds, attain the bliss in heaven and join the company of thy forbears. Be free from all sins and once again may thy spirit acquire (reside in) noble body full of lustre. And once again may thou come to this world to perform noble deeds.

*From Manusmriti:*

"Everything perishes with the death of the body. It is only Dharma (righteousness) that is our real friend, which even after death remains with the spirit. Therefore do not allow the Dharma to perish, for Dhrama (when) perished brings about our (own) destruction."

*From the Bhagavad Gita 11/38:*

Thou are the primal God, the ancient Being. Thou art the final resting place of this universe. Thou art the Knower and That which is to be known and the Ultimate Goal. By Thee is the universe pervaded, O Thou of infinite form.

*From the Bhagavad Gita 2/22:*

Even as a person casts off worn-out clothes and puts on others that are new, so the embodied Self casts of worn-out bodies and enters into others that are new.

*From the Bhagavad Gita 2/20:*

It (the Self) is never born, nor does It ever die, nor, having once been, does it again cease to be. Unborn, eternal, permanent and primeval, It is not slain when the body is slain.

[Note: The Self is destitute of the six kinds of modification inherent in every living thing: birth, subsistence, growth, change, decay and death. The Self is altogether changeless.]

*From the Bhagavad Gita 2/23:*

Weapons cannot cut It (Self or the individual Soul), fire cannot burn It, water cannot wet It, wind cannot dry (wither) It.

[Note: Weapons can destroy an object by cutting it into parts; but the Self is without parts and is therefore indestructible. The same applies to the other methods of destruction. Only a material object consists of parts and is therefore destructible.]

*From the Bhagavad Gita 2/27:*

For to that which is born, death is certain, and to that which is dead, birth is certain. Therefore you should not grieve over the unavoidable (inevitable).

*From the Bhagavad Gita 2/28:*

All beings are unmanifest in their beginning, O Arjuna, manifest in their middle state, and unmanifest again in their end. Why, then, lament (grieve) for them?

[Note: Commentary by Swami Shivananda, Divine Life Society, Rishikesh: The physical body is a combination of the five elements. It is perceived by the physical eye only after the five elements have entered into such combination. After death the body disintegrates and the five elements return to their source. The body cannot be perceived now. Therefore, the body can be perceived only in the middle state.]

*From Yajurveda 2/54:*

May we get in future births again and again the mind, for doing virtuous deeds, for acquiring strength, for longevity, and contemplation of God for long.

The shaving of the head of the male whose near relation has died is customary and practised in many Hindu homes. It may be a voluntary custom because we have not come across reference to this practice in scriptural texts. The period of impurity (Asaucha) or pollution or defilement is generally for ten days (from the day of last rites or cremation) for near relations.

The rules to be observed during the period of impurity are of two kinds-negative (passive) and positive. The negative rules require the mourners to forego the many pleasures and comforts and even the routine business of daily life, thus exhibiting the feelings of grief and sorrow. They forbid certain things such as cutting of the hair and beard; forbid the study of the Vedas (during this period), Grhya offerings etc. The positive rules have also their origin in the aggrieved feelings of the survivors. They enjoin for a period of three days, to observe continence, to sleep on the ground, to live on begged or purchased food, to eat only in the day time etc.

The collection of the bones (a day after cremation of the body) is the ceremony known as 'Asthi-Sanchayana'. These are either dispersed in waters of sacred rivers or buried in the ground.

6

# Life after Death in Hindu Mythology

Many people believe that after death, they will continue to live on in new and different bodies. The theory of Karma and rebirth says that the mental qualities that we possess carry on from one birth to the next. But does this mcan our memories arc accurate? People believe they have memories of reincarnation. Some people, upon experiencing déjà vu, feel that the experience is a proof of existence of former lives. Some think the truth comes out under hypnosis while others believe just from their memory. But is this good evidence to back up the belief of life after death?

The doctrine of karma says that one experiences déjà vu because of reincarnation. But how accurate is this statement? These people have the sense of having visited a place before. Many people argue that this sort of experience is vague in its nature. It might have many possible explanations. Since déjà vu is a feeling, perhaps the feeling arose from something else. Something else in the environment could have caused one to feel like they've been here before. These explanations can be based on childhood memories that are "similar" but not identical. Maybe they saw a place that resembles the place they are claiming to have lived in before. It is also possible they saw a photograph of it. They might feel it is dejavu when in fact they may have forgotten that they have been there before. Another explanation could be the possession of a disorder. Memories of former lives could be the result of an illness they might be suffering from. It can even be a memory disorder and the things they are claiming to be past memories might only be bits and pieces of former memories from their "present" life. Many people claim to have spontaneous or recovered memories of past births. But how do we know this isn't a mere hallucination? They might be seeing things or imagining them. Maybe this is a matter of wishful thinking. The person "wishes" they were reincarnated. Their obsession with it probably drove them to believe it. Fraud can also play a role in such cases. How do we know the person isn't lying?

Alleged memories of past lives are usually obtained by a procedure called hypnotic regression. Subjects are asked to recall experiences they had from present to past. They are then asked to recall events that happened before they were born. This produces memories of past reincarnations. But how do we know this is correct? The subjects could have invented such stories out of a natural desire to please the hypnotist or perhaps they don't know they are lying. People can also have false memories of past births/events because of the hypnotist himself. A hypnotist can instill false beliefs in easily affected subjects. It is possible that a hypnotist could induce the mind to generate a general type of fantasy that "feels" real. The hypnotist could make you believe you had a previous life. Thus, you can't fully believe that under hypnotic regression, the recalled memories are true.

But now, let us suppose the story of a past life seems to be accurate. How do we know it is really accurate? What proof do we have? The subject must have obtained the details either consciously or subconsciously. He may have obtained it from books, documents or other historical material. You need proof in order to say that an argument for life after death is based on memories of former lives. Critics might say that you don't need proof in order for something to exist. But until there isn't proof that these memories are real, you can't say that life after death can be based on memories. Let's suppose the subject's account of experiences in a past life is demonstrated to be 100 per cent accurate, and they couldn't have obtained details and facts about them. Then how can we be sure that this person is the same person whose experiences have been recalled? They could be memories of someone else's former life. This, then, shouldn't be used to prove the existence of life after death. Without proofs that what the subject believes is true from a former life, you don't have to believe it. One might believe that maybe it's possible that no one knows about this small detail which a subject has recalled as a past memory. But the subject still, could be making it all up. It is also possible that he might be making it all up for attention.

One might remember having no talents in a past life. And now that in this life they are born with extraordinary talents, they are sure they have been reincarnated. They believe they did good deeds in their former lives, and as a result, they have extraordinary talents in life. This can, though, be due to their environment, or maybe it just happened. It can be a matter of coincidence too. Maybe believers of the theory of life after death feel that if they meditate and think about their past lives, they will remember. But these people usually focus their attention on one simple, repetitive thought. The more they think about it, the more they are likely to begin to hallucinate. Maybe one might remember speaking another language in the past. Upon hypnosis they recite some lines of that same language. They might be certain that they have learned this language in the past life. But maybe they just remember hearing it in their present life. You can't speak a language you never learned before. But just because you can speak another language doesn't mean that you know it.

The theory of karma and rebirth say that qualities from our mental character continue on from one birth to the next. These qualities include talents, likes and dislikes, ones emotions, and, etc. If this is true, then what about the people who claim to remember having certain qualities in their former life, but don't have these qualities in their present life? What about these subjects who claim to remember liking and disliking certain things, yet in this life, these likes and dislikes aren't the same? If these qualities change, then what is the proof that the subject is the same person as who he claims to be? People may recall dying of an illness, accident or other diseases. Such things as accidents, drugs, surgery, shock treatments, strokes, tumors, and, etc., might have destroyed parts of their brains.

If so, then how do we measure the accuracy of what they are presently saying? It is possible to lose memory, talents, likes and dislikes and many others because of head injuries. There is no need, then, to have faith on their memories if there are possibilities that parts of their brains might have been severely damaged.

Although people may claim to remember things from their past lives, people need not believe them. Without proof that the past even occurred, we don't have to believe it happened. If there is no way to distinguish the statements of memory from the statements from imagination, then there is no reason to believe that there is a life after death.

## After Life

The Buddhism belief of death and after death is very different from any I have ever heard of. They consider the after death just as important as the person's time on earth. Buddhist believe that in your lifetime, nothing that you posses other then your "karma" follows you after death. In saying this, Buddhist people believe that if you live your life honestly and positive, then good thing will follow for you in your "resurrection" which may be the result of coming back to life as God, or something very beautiful. Contrary to that, if you cheat people out, and live a dishonest and negative life, you may resurrect into the "hells", or come back as a deformed and ugly person or animal.

The Jainism view life as an endless reincarnation, as the Buddha's do they are born, live their lives as long as they are given and then they are born again. Jains base their religion around karma, and if you have good karma then you will be given a good life and when you die you will receive a good fortune in your second life, or as they call it the Circle of Births. I think that if everyone based his or her life around having good karma we would be living in a pretty good world. I like this approach to life, what you practice in your life results in your outcome after to die.

Christianity again, is something again very different from the above afterlife beliefs. Within this religion, it is believed that when one person dies, depending on how honest and truthfully your life was lived, you will go to either "heaven" or "hell". Heaven is said to be "up in the clouds" where your soul raises, and where all bad becomes good. This is where you may "achieve your eternal happiness". Hell on the other hand, is stereotyped as a place where the "devil" is. It's a place where you will be "burned" in the devils fire.

## Mourning Practices

Mourning practices for the Buddhism religion comes accrossed to me as being very extraordinary. They want to ensure that the persons after life is secure and they are ready to move on.

They diseased body is cremated after eight days, following that, Buddhist people prayer for the diseased person for forty nine days after they day, in preparation for that person's death, and also to allow that person to seek the best possible after life that is possible. They spend several weeks after a person's death talking to them and reading from their holy scriptures. The way they take forty-nine days to make sure the person is ready for their new life is very difficult for me to understand.

Jainism look at life as their are two things: Soul & Matter, they say that soul is life, and how you value you life. If you value your life and other living creatures then you have good soul. They say that matter is lifeless and is not good. Matter is evil and is what results in a bad outcome in the circle of births. If a person has bad karma or bad matter it goes and affects the soul.

Christianity follows the mourning system that many of us are probably used to. A person dies, and within a couple days their death is celebrated for family and friends by having a "wake" and a "funeral". At these ceremonies the diseased loved ones get their final chance to see them. After this, the person is either buried or cremated (depending on choice), and then put underground in a graveyard, with a gravestone. Many times loved ones will visit the gravestone to pray and leave flowers.

## Traditions and Other Beliefs

There is a famous book that the people of the Buddhist culture study. The book is called Bardo Thodol, meaning the book of the dead. This book even dates back to having pre-Buddhist teachings in it. It preaches that the human soul abides for forty-nine days in a dream like state. This state is called Bardo. In this book they explain that this little device that is actually called a prayer wheel. This wheel is carried around by many Tibetan monks and is said to contain written prayers that are activated by movement.

Another interesting aspect of the Buddhist religion is that these teachings were carried into China soon after they became popular in India. I had no idea that this religion was carried to other countries. Our group would have never guessed that it would spread across several different countries.

People of the Jainism religion can be "released from the circle of births", to do this which is considered a bad thing and will not receive any prayer or warship.It occurs from not believing in the religion or going against the religion such as bad karma, or killing innocent, or affecting others.

The Jains are very pro life, they even will not harm a living creature, as they think it might go against their karma, they care so much about animals and will not eat meat if it has to be cooked.

Christianity began when communication was slow and authority was rather decentralised, they were looked upon for guidance and authority.

Some of the beliefs that Christianity followed were as follows: "we believe in only one God, the Father Almighty, maker of all things visible and invisible. And in one Lord Jesus Christ, the son of God, begotten of the Father, the only-begotten; that is, of the essence of the Father, God of God, Light of Light, very God of very God, Begotten not made, being of one essence with the Father; by whom all things were made, both in heaven and on earth; who for us men, and for our salvation, came down and was incarnate and was made a man."

Some of the traditions of the Christian faith are that they celebrate the Eucharist on Sundays, and prey the word of the Lord. Take the body of Christ and reflect to your self-kneeling by your seat. You give a sign of peace through a handshake and rejoice with everyone around you. When you walk into a Christian church you will become overwhelmed with great art work, and beautiful music and himms of rhythm. These are the visual components of attending mass combined with prayer. In my opinion I believe in this faith because that is the faith that I have been brought up to believe, therefore I will support all notions and practice all of their traditions.

## Hindu Death Rituals and Beliefs

There is one thing that is certain in this lifetime: eventually we all must die. A belief in the cyclical reincarnation of the soul is one of the foundations of the Hindu religion. Death is viewed as a natural aspect of life, and there are numerous epic tales, sacred scriptures, and Vedic guidance that describe the reason for death's existence, the rituals that should be performed surrounding it, and the many possible destinations of the soul after departure from its earthly existence. While the ultimate goal is to transcend the need to return to life on earth, all Hindus believe they will be reborn into a future that is based primarily on their past thoughts and actions.

The first mortal to meet his fate with Death was named Yama. This dubious honour makes him uniquely qualified to lead the way for others after death. The sacred scriptures of the Rig Veda, which call him King Yama, promise that all who have been good will receive "admission to Yama's paradise and the everlasting enjoyment of all the heavenly pleasures, include the restoration of a sick body, the maintaining of family relations and the highly desired apotheosis". Yama is aided by two killer guide dogs that are described as the "four-eyed keepers of the path, who watch over men." These "two dark messengers of Yama with flaring nostrils wander among men, thirsting for the breath of life". Yet, once they have secured their prey, they lead them back to their heavenly realm, where Yama directs them to their destiny.

Cremation is a ritual designed to do much more than dispose of the body; it is intended to release the soul from its earthly existence. "Hindus believe that cremation (compared to burial or outside disintegration) is most spiritually beneficial to the departed soul." This is based on the belief that the "astral body" will linger "as long as the physical body remains visible." If the body is not cremated, "the soul remains nearby for days or months" The only bodies that are not generally burned are unnamed babies and the lowliest of castes, which are returned to the earth.

The standard cremation ceremony begins with the ritual cleansing, dressing and adorning of the body. The body is then carried to the cremation ground as prayers are chanted to Yama, invoking his aid.

It is the chief mourner, usually the eldest son, who takes the twigs of holy kusha grass, flaming, from the Doms' (the untouchable caste who tend funeral pyres) eternal fire to the pyre upon which the dead has been laid. He circumambulates the pyre counterclockwise—for everything is backward at the time of death. As he walks round the pyre, his sacred thread, which usually hangs from the left shoulder, has been reversed to hang from the right. He lights the pyre. The dead, now, is an offering to Agni, the fire. Here, as in the most ancient Vedic times, the fire conveys the offering to heaven.

After the corpse is almost completely burned, the chief mourner performs the rite called kapalakriya, the 'rite of the skull,' cracking the skull with a long bamboo stick, thus releasing the soul from entrapment in the body. After the cremation, the ashes are thrown into a river, ideally the Ganges river, and the mourners walk away without looking back.

The death ritual does not end with the elimination of the body. There is still the safety of the soul to look after. To ensure the passage during its voyage to the Otherworld, an eleven-day ritual called shraddha is performed. It "consist(s) of daily offerings of rice balls, called pindas, which provide a symbolic, transitional body for the dead. During these days, the dead person makes the journey to the heavens, or the world of the ancestors, or the 'far shore.'" "On the twelfth day, the departed soul is said to reach its destination and be joined with its ancestors, a fact expressed symbolically by joining a small pinda to a much larger one" Without these rites, the soul may never find it way to Yama's realm.

Those who have been "meritorious," but have not quite attained liberation through Self-knowledge, are sent to a heavenly realm to await their fate. "There the Gandharvas (demigods of fertility) sing to them and the bevies of celestial nymphs dance for them." Since there is no need for punishment, "they go forth immediately on very high divine carriages. And when they get down from those carriages, they are born in the families of kings and other noble people." There they "maintain and protect their good conduct" and live out their days before they are reborn enjoying "the very best of pleasures".

The fate for those who have participated in less honourable thoughts or actions is far less pleasant. The Arthasastra, a Hindu textbook from the second century BCE, offers a detailed description of some of the more frightening realms. Yet before reaching these dangerous destinations, one must first endure a miserable journey. "The hard-hearted men of Yama, terrifying, foul-smelling, with hammers and maces in their hands" come to get the deceased, who tremble and begin to scream. Filled with terror and pain, the soul leaves the body. "Preceded by his vital wind, he takes on another body of the same form, a body born of his own karma in order for him to be tortured."

The evil man becomes born as an animal, among the worms, insects, moths, beasts of prey, mosquitoes, and so forth. There he is born in elephants, trees, and so forth, and in cows and horses, and in other wombs that are evil and painful. When he finally becomes a human, he is a despicable hunchback or dwarf, or he is born in the womb of a woman of some tribe of Untouchables. When there is none of his evil left, and he is filled with merit, then he starts climbing up to higher castes, Sudra, Vaishya, Kshatriya, and so forth, sometimes eventually reaching the stage of Brahman or king of men. With so many unpleasant possibilities, it is easy to understand why reincarnation is not the only goal of every Hindu.

Those who lead a life of austerity, meditation and grace can look forward to the possibility of reaching Brahmaloka. This is the "highest among the heavenly planes" and the dwelling place of Brahma himself. "This is a place of intensely spiritual atmosphere, whose inhabitants live, free from disease, old age, and death, enjoying uninterrupted bliss in the companionship of the Deity."

There is no need for them to return to earth because they have freed themselves "from all material desires." While they do experience a sense of individuality, they also experience a oneness with Brahma. This is the realm of immortality.

There is one other way to achieve liberation from samsara. This is to die within the city of Benaras, on the Ganges. "Death, which elsewhere is feared, here is welcomed as a long-expected guest." A city of many names, it was known in ancient time as Kashi, the city of light, and the Mahabharata refers to it as Varanasi. The funeral pyres, which are located on the river, burn nonstop. "Death, which elsewhere is polluting, is here holy and auspicious." People travel from around the country and the planet to spend their last days in Benaras because, "Death, the most natural, unavoidable, and certain of human realities, is here the sure gate to Moksha, the rarest, most precious, most difficult to achieve of spiritual goals".

For those who are unable to die in Benaras, cremation on the banks of the Ganges or the spreading of the ashes in her waters is the next best thing. Referred to as the "River of Heaven" or the "goddess and mother," she is considered to be sacred from her source in the Himalayas, all the way to the sea in the Bay of Bengal. Her power to destroy sins is so great that, people say, "even a droplet of Ganges water carried one's way by the breeze will erase the sins of many lifetimes in an instant".

***Mourning, Burial at Sea:*** It must be understood that while this information was furnished by reliable sources, there are many different opinions between those of Hindu faith, and any Hindu contemplating cremation or burial at sea must seek the advice of a trusted priest.

Hindu death rituals in all traditions follow a fairly uniform pattern drawn from the Vedas, with variations according to sect, region, caste and family tradition. Most rites are fulfilled by the family, all of whom participate, including the children, who need not be shielded from the death. Certain rites are traditionally performed by a priest but may also be performed by the family if no priest is available. Here is a simple outline of rites that can be performed by Hindus in any locality. Variations are noted and suggestions made for Hindus in Western countries.

***As Death Approaches:*** Traditionally, a Hindu dies at home. Nowadays the dying are increasingly kept in hospitals, even when recovery is clearly not possible. Knowing the merits of dying at home among loved ones, Hindus bring the ill home. When death is imminent, kindred are notified. The person is placed in his room or in the entryway of the house, with the head facing east. A lamp is lit near his head and he is urged to concentrate on his mantra. Kindred keep vigil until the great departure, singing hymns, praying and reading scripture. If he cannot come home, this happens at the hospital, regardless of institutional objections.

***The Moment of Death:*** If the dying person is unconscious at departure, a family member chants the mantra softly in the right ear. If none is known, "Aum Namo Narayana" or "Aum Nama Sivaya" is intoned. (This is also done for sudden-death victims, such as on a battlefield or in a car accident.) Holy ash or sandal paste is applied to the forehead, Vedic verses are chanted, and a few drops of milk, Ganga or other holy water are trickled into the mouth. After death, the body is laid in the home's entryway, with the head facing south, on a cot or the ground—reflecting a return to the lap of Mother Earth.

The lamp is kept lit near the head and incense burned. A cloth is tied under the chin and over the top of the head. The thumbs are tied together, as are the big toes. In a hospital, the family has the death certificate signed immediately and transports the body home. Under no circumstances should the body be embalmed or organs removed for use by others. Religious pictures are turned to the wall, and in some traditions mirrors are covered. Relatives are beckoned to bid farewell and sing sacred songs at the side of the body.

***The Homa Fire Ritual:*** If available, a special funeral priest is called. In a shelter built by the family, a fire ritual (homa) is performed to bless nine brass kumbhas (water pots) and one clay pot. Lacking the shelter, an appropriate fire is made in the home. The "chief mourner" leads the rites. He is the eldest son in the case of the father's death and the youngest son in the case of the mother's. In some traditions, the eldest son serves for both, or the wife, son-in-law or nearest male relative.

***Preparing the Body:*** The chief mourner now performs Aarti, passing an oil lamp over the remains, then offering flowers. The male (or female, depending on the gender of the deceased) relatives carry the body to the back porch, remove the clothes and drape it with a white cloth. (If there is no porch, the body can be sponge bathed and prepared where it is.) Each applies sesame oil to the head, and the body is bathed with water from the nine kumbhas, dressed, placed in a coffin (or on a palanquin) and carried to the homa shelter. The young children, holding small lighted sticks, encircle the body, singing hymns. The women then walk around the body and offer puffed rice into the mouth to nourish the deceased for the journey ahead. A widow will place her tali (wedding pendant) around her husband's neck, signifying her enduring tie to him. The coffin is then closed. If unable to bring the body home, the family arranges to clean and dress it at the mortuary rather than leave these duties to strangers. The ritual homa-fire can be made at home or kindled at the crematorium.

***Cremation:*** Only men go to the cremation site, led by the chief mourner. Two pots are carried: the clay kumbha and another containing burning embers from the homa. The body is carried three times counterclockwise around the pyre, then placed upon it. All circumambulating, and some Aarti, in the rites is counterclockwise. If a coffin is used, the cover is now removed. The men offer puffed rice as the women did earlier, cover the body with wood and offer incense and ghee. With the clay pot on his left shoulder, the chief mourner circles the pyre while holding a fire brand behind his back. At each turn around the pyre, a relative knocks a hole in the pot with a knife, letting water out, signifying life's leaving its vessel. At the end of three turns, the chief mourner drops the pot.

Then, without turning to face the body, he lights the pyre and leaves the cremation grounds. The others follow. At a gas-fueled crematorium, sacred wood and ghee are placed inside the coffin with the body. Where permitted, the body is carried around the chamber, and a small fire is lit in the coffin before it is consigned to the flames. The cremation switch then is engaged by the chief mourner.

***Return Home; Ritual Impurity:*** Returning home, all bathe and share in cleaning the house. A lamp and water pot are set where the body lay in state. The water is changed daily, and pictures remain turned to the wall. The shrine room is closed, with white cloth draping all icons. During these days of ritual impurity, family and close relatives do not visit others' homes, though neighbours and relatives bring daily meals to relieve the burdens during mourning. Neither do they attend festivals and temples, visit swamis, nor take part in marriage arrangements.

Some observe this period up to one year. For the death of friends, teachers or students, observances are optional. While mourning is never suppressed or denied, scriptures admonish against excessive lamentation and encourage joyous release. The departed soul is acutely conscious of emotional forces directed at him. Prolonged grieving can hold him in earthly consciousness, inhibiting full transition to the heaven worlds. In Hindu Bali, it is shameful to cry for the dead.

***Bone-Gathering Ceremony:*** About 12 hours after cremation, family men return to collect the remains. Water is sprinkled on the ash; the remains are collected on a large tray. At crematoriums the family can arrange to personally gather the remains: ashes and small pieces of white bone called "flowers." In crematoriums these are ground to dust, and arrangements must be made to preserve them. Ashes are carried or sent to India for deposition in the Ganges or placed them in an auspicious river or the ocean, along with garlands and flowers.

***First Memorial:*** On the 3rd, 5th, 7th or 9th day, relatives gather for a meal of the deceased's favorite foods. A portion is offered before his photo and later ceremonially left at an abandoned place, along with some lit camphor. Customs for this period are varied. Some offer pinda (rice balls) daily for nine days. Others combine all these offerings with the following sapindikarana rituals for a few days or one day of ceremonies.

***31st-Day Memorial:*** On the 31st day, a memorial service is held. In some traditions it is a repetition of the funeral rites. At home, all thoroughly clean the house. A priest purifies the home, and performs the sapindikarana, making one large pinda (representing the deceased) and three small, representing the father, grandfather and greatgrandfather. The large ball is cut in three pieces and joined with the small pindas to ritually unite the soul with the ancestors in the next world. The pindas are fed to the crows, to a cow or thrown in a river for the fish. Some perform this rite on the 11th day after cremation. Others perform it twice: on the 31st day or (11th, 15th, etc.) and after one year. Once the first sapindikarana is completed, the ritual impurity ends. Monthly repetition is also common for one year.

***One-Year Memorial:*** At the yearly anniversary of the death (according to the moon calendar), a priest conducts the shraddha rites in the home, offering pinda to the ancestors. This ceremony is done yearly as long as the sons of the deceased are alive (or for a specified period). It is now common in India to observe shraddha for ancestors just prior to the yearly Navaratri festival. This time is also appropriate for cases where the day of death is unknown.

Hindu funeral rites can be simple or exceedingly complex. These ten steps, devotedly completed according to the customs, means, and ability of the family, will properly conclude one earthly sojourn of any Hindu soul.

Religions such as Hinduism offer our own immortal souls satisfying answers to questions of life and death. Their ancient mythic texts provide real reasons for our existence here on earth. They also demonstrate that death is something that can be prepared for instead of being feared. In addition, they offer the possibility of something to look forward to, so we need not dread our last days on this planet. A true hindu shall love death as he loves this life.

## The Wheel of Birth and Death

*Reflection has taught me that there is nothing mightier than Destiny... Zeus bows to her power. She surpasses iron in hardness. —Euripedes' Alcestis.*

*Heredity is a condition, not a destiny. —Bjornson.*

*As a man casts off worn-out clothes, and puts on others which are new, so the embodied casts off worn-out bodies, and puts on others which are new.—Bhagavad Gita.*

The crucial feature of the Greek conception of life was the dramatic distinction which it made between will and the conditions with which will had to cope. Just as surely as our birth on the planet Earth gives us a place, definite, however infinitesimal, in the solar system, relating us in our degree to all that occurs within the orbit of the farthest satellite, so it is clear that our position, geographically, ethnologically, historically, upon that planet, places us from the beginning at definite points on lines of cause and effect, to which, as human beings, we can but exercise the function of acceptance. This Not-to-be-refused, which modern science calls natural law, was simply to the Greek an unexplained and unexplored Necessity or Fate.

To the ancients, a curse, for example, was no exercise of the volition of the speaker. It was in no sense a threat. Our own more frivolous use of the word is a case of degradation by the death of a conception. To the old Greek, as indeed to the Hindu and the Norseman, a curse was entirely a prophecy. It was pronounced by way of warning or revelation that upon a certain act certain results would be found to follow Apollo perceives that if Laios begets a son, disaster will result. He does not determine that it shall be so. Evidently, will is regarded as free up to a certain point, or we should not have the alternative imagined, of begetting no son.

This fact the Greek mind appears to accept without further inquiry For it, overwhelming interest attaches, not to an analysis of the nature and conditions of fate, but to the spectacle of the human will in spiritual conflict with it. This spectacle is the theme of the whole of Hellenic tragedy. The Christian doctrine of grace introduces something confused and miraculous into the European idea of life, and for centuries the pursuit of the knowledge of things as they are is thwarted by a supernatural-metaphysic of things as they ought to be, and are not. With the Renaissance, however, the intellect of Europe springs back sharply to the Greek position. Macbeth and Othello are in some ways as completely Hellenic as anything of Aeschylus. Temptation is once more placed outside a man; true and false incentives are inextricably blended; and the will is shown as the mere plaything of its own blindness. On these points, and in the feeling of vastness with which he covers his subject, Shakespeare's delineation is all Greek.

In Macbeth, it is true, a sense of ethical suffering somewhat blurs the outline. But nothing dims the perfect beauty of Othello. Untortured by misgiving its heroic figures move from the dawn of their love to the noontide of supreme vindication of its purity in death. The particular problem is not antique. Its delicacy of tint is somewhat modern, but in simplicity and grandeur, in the conviction that life is a mere straw swept along on the current of necessity Othello is an ancient drama.

One great difference between the Hellenisms of antiquity and of the Renaissance lay in the fact that organisation was at the disposal of the modern. Isolated genius writes dramas, elabourates philosophies, or carves statues: organised genius produces scientific inquiry. In some sense modern science is nothing but the efficient development of the Aristotelian and Alexandrian elements of classical thought. The human will itself, however, is the one thing eternally baffling to human research. There is no crucible in which it can be melted. All science, therefore, resolves itself into the old problem of the Greek dramatist—the problem of due observation of the conditions which confront the will; and it is by a strictly logical development of the thought of the ancients—a thought which scarcely dreamt of any distinction between a man and his body—that we arrive at the modern conception of body-and-brain as the last and crucially important element of destiny.

Its naïveté is at once the strength and weakness of European thought. The springs of modern fiction are still brackish with the salt of our enthusiasm about heredity. Recent talk of degeneration is little more than the bitterness left within a cup. Like every single truth mistaken for the whole, heredity would impose as great a bondage on the human spirit as any system of fatalism. Of what use the fight against the weakness or ignorance of one's ancestors? What hope of victory over the taint that is in the blood? And yet, high over all law and all instruments rose, rises, and shall for ever rise, the human will, its brow bright with the sunshine of freedom, its foot on the foe that our subtle criticism had pronounced invincible, serene in the knowledge of its own power to defy alike heredity and the nature-of-things, and make for itself out of the web of failure the mantle of a supreme victory.

But this will so often seems asleep! Unaroused, or ignorant as a child, it has turned aside perhaps for every wayside flower, for any shining pebble, and in the hour of the crisis is simply missing. Or it may be that it suffers from some base intoxication of falsehood or desire, and has fallen down to kiss the feet of evil as though it were good, courting slavery and defeat as maidens to be caressed. Surely here, and here alone, is the crux of things, in the difference between the enlightened and the unenlightened will. Necessity is but the sum of the conditions. Heredity is but one, though the most critical, of those conditions. In the setting of the will itself towards bondage or towards freedom lies the secret of the unity of life.

There are thus three factors in the interpretation of human life, and it has been the distinction of Asiatic thought to have recognised all three. A profound certitude that cause must sooner or later be followed by effect, while effect has as surely been preceded by cause, gives to the Indian temperament an air of quiet resignation which is far from being the inactive fatalism so commonly supposed. For there is surely the difference of extremes between a dignified acceptance of things because they are unaccountable and not to be interfered with, and a similar dignified acceptance because they are so entirely accountable that events require no acceleration!

That India understands the doctrine of heredity is demonstrated by caste. There alone, amongst all the countries of the world, it has been held for ages an unpardonable social dishonour to allow the diseased or deformed or mentally alienated to marry. For such, the quietly enforced decree of caste has been always—no posterity. But more than this, the very meaning of the institution is, amongst other things, the attempt to develop still further the brain of the Brahman, the hand of the toolbearer, and every form of expert faculty.

It is true that it rejects the crossing of blood as a means to this end, but it looks to the cumulative influence of careful selection from generation to generation, to that of the occupational environment, and to the inheritance of the effects of clean-feeding. The last is held specially important to the user of the brain: hence the Brahman represents more than any other the fiber produced by countless generations of care in this respect, and the lower we go in society the less do we find of such transmission.

But the Indian comprehension of the nature of things and of heredity as complementary elements in the scheme presented to the will has never meant blindness to the last and most important consideration of all—the efficiency of the will itself. If this were not the determining factor, India would say, it would not be possible, as it is, to watch two brothers, with the same inheritance, the same material opportunities, and the same moral environment, journey, one to glory and the other to shame, by a common road.

And if it were not also the ultimate standard of success or failure, the Greek story of Aristides, for instance, would lose all its pathos" For we all know how, when an ignorant man asked his help in casting his vote for the condemnation of Aristides, the great man first complied with his request, and then, on mildly inquiring its reason, was answered, "I am tired of hearing him called 'the just.'"

Is it here, or in the story of Dives and Lazarus, that we catch a glimpse of inequality? Which is the crueler perplexing of our sense of justice—that one man receives wealth and another poverty, or that one cannot wish well, nor another ill?

The answer of India is not doubtful. There is one tool and only one, she says, that is finer than the most perfect human brain, and that is the tool of a noble intention. No more than other delicate instruments is this, she claims, immediately producible wherever we may wish to see it. Just as faculty grows from feeble and unrationalised to its perfection, just as organisms progress from minute and simple to large and complex, so must we suppose that will passes through all the stages of egotism till it reaches that illumination which we know as perfect charity. At each stage the possibilities of aspiration are limited, though they become less and less so as the goal is approached. The whole Hindu outlook is thus critical and scientific. There is no longer a vague horrible something called sin: this has given place to a clearly defined state of ignorance, or blindness of the will. Nor is this ignorance conceived of as a stationary or fixed quantity.

So surely as trees grow and rivers seek the sea will it sooner or later give place to knowledge, in every human soul; and then a man's mere forgetfulness of his limited personality and its aims may look to others like nobility: to himself it will not even be apparent, lost in the larger yearning of more universal life. Thus a great and generous thought is like a position near the river-mouth to the water springing at the source, not by any means to be reached without traversing the complete distance. The supreme good fortune possible to man would consist of a noble intention, joined to a great brain, joined to an external position of mastery and freedom an advantageous point, that is to say, on some line of cause and effect. Such, we may take it, to Gautama the Buddha, was the opportunity of his birth. Most lives, however, represent every possible degree, and combination of degrees, of the three conditions. We see the great position made the background of stupidity and meanness, We see the kind wish rendered futile by feebleness of intellect. Very occasionally there is no discord between person and circumstance; but now and again the discrepancy takes the acute form of the lion caught in the net, or the common criminal wearing an emperor's crown. Whence have these anomalies arisen? In what firm order do they stand rooted?

The Hindu mind seems always to have been possessed of the quiet confidence that all phenomena will yield themselves to a rational explanation. Since "that which exists is one," it is absurd to suppose an ultimate contradiction between the human reason and the universe. The mind that is normal and right amongst its fellows is normal and right in its relation to things. If we see and hear and taste, it is because in primal vibration there is something correspondent to sight and sound and the rest, of which our human sense has been the necessary outcome.

Our faculty, that is to say, may be feeble, but we must assume it to be true. If thirty years of life can impress us with a sense of terrible duration, utterly disproportionate to their relative importance, it is because in the Absolute there is no passage of time, all the infinite eternities of consciousness lying in the Now. If human love can oppress us with a vastness undreamed of, suddenly opened before us, it is because in it we have approximated to a state which transcends all limit and all change.

Whatever be the nature of the Real it must include, not exclude, consciousness. This being so, we must take it that the order of things as we see them—time, space, and causation—applies to life itself as naturally as to all that within the limits of life we perceive. Our appearance here from birth to death is a simple case of the sequences that every moment of our stay brings to our notice. It is the effect of some cause which could no more have failed to find its fulfillment in time and space than the self-striking of a bird's wing could fail to be accompanied by flight. Everything, again, within the general effect, is a subordinate effect conditioned by its own subordinate cause. Physical, mental, and moral, are only terms denoting so many dimensions, as it were, within which the seed has germinated and come to its fruition. So much for the effect.

Do things, as we see them, give us any hint as to the nature of the cause? Yes, there is one force—the force of desire—that we see at work daily, making, cherishing, gathering, action and its fruits. Without this as creative antecedent it will be found on examination that nothing that we know of comes to pass. Hence if life as a whole be regarded as but a phenomenon similar in kind to those which it encloses, we are impelled to the conclusion that of it also the efficient cause has been the human will. We dreamed of ourselves as bodies. Falling into some strange error, we longed for the sweets of sense. And we awoke and, without knowing it, found ourselves in prison, there but to continue adding to the energy of those desires, each of which was already a fetter binding us the faster. Such is the Hindu interpretation of our presence here. Of what led to our self-deceit he attempts no account, conceiving that his right to a rational theory applies only to the phenomenal, meaning those things that are perceived within the play of reason.

Thus, life is a harvest reaped at birth. It is also the sowing of fresh harvests for the painful reaping of the future. Every act is as a seed, effect of past cause, cause of effect to come—Karma. The unending wheel of birth and change and death. For the Hindu does not consider that a single life alone is to be accounted for. The very constitution of our minds forces on us the idea that phenomena are cyclic; that appearances recur; that the starry Universe itself blooms and will wither like another flower. Clearly then the causes that have placed us here today must bring us again; must, in the circling of infinite ages, have brought us infinite times before. This is the doctrine of Reincarnation. Our ignorance now tells of a deeper ignorance in the past. The desires that burn within us are but our subjective apprehension of what is yet to be. For that which we long for must come to our hand. The Karma of each birth is only the harvest of our ancient wishes.

What the victim of desire so constantly forgets, however, is the twofold nature of things, and their constant state of flux. Good brings evil; wealth is succeeded by poverty: love is but a messenger sent before the feet of sorrow. In fact, the seeming benefits of material things are in reality scourges, sooner or later to lash the very back of him who drew them to himself. None, for instance, could be so puerile as to declare palaces, jewels, and horses as good in themselves, so that their chance possession now and again should be any compensation for the suffering of requiring them. It is little more exalted, says the Hindu, to claim love, intellect, and salvation, as necessities. The world of Maya consists of the perpetual alternation of opposites. Every desire carries its fulfillment, its decay, and its retribution hidden within itself. That what we would have we must first give, is the lesson of austerity.

The Karma of an individual, then, consists of a given condition of taste or knowledge, a given physical equipment, and a given share of material fortune or misfortune. Taste sometimes rises to genius, or sinks to brutish appetite. The physical equipment may include a mathematician's brain, a violinist's hand, or a body tortured by perverse temptations. In any case, according to the theory, the will that has come to administer, earned exactly that endowment, and in this respect life is justly distributed. It is thought not unnatural that the soul of a Bach should seek incarnation in a family of musicians, since here it could best find the conditions it demanded.

With regard to such matters, a vast lore has been accumulated, into which it is interesting to dip. There is a popular belief amongst Hindus that marriage is always contracted between the same two persons, and that the merit of either is divided equally with the other. However this may be, love at first sight—an occasional experience the world over!—is held a sure proof of past friendship and acquaintance. Very perfect relationships, by which is meant, amongst other things, those that are complex in their quality, would be considered in the same way, to be long-rooted. The religious life is one of the most fascinating subjects of speculation. It will sometimes happen that the stern ascetic in the midst of his austerities yields to, or at least harbours, some vain desire. This is enough to precipitate him once more into the world, where his position and power will be exactly equal to the severity of his past renunciations. He may thus very easily become a monarch, and it is believed that a faint memory of the religious habit often haunts the throne.

The great Akbar of Delhi told of such a reminiscence in his own case. He had been a monastic novice, and had fallen in love! When sovereignty was exhausted, however, he would return to his prayers and gain freedom, without another fall. An impression of this kind about Queen Victoria was the real secret of the influence of her name in India—an influence, be it added, which would have been much deepened had she succeeded in abdicating some few years before her death, in order to devote the rest of her life to God.

We must remember, however, that the Oriental, born to the idea of re-incarnation, rarely becomes so infatuated with it as to make it his sole dependence in interpreting life. He does not lose his head over it, as may one who hears of it for the first time. He is well aware that, on his own hypothesis, we are engaged in the sowing of seed, as well as the reaping of grain. He will not therefore attempt to explain every new introduction from an imaginary past. This life is to him but one measure in a long passage of music. The great majority of its tones gain all their beauty and meaning from the fact that they wet e prepared beforehand and will be resolved after, but some nevertheless are new. That we do not, as a rule, remember our pasts is, he argues, no disproof of their existence, since neither do we remember our birth and infancy.

It is this clearness of logical speculation that lends its terror to the Indian notion of existence. To the wise man, frankly, life is a bondage, and the only question how to be freed from it. Suicide cannot solve the problem. The reasons for this act may be frivolous or weighty. It is an instrument as much within a man's own power as the tools of his calling or the weapons of self-defence. Only, it offers no escape from the misery of existence. Can the schoolboy make progress in arithmetic by wiping from his slate the sum he could not work? Will not that particular difficulty recur whenever he would take an onward step, confusing, taunting, and blinding him, till it is conquered? Even so is the lot of the suicide, thinks the Hindu. He desired to escape the rope of justice? Then in some future incursion into life it will become his Karma to stand on the scaffold and undergo the extreme penalty, for a crime he has not committed.

He would flee from a dishonour he had not strength to endure? No coward's self-banishment shall suffice to save him. Sooner or later the ordeal must be met and faced. Or was it the abstract hatred of life that used his own hand to slay the man? Fool! saw he not that the act was part and parcel of an extreme self-indulgence, and must bring its terrible consequence of exile from all that could make existence beautiful and blessed?

Desire, in short, is the ego-centripetal, the self-assertive, self-regarding force. The current must be turned out deliberately, not drawn inward. The passion for self must be destroyed in the thirst for service. Desire must be burnt to ashes in the fires of renunciation. Then, and then only, will there be escape from the incessant turning of the wheel. Then alone can the victim become the conqueror, and the slave master of the world.

This is the "cosmic suicide" of Schopenhauer, the much talked-of "pessimism" of the East. It is indeed a familiar conception to all Hindus, so familiar as to be an integral part of language. But it is hardly "pessimism." Does the prophecy of victory carry with it sadness? the certain promise of his freedom embitter the slave? There is a sense in which, if Hindu philosophy be not optimistic, it is difficult to know what the world means by optimism. Taking the doctrine of reincarnation as a whole, we find it so necessary to the theory of Maya that even the Buddhist formulation could not exist without some version of it. At the same time, a clear understanding of it is a valuable corrective of slipshod misconceptions as to the philosophy of illusion. That this involves no lazy intellectual uncertainty regarding phenomena we have seen, since the whole doctrine of Karma is based on the Hindu's implicit conviction of the entire calculableness of law.

It cannot be too clearly understood that the argument of Maya is compatible with, and tenacious of, the severest scientific research, and that to Oriental thinking, only that man who has in his own person, by some method of self-discipline, achieved a realisation, compared to which all that we know through the senses is unreal, has a right to speak of the phenomenal universe as, to him, fundamentally an illusion. The effort to reach this vision remains, nevertheless, to the Oriental mind the one end and justification of existence, the one escape from the wheel of life, and mankind is for ever divisible into those who see and struggle towards such a goal, and those who are engaged in sowing the wind, and reaping the whirlwind, of Desire.

The battlefield of Kurukshetra lies silent these many centuries, yet still to the ear of the wise man it echoes the doom of Humanity in the terrible words "of that which is born, death is certain of that which is dead, birth is certain."

## Love Strong as Death

As to the skies their centre is the Polar Star, so to the Eastern home the immovable honour of its womanhood. Here is the secret of that worship of the mother in which all union of the family and all loyalty to its chief are rooted. Woman in the West may thirst for the glory of love or the power of wealth: in Asia, her characteristic dreams are of perfectness and purity and faith. Woman in the West is a queen, exposed to the fierce light that beats upon a throne, putting to good or evil use the opportunities of sovereigns. Even queens in the East are too sacred to be looked upon by common eyes. They grow, like the tall white lilies of annunciation, set in the dimness beside some altar, screened from the very glances of the faithful at their prayers. The long silken tent through which such ladies move from palace-door to carriage-step is no vulgar prison, but a shrine. Bereft of its concealment, they would feel dishonoured, unprotected, as does the widowed gentlewoman, compelled to fight for bread, amongst the struggling crowd.

The very possibility of this blaze of publicity shed on delicate high-bred womanhood is repugnant to the Oriental mind. Remoteness and shadow, silence and obscurity, seem to it the true environment of holiness. And woman is held to be so much a sacred mystery that no man may even mention the name of another's wife to him. "Are they at home all well?" is the guarded form which the necessary inquiry for her health has to take. The outer courts of the house, where the men pass the day, the verandah and the stoop, where neighbours meet and chat, these are but public places. Here the intellectual life may be lived, and civic affairs transacted. But it is by the cool grey threshold of the inner, the women's rooms, that the world of home is entered. And what an ocean of passionate loving surges through the quiet walls! Here the wife listens for the feet of the returning husband. Here the widow sobs for him who will return no more. Here scamper home the babies to find mother or aunt, grave elder sister, or twin-souled younger comrade. Here youth lays its plans and brings its perplexities, while old age looks on, with the quiet eyes of experience and of faith. Here passes, in short, all that mingling of smiles and tears, of laughter and prayer, of charm and weariness, that goes to make up the bitter-sweet sacrament of daily life. Only the art of medieval Holland speaks a passion for home as ardent as this of the Orient, which as yet has found no voice!

Standing without in the noonday hush and looking into the semi-darkness of the women's apartments it is as if one caught a glimpse of some convent garden, full of rare and beautiful flowers. This is the women's hour. Their natural guardians are all absent, sleeping, or at business. Only in the outer court a drowsy servant guards the entrance. An air of innocent raillery, of delicate gaiety, pervades all. Friendly confidences and gentle fun are being exchanged. It is now that the long melancholy cry of the peddler is heard, with his "Bracelets and bangles—who wants?" or "Good, good cloth!" or what not. And the wandering merchant may be called in, to add amusement to the moment by his baiting and bargaining.

Noonday passes, and slender widows in their long white veils fall to telling their beads, unnoticed and absorbed. Here and there a mother glides away to prepare for the children's coming home from school. The sound of laughter and talk dies gradually down; and afternoon wears on to evening, and the hour of prayer. So passes the day's drama, with all its blending of subdued tints, from dainty rose to ashen grey. Yet almost all the windows of the home look inwards and four blank walls enclose the whole. True indeed is it that silence and shadow are the ideals of this, the life of Eastern womanhood.

But the ideal itself, that it may be fixed and perpetuated, requires its culminating types and centres, its own duly consecrated priesthood, whose main task in life shall be to light its lamp and wait upon its altar. And such persons, in the world of Indian women, are the widows. Literature consists largely of man's praise of woman in relation to himself; yet it remains eternally true that this heroine of man—Helen, Desdemona, Beatrice—is but one modification or other of her who goes unseen, unrhymed, unnamed, the woman of solitude, the woman who stands alone.

Neither Europe nor the modern spirit can claim the glory of having created the idea of woman as an individual. Queen Hatasu had it, in ancient Egypt. In still older Chaldea, Semiramis had it. In the sagas of the North, it is true, no woman goes unwed. But no sooner does Christianity—the Mission of the Asiatic Life—appear amongst us, than medieval history blossoms into its Hildas, and Teresas, and Joans, its Saxon Margarets and its Spanish Katherines. It is the self-protecting woman only, who is born perhaps of the nineteenth century. Of old it was held by Frank and Saxon, by Latin and Teuton, that she who did not marry needed the protection of the Church. And in Asia to this day it is believed that she requires the sanction of the religious life itself, though that life belived for the most part within the community-house. For the only unmarried woman in India is the widow, and especially the child-widow—that is, one whose betrothed has died before actual marriage.

A kind of faithfulness is implied in this, which is quite different from the faithfulness of the West. There, it is counted for great fidelity if amidst the growing complexities of life there run the stream of a strong and constant memory; if the bereaved wife be true to the idea for which the husband stood; if she carries his name as a banner, whose new adherents are won by the power of her own consecration. In India, no growth of complexity can be permitted. Where the life stood when its companion was smitten down, there it must remain, till a second death completes the releasing of that one being who only seemed to others to be two.

How wonderful is death! So cold, so still! The mind is withdrawn from the senses, and steadied, that enters its presence but for a moment. They who dwell there find release into a great calm. The Hindu widow lives out her life with her soul ever present at the burning-ghat. Her white sari, unbordered, her short hair, her bareness of jewels, her scant food and long prayers, her refusal to meet guests and join in festivities,—all these things are but the symbols of its abiding lights and shadows. She has found her vocation, so to speak, and as a nun must henceforth direct her life. If she be a child-widow, this is only the more true. Then, the church in which she lingers is more apt to be the thought of the Divine itself. But if in her widowhood she can remember what it was to be a wife, her altar will be the name of the dead husband, and her austerities will carry with them the unspeakable gladness of the memory that half of all their merit goes to him. This belief in a mystic union of souls was the motive of suttee,—a sacrifice that was supposed to lift the husband's soul at once into bright places, and brings his wife to enjoy them beside him for thousands of years. Who, with such an idea deep-ingrained, could not laugh at fire?

It is clear that this scheme of the widow's life is inherent in a great simplicity. A marriage which had but one duty could alone have led to this bereavement which has but one thought. And yet we must understand that it is in this terrible blight of love that the strong woman finds her widest individual scope.

It is told of Bhashkaracharya, the mathematician that he had but one child, the maiden Lilavati. Casting her horoscope carefully, he discovered that there was only a single moment in her life when she could be married without fear of widowhood. Preparations were made for the wedding accordingly, and the father himself constructed an instrument by which to regulate the time of the ceremonies. Water would be admitted drop by drop through a certain hole, from one pot to another, and its reaching a given height was the signal for the sacramental act.

The marriage-rites began, but the child Lilavati grew tired, and went wandering from room to room in search of amusement.

In some obscure corner she came upon an unaccustomed-looking pot, and leaned over its edge to watch how the inner section was gradually sinking in the water which it contained. As she did so a tiny pearl fell all unnoticed from her wedding crown, and stopped the hole through which the water passed! Time went on, but the vessel sank no further. "Ah!" exclaimed Bhashkaracharya sorrowfully, when, the hour already past, he found the jewel that had frustrated all his caution, "it is useless for a man to fight against his destiny!"

Within some few weeks or months the little bride was left a widow. But now her great father resolved to make of her a woman so learned that she should never sigh for earthly happiness—a resolve in which he succeeded to such an extent that to this day it is not known whether the abstruse treatise named "Lilavati" was merely dedicated to her, or whether she asked the questions to which it contains the answers.

This story is historic. But simple instances abound in every village. The kind widowed aunt who lived in the opposite house to ours, did she not count every soul in the Calcutta lane, together with her brother's children, as her own? "Do not leave this country," she would say to some member of our household every now and then, "for you know I count you all my bairns!" When the man in the next house died of cholera, it was not we, the European neighbours, but this Pishi-ma of ours, who was first on the scene with disinfectants. When the immediate necessity of cleansing the whole house was explained, it was still another and older widow lady who listened, and carried out the work with her own hands. Indeed, wherever one is called in time of need, one finds a group of widow-women already present. There is no act of nursing that these are not ready, and even eager, to perform; no disease so loathsome or dangerous that they will not gladly take a sick child into their arms; no injury so bitter that it will prevent their weeping sorrowful tears of sympathy with the injured in his hour of pain and loss.

It is quite natural that widows should he more free for the civic life than other women. Wives have their husbands' comforts to attend to, and mother their thousand and one maternal cares. But the widow, and above all the childless widow, in her agony of solitude, can hear the sobs of children not her own, can stretch hands across the desert of her own mourning to those who are ill, or in poverty, and desolation. In the last generation lonely women had still more scope than they have now. I have heard of one who never sat down to the mid-day meal till a servant brought her word that every soul in the village had already eaten. Almost every family can remember some aged dame of its own who was famed for her skill in all sorts of remedies for man and beasts.

The very cow-goddesses, who are worshipped in Himalayan villages in time of cattle pestilence, may have been actual Hindu women of this type, raised to the rank of deities. But the last half-century in India has been rapidly accomplishing the decay of the middle classes; and with this decay, brought about by the shrinking of wealth in its old channels, the fall of woman, in social and material power, proceeds apace. Yet still the widows represent the intellectual centres amongst women. The more modern they are, the less likely is it that they can reel off Sanskrit verses, but the more probable that they read books in the vernaculars. In any case, they produce the saints; and the position of a woman-saint in India is such that no man in her neighbourhood will venture on a journey without first presenting himself before her veiled form, taking the dust of her feet, and receiving her whispered blessing.

Widows have constantly distinguished themselves, especially in Bengal, as administrators of land and wealth. Of this pattern was the great Mahratta Queen of Indore, Ahalya Bai. Her husband died while waging war with Scindia and another, and her first act was to disband her armies, and send word to the sovereigns that she was at their mercy, a defenceless woman. The expected result followed in the complete abandonment of all hostilities. After which, Ahalya Bai Rani lived and reigned for many a long year eating the Hindu widow's handful of rice of her own cooking, and spending her great revenues in public works on the largest scale.

For the wife becomes regent when a man dies during the minority of his son; and even if the latter be already of age, his ownership of an estate is by no means free and complete during the lifetime of his mother. The whole world would cry shame if he acted without her occasional advice, and, indeed, the Indian woman's reputation for business capacity is so like the French that it is commonly said of encumbered property that it needs a widow's nursing.

In such a case there is, however, for the wealthy woman one temptation. Throughout her married life her relation with her father's house has remained close and intimate. At least once a year, if not oftener, she has returned to it on visits. Her eldest child was born there under her own mother's care. Her girlhood's friends have perpetually renewed her youthful memories by hastening to see her on her arrival, and talk over old times. It was many a year before the revival of familiar associations ceased to make her wholly a child again, so that she would run bare-headed down the lane to a neighbour's house, rejoicing in the unaccustomed freedom of the fact that the only men she was likely to meet were practically her own brothers, for she had played with them in babyhood.

But if the relation to her early home and to her past be thus deep and exquisite, what are we to say of the bond that knits together the Hindu sister and her brother? Here is the tie that offers to the woman of responsibilities her great temptation; for it is considered hard and yet essential, for one who administers a dead husband's wealth not to bestow it in these channels, not to submit to management and direction, not to transfer possession gradually from the one house to the other. And the very insistence upon the dishonour of such a course is in itself testimony to the affection that tempts. The perfect wife is she who loves her husband with a love that forgets even father and brothers if need be. But how arduous is such perfection to attain! One day in the Hindu sacred year is known as "The Feast of Brothers," because on it sisters are visited and give their benisons. And so, even about the detached life of the married woman, made independent of her father's care, early associations continue to twine and grow stronger. They never cease to be an organic part of her life; and if the stress of her existence throws her back upon them, she knows that on which she leans, that it will not fail her at her need, or prove a false staff, breaking in her hand.

And yet her natural longing, in the first days of her widowhood, is to remain, unless forbidden by his poverty, in the household of her father-in-law, for herein lies all her loyalty to the dead. Nay, it will often happen that even a child-widow is anxiously retained by her husband's parents, as a token, in some sort, left by him who is gone. All the glory of womanhood lies in such things as these. Even in her own home, too, a widow has the right to be exacting on a thousand little points regarding her dead husband. Do her father and brothers not remember the great days of obligation of the household into which she married? Do they require reminder, instead of hastening to be beforehand with her, in suggesting the gifts and offerings she would do well to send? Ah, then, it is only herself for whom they cease to weary themselves, or do they forget his dignity who should be as dear as their own blood. And for her own part she watches with solicitude all that passes in the family whose name she bears. Is a new bride received among them? From her own diminishing store of jewels will be sent some trifle—may be only a couple of tiny gold jasmine flowers for the ears—by the bereaved to the newly-wedded daughter-in-law. Or she hears of sickness and arrives to nurse. She comes to wait on the aged, or will assume charge of the young while grave elders goon pilgrimage. All this implies a network of social ideals that tends to make it difficult to divert the income arising from alliance.

Over and above her alleged common sense, on the other hand an estate that passes into the hands of a woman ruler enjoys the economic advantage of her freedom from personal extravagance; for the energy with which a widow pursues after abstinence is extraordinary. To this day she lives in an ancient India, created by her own habits. In Calcutta she drinks only Ganges water, holding that the municipal supply is contaminated by European use. She will eat only rock-salt in order to avoid the pollution of manufacturing processes When ill she accepts treatment only from the old Indian doctors, the vaidya or the kaviraj, and pays fantastic sums for their medicines if they come from Benaras or some other seat of classic learning. If well, she eats one meal of cooked food prepared with her own hands at or after mid-day, and only a slight refection of milk, fruit, and unleavened bread at nightfall. Her hair is cut short (or in some parts of India the head is shaved), perhaps originally to remove the temptation of beauty, but, as far as custom knows and questions, only that she may bathe the more frequently and easily—every bath conveying to her the notion of a baptism.

Such is her ordinary routine. Her occasional dissipations consist in a pilgrimage, an extra visit to a temple at dawn or after sunset, or attendance at some ceremony of epic recitation. Is it not well said that she knows no extravagance?

It is because her life is holier than that of others that no hand must touch her food, though she may prepare and serve the meals of any in the house. For the same reason, if questions of precedence arise, she stands higher than married women. Did she not rise before dawn to tell her beads, or to sit for an hour in meditation? Then, when her room was cleaned and ordered, did she not go to the river for the morning bath? Returning with the wet sari that she had washed, according to daily custom, with her own hands, did she not don the silken garment and pass to that ceremonial worship, with flowers and offerings that lasts for at least an hour or more and only when that worship was ended could she begin to think of cooking her meal. With the waning of the afternoon she falls again to telling her beads, right hand and rosary both concealed in a little bag. At the moment of "candlelight," she passes once more into actual meditation. Then an hour's chat, the frugal evening meal, and so to bed, to begin at dawn on the morrow again the daily round.

An incomparable moment in the history of a Hindu family is that of the return to it of a young daughter freshly widowed. Unspeakable tenderness and delicacy are lavished on her. A score of reasons for the mitigation of her rule are thought out and urged. In spite of her reluctance, the parents or parents-in-law will insist. Sometimes the whole family will adopt her austere method of living for a few months, and keep pace with her self-denials step by step, till she herself discovers and breaks the spell. "Well, well!" exclaimed an old father brooding over the ruin of his child's happiness at such a crisis, "it was high time for me to retire from the world; can we not renounce together, little mother?" And while she is supported by her father's strong arm, the mother's wings are open wide, to fold closer than ever before the bird that has flown home with the arrow in its heart. Indeed, this union of theirs has become proverbial, so that if some small son be uncommonly helpful and chivalrous to his mother, friendly neighbours will say, in banter: "But this is no boy This is surely your widowed daughter, mother!" So pass the years, till, it may be, the mother, herself widowed, becomes as a child, falling back upon the garnered strength of her own daughter. Life ebbs: but discipline gathers its perfect fruit, in lives stately and grave and dignified, for all their simplicity and bareness; in characters that are the hidden strength alike of village and of nation; in an ideal of sainthood justified; an opportunity of power created.

In the long years of her mature life we picture the Madonna standing always beneath the Cross. And we are right. But patience! not for ever shall she stand thus. It shall yet come to pass that in high heaven a day shall dawn, on which, wearing the self-same meekness, clothed in self-same humility, the Mother of Sorrows shall be crowned—and that by her own Son!

## The Gospel of the Blessed One

*We worship Thee, Seed of the Universe,*
*Thou one unbroken Soul.*
*We worship Thee, whose footstool is worshipped by the Gods,*
*Thou Lord of the Saints,*
*Physician of the World-disease,*
*To Thy lotus-feet our salutation, O Great Soul!*
*Hindu form of salutation to a Divine Incarnation.*

It is told of a certain Bodhisattva that, all his struggles done and illumination reached, he was about to pass over into Nirvana. But as his feet touched the threshold of supreme blessedness there rose to his ears the sound of the sorrowful crying of humanity. Then turned that great soul back from Nirvana and entered again into life, declaring that till the last grain of dust in the universe had passed in before him, he would by no means go into salvation. And this Bodhisattva is he who sits on the throne of the Dalai Lama in Tibet, watching the world of men with eyes of divine pity from afar off.

Called by various names, arrayed in widely, differing garb, we come constantly in Hinduism on the attempt, as here in the story of the Dalai Lama, to express the idea that in the great Heart of the Absolute there dwells an abiding charity towards men. It would seem as if, to the religious instinct of humanity, the dream of "the pursuit of the soul by God" is a necessity; and the Hindu, well aware of the impossibility of giving it logical expression, veils his effort in mythology. Whence the stories or the Avatars. For our conception of the doctrine of reincarnation is only complete when we understand that now and again the Eternal Love is represented as projecting itself into the sphere of manifestation, taking shape as a man, in order to act as a lamp amidst the darkness of delusion, a counter-magnetism to the attractions of desire.

It is absurd, says the Hindu—whose imagination can never be charged with provincialism—to think that such an Incarnation, supposing it to occur at all, could visit the world only once. Is respect of persons a divine attribute? Or is the need of mankind at any time less than complete? Can we believe, again, that the power of creative energy to assume and throw off the shell of personality is exhausted in a single effort? Rather must the taking upon Himself of mortal form and limitations be to the all-pervasive "as the lifting of a flower's fragrance by the summer breeze," a matter of play; or like the shining of a lamp through the window wherein it is set, without effort—nothing more.

The orthodox Hindu is thus usually in no position to deny the supernatural character of the Babe of Bethlehem. He is only unable to admit that the nature of Christ stands alone in the history of the world, holding that his own country has seen even more than the three—Rama, Krishna, and Buddha—who were His brothers. Still more cogently does he claim sometimes that all these and possibly others of whom he has not heard, are but one soul, one expression of Godhead coming back at different times to lay hold on the hearts of men. And he quotes in support of this contention the familiar words of Krishna: "Whenever religion decays, and when irreligion prevails, then I manifest myself. For the protection of the good, for the destruction of the evil, for the firm establishment of the dharma, I am born again and again."

It is natural enough to the Hindu intellect that around each such forth-shining of the Divine should grow up a new religious system or Church. But each of these is only a special way of expressing the one fundamental doctrine of Maya, a new mode of endearing God to man. At the same time it is thought that every one, while recognising this perfect sympathy of various faiths for one another, should know how to choose one amongst them for his own, and persist in it, till by its means he has reached a point where the formulae of sects are meaningless to him. "For it is good," say the people, "to be born in a church, though it is foolish to die there."

In this sense—somewhat different from the religious partisanship of Europe—the popular and growing belief of the Hindu masses consists of various forms of the worship of Krishna. It is this creed that carries to those who need it, a religious emotionalism like that of the Salvation Army or. of Methodism. In the hottest nights, during periods of "revival," the streets of a city will be crowded with men bearing lights and banners, and dancing themselves into a frenzy to such words as:

*Call on the Lord, Call on the Lord,*
*Call on the Lord, little brother*
*Than this name of the Lord,*
*For mortal man, There is no other way.*

Krishna, like Rama and like Buddha, is considered to be a special incarnation of Vishnu, God the Preserver. It is therefore pertinent to appeal to Him for the goods of life, for consolation in sorrow, for deliverance from fear. He is known as the Holy

Child, born in humility amidst cowherds by the Jumna; the Gentle Shepherd of the People, the Wise Counselor, the Blessed Lord, tender Lover and Saviour of the human soul; and by other names not less familiar to ourselves. It is an image of the Baby Krishna that the Indian mother adores as the Bambino, calling it "Gopala," her cowherd. His name fills gospels and poems, the folk-songs of all Hindu races are full of descriptions of Him as a cowherd wandering and sporting amongst His fellows; and childish literature is full of stories of Him, curiously like European tales of the Christ-child. To the ecstatic mystic, He is the Divine Spouse.

If we dip into His history we shall think it a strange medley. So many parts were never surely thrust upon a single figure! But through it all we note the pre-dominant Indian characteristics,—absolute detachment from personal ends, and a certain subtle and humorous insight into human nature.

His main spiritual significance for India does not, perhaps—with one exception—attach to that part of His life which is related in the Mahabharata, but rather to what is told of Him in the Puranas—works not unlike our apocryphal Gospels. But the one exception is important. It consists of no less an incident than that conversation with the chieftain Arjuna which comprises the Bhagavad Gita, or Song of the Blessed One. Of this little poem—only some three or four times the length of the Sermon on the Mount, and shorter even than the Gospel of St. Mark—it may be said at once that amongst the sacred writings of mankind there is probably no other which is at once so great, so complete, and so short. It provides the worship of Krishna—and incidentally all kindred systems—with that open door upon abstract philosophy without which no cult could last in India for a week. But it is by no means the property of the Vaishnavas exclusively. From Kashmir to Cape Comorin it is bone of the bone and flesh of the flesh of all forms of religious thought.

Its ideas are unmistakably Indian in colour: its feeling is just as unmistakably universal. The voice that speaks on the field of Kurukshetra is the same voice that reverberates through an English childhood from the shores of the Sea of Galilee. We read the gracious words, "Putting aside all doctrines, come thou to Me alone for shelter—I will liberate thee from all sins, do not thou grieve." "Fixing thy heart on Me, thou shalt, by My grace, cross over all difficulties," and we drop the book, lost in a dream of One who cried to the weary and heavy-laden, "Come unto Me." We certainly now understand, and cannot again forget, that for the Indian reader the eyes of the Lord Krishna are most kind, His touch infinitely gentle, and His heart full of an exceeding great compassion, even as for us are the eyes and the hand and the heart of Him Who spoke of Himself as the Good Shepherd.

Like our own Gospels, the Gita abounds in quaint and simple metaphors. "As a lamp in a sheltered spot, not flickering," must be the mind. All undertakings are surrounded with evil, "as fire with smoke." The round of worship is "as a wheel revolving." So great is wisdom that though thou shouldst be "even the most sinful of all sinners, thou shalt cross safely to the conquest of all sin by the bark of wisdom alone." One of the most beautiful, referring to those perceptions which constitute the Universe as we know it, says, "All this is threaded upon Me as gems upon a string." Nothing is mentioned that would not be familiar to the poorest peasant, living on a fertile plain, diversified only by a river and an occasional walled city.

And indeed it was for these, labouring men, unlettered and poor, that the Gita, with its masterly simplicity, was written. To those who had thought salvation and the beatific vision as far beyond their attainment as a knowledge of the classics—to these humble souls the Divine Voice declares that, by worshipping God and doing at the same time the duty of his station, every man may attain perfection. "Better for one is one's own duty, however badly done, than the duty of another, though that be easy." Again and again, as we read the Gita, we are driven to the conclusion that we hear an infinite mercy addressing itself to a people who had imagined the knowledge of God to be the monopoly of priesthoods and religious orders, and bidding them be of good courage, for the true monk is he "who neither hates nor desires," the true worshipper any one who "offers to Me with devotion even a leaf or a flower or a cup of water." No wonder that the Indian people, saluting a Divine Incarnation, call Him the Physician of the world-disease! Never did speech know how to be more interior. "Those who worship Me, renouncing all actions in Me, regarding Me as supreme, meditating on Me with entire devotion, for them whose thought is fixed on Me, I become ere long, O son of Pritha, the Saviour out of the ocean of this mortal world."... "For I am the abode of Brahman, the Immortal and the Immutable, the Eternal Substance, and the unfailing Bliss." We kneel in a vast silence and darkness, and hear words falling like water drop by drop.

Nothing is omitted from the Gita that the unconsoled heart requires. There are even the tender promises of daily bread, so dear to the anxious; "They who depend on Me, putting aside all care, whatsoever they need, I myself carry it to them," runs one verse. Of this a beautiful story is told in the villages. The Brahman sat copying the text, but when the word "carry" had been written, he felt a doubt. "My dear," he said, turning to consult his wife, "thinkest thou not it is irreverent to say 'carry' here? Did not our Lord not mean 'send?'" "Beyond a doubt, beloved," answered his wife, "it is as thou sayest. Let the word be 'send.'" Then the man took his penknife and erased the word he had just written, substituting his own emendation for it. A moment later he rose up to go and bathe. But his wife stood before him with troubled face. "I told thee not," she said, "that there is no food in the house, and naught have I to cook for thee." The Brahman smiled gently. "Let us call upon our Lord to fulfil His own promise," he replied quietly; "meantime, I shall go and bathe," and he passed into the next room. Only a few minutes had he gone, when his wife was called to the door by a beautiful youth, who stood there with a basketful of delicious foods, ready for eating. "Who sent me this?" the woman asked in amazement. "Your husband called me to carry it," said the lad carelessly, putting the basket as he spoke into her hands. But to her horror, as he lifted his arms, the housewife noted cuts and gashes above his heart. "Alas, my poor child, who hath wounded thee?" she cried. "Your husband, mother, before he called me, cut me with a small sharp weapon," was the quiet answer. Dumb with astonishment, the Brahman's wife turned away to bestow the viands he had brought, and when she came back to the door the youth had gone. At that instant her husband re-entered the room, having returned, as she supposed from bathing. Her wonder about the food was forgotten in indignant sympathy. "Why," she cried, "didst thou so hurt thy messenger?" The man looked at her without understanding. "Him whom thou sentest to me with food, as thou didst go to bathe," she explained. "To bathe!" he stammered, "I have not yet been!" Then the eyes of husband and wife met, and they knew both who had come to them, and how they had wounded the heart of the Lord. And the Brahman returned to the sacred text, and once more erasing a word restored it to its original form, for there can be no doubt that the true reading is, "They who depend on Me, casting aside all care, whatsoever they need, I myself carry it to them."

Such are some of the associations which cling to the little image of Krishna that the children about Calcutta can buy for a few farthings. It is made of lime, and painted blue—for just as white, to the dweller amongst northern snows, signifies purity, so blue, the colour of sky and ocean, to the child of the south, is the token of the Infinite. The left hand of the image holds a flute to the lips; the right carries a thin golden scroll, referring to the Gita. The feet are crossed carelessly, like those of any strolling peasant-player, and the head is crowned. Simple toy as it is, there is hardly a detail of the composite figure in which a devotional system does not centre.

"O Thou that playest on the flute, standing by the water-ghats, on the road to Brindaban!" sing the lovers of Krishna, and their hearts melt within them while they sing, pierced as by S. Teresa's wound of seraphic love. Of all its elements, however, there is none which has the unequalled importance to the world of the scroll in the right hand, both as throwing light on Indian habits of thought and as an exposition of the science of religion. The questions, therefore, On what fundamental experience does the Gita base itself? To what does it appeal? What does it single out in life as requiring explanation? What is its main imperative? are of singular interest. That place which the four Gospels hold to Christendom, the Gita holds to the world of Hinduism, and in a very real sense, to understand it is to understand India and the Indian people.

It is believed by Hindus that when great forces are in action, on occasions such as those of battle and earthquake, a certain state of etheric vibration is produced, which makes it easy for minds trembling on the verge of supreme knowledge to vault the barricades of sense and find illumination. Perhaps this is because a great intensity of experience has to be found and transcended. Perhaps the conditions, apparently simple, are really more complex than this. At any rate, the story of the Bhagavad Gita is of the coming of such beatitude to a young soldier named Arjuna, some three thousand years ago.

Incidentally, the opening of the poem presents us with an impressive picture of an ancient battlefield. On the great plain of Kurukshetra, already the scene of the prayers and austerities of saints and pilgrims for hundreds of years, two armies face each other. The leaders of both sides occupy chariots drawn by white horses; over each waves his personal ensign; and each carries a conch-shell, by way of trumpet, to enable him to give signals and enforce attention to his commands. Both armies are represented as great hosts, but indications are not wanting that that of Duryodhana, the usurper, under the leadership of Bhishma, is the larger and stronger. And this is natural, since Duryodhana, rightly or wrongly, is still suzerain of the whole country, while the five Pandava brothers, his cousins, are only bent on the recovery of their rights from him. We have to call to mind that this is an ancient battle, consisting of an immense number of small fights, before we are able to give our thoughts calmly to the narrative, for we are told that from all parts of the field and on both sides the white conch-shells have been blown, giving the signal for assault, and that already "the discharge of weapons" has begun, when Arjuna requests Krishna, who is acting as his charioteer, to drive him into the space between the two hosts, that he may single out those with whom he is to enter into personal combat during the fray.

The sight of the foe, however, has an extraordinary effect on the mind of the chieftain. Instead of looking on his enemies with an accession of faith in the justice of his own cause and a heroic determination to struggle to the last in its defence, he seems to realise for the first time the consequences of the attack. Amongst the foe stand all he has ever loved or honoured—Bhishma, the head of his house, the adored grandsire of his childhood; Drona, to whom he owes his education, and for whom he cherishes a passionate reverence; and cousins and relatives innumerable besides, of whom the very worst is an old playfellow or a gallant combatant in tourney.

The path to victory lies through the burning-ghat of the dead! The ashes of all he loves are scattered there! As he realises this, Arjuna's great bow slips from his hand, and he sinks to the floor of his chariot in despair. We must remember that this is no mere failure of courage. The soldier has been tried and proved too often to be open for a moment to such an imputation. Neither is he represented as entertaining the slightest doubt of ultimate triumph. To the fortunes of war he gives not a thought, assuming, as do all brave men, that they must follow the right. He simply realises that for the sake of a few years of dominion he is about, with his own hand, to rid the earth of everything he loves. He realises, too, that this widespread slaughter will constitute an enormous social disaster.

This feeling of Arjuna's finds religious expression. "I desire not victory, O Krishna, neither kingdom nor pleasures.... It would be better for me if the sons of Dritarashtra, arms in hand, should slay me, unarmed and unresisting, in the battle." Surely the moral situation is finely conceived! A prince, of the proudest lineage on earth, is eager to be offered up as a sacrifice rather than accept empire at the price to be paid for it. On the battlefield of life does any case need better stating? Yet this thirst for martyrdom, which looks so like renunciation, is really quite another thing. "Thou art grieved for those who require no grief, yet thou speakest words of wisdom," says Krishna. For, instead of the actual indifference to the world and to his own part in it, of one who perceives that all before him is unreal, Arjuna is betraying that determination to maintain things as they are which belongs to those who hold that affection at least is a very actual good. It is on this distinction that the whole treatise is based.

At first, indeed, the charioteer affects to meet the chieftain's hesitation with all the contempt of knighthood for panic. "Yield not to unmanliness, O son of Pritha!" he exclaims. "Ill doth it become thee. Cast off this base weakness, and arise, O terror of foes." It is not till Arjuna, with a touching acknowledgment of grief and confusion, makes a supreme appeal for intellectual enlightenment, that Krishna, in the character of divine teacher, enters on that immortal pronouncement regarding the Real and unreal, which ends by sending the knight back to the duty of his birth, unshrinking, with the words: "Firm, with undoubting mind, I obey Thy word."

As the dialoguc proceeds, the dramatic element disappears. The echoes of battle die away. We are standing alone in some chamber of the soul, holding that colloquy between human and divine, finite and infinite, which never ceases during life for any one of us, however little able we may be to disentangle it from the voices of the world. At the culminating moment of the interview, when the worshipper receives the sudden revelation of all existing in and by the Lord Krishna, as mere multiform expressions of His sole energy, even at this moment, and during the rapt and broken praise which follows it, we find nothing discordant in the mise-en-scène. A chariot of war has become, as only a Hindu pen could have made it, silent as any cell of meditation. The corner of a battlefield has grown as remote from the whirl of life as the inmost recesses of a heart at prayer.

The main argument is, as we might expect, that as all appearances are delusive, action is to the wise man indifferent, and should be performed, once he is sure that he is called to it, without fear of consequences. "Him the wise call a sage—the man whose undertakings are all devoid alike of objects and desires, whose acts have been burnt to ashes in the fire of wisdom." "Never did I not exist, nor thou, nor these rulers of men; and no one of us will ever hereafter cease to exist." Therefore, "Free from hope and from selfishness, without any anxiety of mind, plunge thou into battle!"

The words are addressed to one who is preeminently a man of action, a soldier—supposed, saving a due regard for his military honour, to be swayed by the passion for justice, and the impulse to defend it. These things being the stake, throw for them, and throw boldly, says Krishna, and as results, take whatever may chance to come. "Man has always the right to work: man has no right to the results of work," is as much the heart and core of the Gita, as "Thou hast no right to success if thou art not also equal to failure," is of Stoicism. In application the two doctrines seem identical, but we have only to read, in order to see the advantage which the idea of Maya gives to the Indian thinker. Clear, sharp, incisive as chisel-strokes, are the utterances of Epictetus: like thunderbolts out of a tropical night the words of Krishna.

The Gita, however, does not consist of a single chain of reasoning, moving in definite progression from beginning to end. Rather is the same thing said over and over again, in as many different ways as possible. Sometimes even a form of words is repeated, as if nothing mattered save to make the meaning clear. There is ample scope here for the digressive energy of ages, of which the outcome is the richly-woven texture, set here and there with those strangely-cut Oriental jewels, which must remain amongst the greatest recorded words of religion to all time.

But readers will completely miss the sense of the Gita who permit themselves to forget its first ringing words: "Yield not to unmanliness, O son of Pritha! Ill doth it become thee. Shake off this base weakness, and arise, O terror of foes!" The book is nowhere a call to leave the world, but everywhere an interpretation of common life as the path to that which lies beyond. "Better for a man is his own duty, however badly done, than the duty of another, though that be easy." "Holding gain and loss as one, prepare for battle." That the man who throws away his weapons, and permits himself to be slain, unresisting, in the battle, is not the hero of religion, but a sluggard and a coward; that the true seer is he who carries his vision into action, regardless of the consequences to himself; this is the doctrine of the Gita, repeated again and again. The book is really a battle-cry. Spirituality is with it no retreat from men and things, but a burning fire of knowledge that destroys bondage, consumes sluggishness and egoism, and penetrates everywhere. Not the withdrawn, but the transfigured life, radiant with power and energy, triumphant in its selflessness, is religion.

The Gita is today the gospel of the Indian Revival. And never was book so well suited to such function. For its eighteen chapters are the expression of an overwhelming national vitality. It is as true of peoples as of individuals, that when the age is full and rich, living is apt to outrun knowing. It is then that large questions press for solution. Great areas of experience require to be related to their common centre and to each other. And so pre-eminently does the Gita do this, that the Muslim and the Christian can sit indifferently with the Hindu to gather its interpretations.

The nature of all faith, the relation of all worship to worshipped and worshipper, the dependence of knowledge on non-attachment under all its forms: it is with problems like these, and not with any particular Credo, that the Gita concerns itself. It is at once therefore the smallest and most comprehensive of the scriptures of the world.

That indifference to results is the condition of efficient action is the first point in its philosophy. But there is no doubt that the action should be strenuous. Let every muscle be hard, every limb well-knit, let the mind sweep the whole horizon of fact; with the reins in hand, the fiery steeds under control, with the whole battlefield in view, and the will of the hero lifted high to strike for justice, "Arise!" thunders the voice of Sri Krishna, "and be thou an apparent cause!"

It is the supreme imperative. Play thy whole part in the drama of time, devoting every energy, concentrating the whole force. "As the ignorant act from selfish motives, so should the wise man act, unselfishly."

Just as the child sees the sun above his head, and the earth beneath his feet, distinguishing himself from both, while to the man of science, sun, planet, and child are all single points in a great ocean of force-matter, absolutely continuous from its centre to its farthest bounds, so to us all, in the sense-plane of thought, God, soul, and relation exist. Having reached that truth, however, which is the Beatific Vision, any one of them will seem the whole, for all conception of limitation will be blotted out. As we ourselves are seen to be but light transformed; as thought and perception, life and motion, sun and planet, are all but different manifestations of a something that we call Solar Energy, so God, self, and universe, are now known to be only distinctions made by sense in that one, Brahman, "the immortal and immutable, the eternal substance, and the unfailing Bliss."

An account of such a vision gives us the culminating chapter of the Gita. Krishna suddenly bursts forth on the sight of his astonished worshipper as the Universal Form, in Whom all that exists in one. Characteristically Indian in expression, full of the blaze and terror of the cosmos, this great scene can only perhaps be thoroughly appreciated by a Western mind if it has first understood something of the craving that it fulfils, caught some flash maybe of the radiance it describes. Yet if the rest of the Gita were destroyed, this one chapter might take its place, for it makes all its logic actual. Arjuna's single sight becomes the sacrament of a whole world's hope.

It was midnight when I reached Thaneswar. The fierce white light of a tropical moon bathed the great common in front, where only trees and bushes, with their coal-black shadows, could be seen, and not a single human habitation was in sight. Behind, the dak-bungalow lay in darkness, and the train by which I had come had passed on long ago into the night. One was alone on the Plain of Kurukshetra with three thousand years.

But the silence did not remain unbroken. Clear and distinct on the still air rose the accents of the immortal dialogue. "Man has the right to work: man has no right to the fruits of work," said, once more, the divine Charioteer. Yet many a memorable battle has been fought, India herself has heard a thousand dialogues, preaching the truths of the Bhagavad Gita. Why, asked my heart, does one come to this spot? For what thing, above all others, does the world remember Kurukshetra? And then I saw why, never to forget. Kurukshetra was the place of the Great Vision, the field of the Divine Illumination of Arjuna.

## On the Loom of Time

The essential differences between countries of the Asiatic and European types are as yet but little understood, and a main difficulty in the growth of an understanding is the absence of elements in the English language, embodying any wide power of social survey. The disciples of Auguste Comte have done much to popularise certain important words and conceptions, but the hearts of angels and the tongues of poets would be too little to meet all the necessities of the task.

The word theocracy, for instance, which is essential to an understanding of Asia, either territorial or historic, has but an ambiguous sound in English. To the learned Positivist it means "the social system built up on theism"; to the vulgar, it indicates some fabulous scheme of divine monarchy, such as is popularly attributed to Israel before the days of Saul, or to England in the dreams of Oliver Cromwell.

To persons thinking in the latter fashion, the two statements that India is a theocracy, and that it is at present occupied by the British Raj, seem incompatible. It is clear that only detailed and penetrative knowledge of concrete examples can build up in our minds such a conception of the essentials of a theocratic system as shall give us the power of handling the term as confidently and intelligently as we now feel capable of using more purely political expressions. And of such examples it will be found best to take the nearest first.

In the history of the world, the city of Rome occupies a unique position, as the Occidental cradle and battle-field of two opposing forces, the Imperial and the Theocratic, or, as one may prefer to call them, the European and the Asiatic ideas. For it was Rome that first imposed upon the West that notion of organised force which is almost all that is at present meant by the state-empire. And through all the feuds and disorders of the Middle Ages, it was the Roman impulse that was working itself out by the energy of barbarian peoples, to its perfect triumph in the nineteenth century. Caesar conceived, Napoleon completed, the imperial scheme. Alexander as an individual may have seen what they saw: but Greece was far too near to Asia, and his military designs could but evaporate before their time into mere learned observations and the exchange of interesting thought.

It was left to Rome to elabourate into fixity of precision that destiny which could not perhaps have been avoided by the peoples of a coastline, kept militant by the daily conquest of Nature, tempted to aggression by the very habits of their life. For empire in the European sense is a very different thing from the marauding hosts of the East going nut to warfare headed by a commander of brilliant prowess. Rome instituted, and modern Europe has inherited, the idea of one people exploiting another, under rights strictly defined by law, with an appearance of order which would deceive the very elect. The Caesars failed by the strength of the inassimilable elements which their Empire had to meet. Napoleon failed because those whom he temporarily subdued were as strong to re-act in imitation as to be assimilated. Today the Roman Empire is represented by some eight or ten emulous peoples and princes, all armed to the teeth, all bent on appropriating the world. But it is the Roman Empire still.

And yet Rome herself is the one character whose part in the drama is completely transformed. For no one yet thinks of her as the metropolis of the juvenile kingdom of Italy. To the imagination of humanity she is still the city of the Church. St. Peter's and the Vatican still form her central point. The Pope still rules. This contrast between her first and second selves is much more startling than the transition by which the brigand-chief becomes the sainted ancestor. Before it happened, it would have seemed far more absurd than it would be today to propose to make the name of Oxford or Benaras a synonym for the vulgar competition of trade. For Rome, the supreme, the invincible, has actually been conquered by the ideas of the East.

The poor and the lowly have taken her by storm. Henceforth is she to be in Europe not the voice of domination, but of renunciation; not the teacher of aggression, but of self-sacrifice; royal in her rank and her prerogatives certainly, but far more deeply and truly the friend of the people than of kings. Henceforth, those who are in a special sense her children will live sequestered from the world, pursuing after poverty instead of riches, after self-mortification instead of self-indulgence; men and women apart, as in the Eastern household. Every simple act that she enjoins will possess a sanctity out of all proportion to its intrinsic value. Her customs will become rituals. Her journeys will be pilgrimages. The simplest ordinances of life, administered by her, will now be sacraments. The expression of her forgiveness will be absolution; of her affection, a benediction. Her very rulers will claim no personal right to their high places, but will declare themselves simple executors of the divine will. "Servant of the servants of God" will be, to the thinking of the world, their proudest title.

In the eyes of the Church, henceforth, all men are to be equal, at least until one has made himself a saint, and another Judas. The differences of rank established by the world are to be as nothing before her, and even ecclesiastical gradations are to be merely as conditions on which grace can work. Many of the saints will be humble and unlearned. Many a bishop will reach the lowest hell. Rank, at least theoretically, is nothing to Rome. Her children are all to be the sharers of a common supernatural life, of which a religious banquet is the token. A great responsibility is to rest upon them, of living worthily of the name by which they are called. Their life, as related to each other and to her, can be expressed only in terms of the exploration and manifestation of certain ideals, laid down broadly in authoritative writings, known as Scriptures, and with less clearness and power in secondary writings and teachings, called traditions.

In other words, the Imperial city has transformed herself into a pure theocracy. If we blot out the idea of birth by a sacramental rite, and substitute that of a chosen place and race, keeping everything else approximately the same, the Church is re-transmuted into any one out of half a dozen Eastern countries—ancient Egypt, Judaea, Arabia, modern

India—under the government of the religious idea. Here, too, the priesthood dominates all classes equally, and the priestly interpretation of life prevails—the very gifts one brings home from a journey are explained as temple-offerings. Here, too, the political system is extraneous: custom is sacred, so that a grammar of habit takes the place of legislation; men and women live apart; merit is the sole real condition of social prestige; and so on.

It is due to the purely natural character of the great complexus, that we have in India the—to us so extraordinary—spectacle of a society handed over to the power of a priesthood, without in any way losing its sense of the universal sacredness of learning and freedom of thought. In the case of Rome, where an artificial system was created on the basis of a foreign experience, the crude temper of the old imperialism betrayed itself primarily against mind and thought, which it conceived as the legitimate sphere of its authority. In Catholic Europe, a man might scarcely venture to believe that the earth moves; must apologies for enjoying the cosmic speculations of La Place; could hardly study Plato without grave suspicion.

In India, atheism itself might be preached on the very steps of the temple. All that the people would demand of the preacher would be sincerity. In Christendom, knowledge has been so much feared that men have again and again suffered torture and death for no other crime. In India, knowledge has always been held to be beatitude. Abundance of words, in every Indian language, testify to the honour paid to scholars. Persian and English books are held as sacred as the Sanskrit. And we should seek in vain, throughout history and language, for any trace of limitation imposed, or suggested to be imposed, upon the mind of man.

Even the vexed question of the right of literature to reveal more than is permitted to conversation, was foreseen long ago and settled in a flash of wit by the legislator who, writing of defilement by the touch of the mouth, makes three exceptions, in favour of "the beaks of birds, the lips of women, and the words of poets."

In fact opinion is so free that religious propaganda is actually discouraged by Hinduism, lest zeal, outrunning discretion, prove mischievous to society. "A man has a right to hold his own belief, but never to force it upon another," is the dictum that has made of India a perfect university of religious culture, including every phase and stage of thought and practice, from that of the kindergarten, where all is concrete, to that of the higher research student, who has direct visualisation of the solutions of problems which most of us cannot even understand.

But freedom of thought in the East has not been the prerogative of religion alone. The deeper we go into the history of Hindu philosophy, the more perplexed we are that with its obviously scientific character it should never have created a scientific movement of the prestige and éclat of that of the West. Patanjali, who wrote his great psychology in the second century B.C., was obviously a physiologist, studying the living body in relation to that nervous system which in its entirety he would call the mind. The action and inter-action of the living neuropsychosis is a question which modern science, content with a more static view of human structure, has hardly yet ventured to tackle, and students of Patanjali cannot be controverted if they hold that when it is reached, it will only be to corroborate the ancient investigations step by step.

But a still more interesting feature of Patanjali's work lies in the fact that it is obviously the final record of a long research, carried out, not by a single individual, but by a whole school, experimenting continuously through many generations. Each man's labour was conditioned by the fact that he had no labouratory and no instruments outside his own body, and there can be no doubt that life was often sacrificed to the thirst for knowledge. The whole, therefore, is like a résumé of two or three centuries of the conclusions of some English Royal Society, or some French Academy of Sciences, dating from two to three thousand years ago. And we must remember that, if the terminology of this old science has a certain quaintness in our ears, this is probably not greater than that which our own talk of forces and molecules, of chemical affinities and sphygmographic records, would have, if it were suddenly recovered, after a lapse of two thousand years, by a new civilisation, stationed, say, in Mexico.

What is true of the psychology is equally true of Indian mathematics, astronomy, surgery, chemistry. The Oriental predilection for meditative insight is an advantage in the field of mathematics, where deduction is a necessity. But at the same time its fundamental solidity and originality are shown by the fact that highly abstruse problems are stated by Hindu thinkers in concrete, and even in poetic terms. And it will be remembered that less than a hundred years ago, De Morgan celebrated the solution at sight of certain hitherto uncompleted problems of "Maxima and Minima," by a young Hindu called Ram Chandra.

The law of gravitation itself was enunciated and discussed by Bhashkaracharya in the twelfth century. And the antiquity of the Sanskrit word shunyo, for nought, together with the immemorial distribution of the system all over the country, conclusively proves that our decimal notation is Indian, and not Arabic, in origin.

How is it, then, we repeat, that a more imposing scientific activity has not been the result of a faculty so undeniable? Many considerations may be adduced in explanation. There is a vast international organisation of scientific effort in Europe today, operating to make an incomparable sum of results. Ancient India knew what was meant by scientific cooperation, but by organisation scarcely. And no one nation, working alone, could have produced the whole of what we know as Modern Science, or even one division of it. Ancient Greece gives us the first word on electricity. What a leap from this to Volta and Galvani! Where, again, had these been without the German Hertz, the French Ampère, the Hindu Bose? And then Italy for a second time takes up the thread of inquiry, and produces the apparatus for wireless telegraphy.

Again, we must remember that in Europe today we have renounced almost everything for science. Art and letters are almost at a standstill. In these departments—at least, in every country outside France and Russia—we are living almost entirely on the treasures of the past. In religion we see the same superficial eclecticism, the same absence of genuine contemporary impulse. But India never was in this position. Side by side with the learned man, speculating or experimenting on the secrets of Nature, the builders were raising the village temple, the shuttle flew to and fro in the loom, the clink of the tools was heard in the brass-smithy, the palace pandits busied themselves with their collection of ancient texts, the saints poured forth the rapture of their souls, the peasant waked and slept in the good company of Nature, rice-field and palm-tree, cattle and farmstead. Faith, art, and industry lived on undisturbed.

After all, is it not possible that we deceive ourselves? The true secret of our elimination of every other intellectual activity in favour of science, is it really the depth of our enthusiasm for knowledge, or is it not rather our modern fever for its mechanical application? How far is the passion for pure truth unimpaired by commercial interests? How far is our substitution of specialisms for synthesis conditioned by finance merely? When our utilitarian ingenuity draws nearer exhaustion, when the present spasm of inventive ability has worked itself out, then, and not till then, will come the time for estimating the actual profundity and disinterestedness of our scientific ardour. Will our love of knowledge continue to drive us on to a still deeper theoretic insight, or will our investigations languish in our hands, lingering on as a mere fashion in learning, even as Aristotle lingered on through the Middle Ages? Till such questions are nearer finding their answer we are in no position to assume that the present period is, or is not, ultimately scientific.

Meanwhile, in India this danger of a mercenary science was always foreseen, and viewed with perhaps an exaggerated horror, so that from the beginning the disciple has been required to seek knowledge for its own sake, renouncing all ulterior motive. The value derived at the present stage of development from incorporating a progressive science in a progressive civilization was thus lost; although we must remember that in a very real sense such a transition, shorn of its lower elements, has occurred in the East from pre-historic times, whenever new plants and animals were to be domesticated, or new tools invented. On the other hand, it is still open to India, facing the actual conditions of the modern world, to prove that the innate capacity of her people for scientific work and inquiry has been in no way lessened by this long abstention from its vulgar profits. In spite, nevertheless, of the relative non-development of natural science in India, it is the perfect compatibility of the Hindu religious hypothesis with the highest scientific activity that is to make that country within the present century the main source of the new synthesis of religion for which we in the West are certainly waiting. Several nations cannot suddenly come into contact by the use of a common language without a violent shock being given to their prejudices in favour of local mythology. Such an occurrence was inevitable in English-speaking countries under present circumstances, and has been accelerated, as it happens, by the agnosticism born of scientific activity. Christianity, moreover, has been further discredited by the discovery that its adherents possess no ethics sufficiently controlling to influence their international relations, and finally by that worship of pleasure which an age of exploitation necessarily engenders.

Thus neither the sentiment of childhood, the reasoning of theology, the austerity of conscience, nor the power of idealism, has been strong enough to maintain the creed of the West against the assaults to which the age has seen it subjected. Everything seems to be going through a transition. Social morality, intellectual formulas, legal and economic relationships, all have broken loose from their old moorings, and are seeking for readjustment. The first agony of the loss of belief is now over, but it has only given place to a dreary hopelessness, a mental and spiritual homelessness, which drives some in whom heart predominates into the Church of Rome, while others in whom the faculties are more evenly balanced, try to forget their need in social service, or in the intellectual and artistic enjoyments of an era of resumes.

Protestantism has at last delivered herself of a genuinely religious product of the highest order, in that love of naked truth which finds its voice and type in modern science. For all other forms of non-Catholicism are more or less compromises, mere halfway-houses on the road to this. But, even in this, the environment of spirituality and the communion of saints are apt to be left behind with the Medieval Church. Is there no way to combine these things? Can the devotional attitude receive no justification from the clear and unbiased mind? Does religion, which has made so much of faith, want less than absolute conviction as its basis? Is that sentiment which has produced all the greatest art, and almost all the greatest conduct, to be relegated to the mental lumber-room, as, after all, only a superstition? Surely, if so, there is an eternal in harmony and divergence between the creative and the inquiring faculties of man.

But the very constitution of our minds forbids us to accept this paradox. It may be that we are no longer able to believe in the exclusive authenticity of any single religious system. But we are fast inclining to the opinion that even here there must be some observable sequence; that creeds and mythologies must be as genuine a product of the Unity-of-Things as the animals and the plants; that order and meaning there must be, in the one case as in the other. Instead, therefore, of a contemptuous disregard of all faiths as equally untrue, we are beginning to adopt to all alike an attitude of respect as equally significant.

Only in India has this recognition of law in religious conceptions ever been held in its completeness as a part of religion itself. Only in India have inspired teachers been able to declare that the name of God, being also an illusion, differed only from worldly things in having the power of helping us to break our bondage to illusion, while they, on the other hand, increased it. Only in India has it been counted orthodoxy to believe that all is within the mind that the forms of gods are but objectifications of our own sense of what is best to be attained, that prayer is only the heightening of will. And therefore it is from India that we shall gather that intellectualisation of belief which is to re-establish, in the name of a new and greater synthesis, our confidence in our own past. In this new synthesis every element of our own thought must find a place—the conception of humanity and the worship of truth, of course, because without these it would have no raison deter. But even the emotionalism of the negro must not go unplaced, uninterrupted, any more than that wondrous mood in which the explorer of knowledge finds himself launched on a vision of Unity that he dare not name. Neither the Catholic organisation of monasticism nor the Protestant (taken from the Muslim) inspiration of common prayer can be left out. There must be a religious consciousness strong enough to recognise the anguish of denial as its own most heroic experience, and large enough to be tender and helpful to the ignorance of a child.

In that other synthesis which grew up under the Roman Empire, all the Mediterranean peoples and those originally related to them found a part. The doctrine of immortality came from the desert; resurrection, mediatorship, and personal consciousness of sin from ancient Egypt; many elements from Persia and Syria; purity and asceticism from the Asokan Essences; the basis of ethics to be transcended from Judea; the spirit of inquiry and the necessary feeling of an intellectual void from Greece, or at least from the Greek elements in Mediterranean society; the instinct of organisation from Rome; and the all-absorbing renunciation and compassion for the world that alone can give sufficient nucleus for a new religion from one sweet central Personality, in whom each of these various hungers found its own Bethlehem—its house of bread.

Similarly, in the new up-growth of our own days, many preparatory influences now at work are to find fulfilment. All who have felt the love of the disinherited and oppressed, all who have followed truth for its own sake, all who have longed to lose themselves in a paradise of devotion and been refused by the armed reason standing at the gate, all who have felt out for a larger generalisation, as they saw the faith of their babyhood falling away from them,—all these have helped and are helping to build up the new consciousness, to make the faculty that is to recognise and assimilate the doctrine of the future. But the evangel itself will be mainly drawn from India.

And then, having thus renewed the sources of the world's inspiration, we may be pardoned if we ask, What of India herself? The Egyptian delivered up his whole treasure, and where is he now? Buried under many a layer of foreign invasion; tilling the soil as patiently and hopelessly as one of his own oxen; scarcely remembered, even as a name, by those who make so-called plans for the country's good, and are wakened only to a stupid wonder, as at the sound of something familiar from books, when they hear that to kill a cat today in the bazaar in Cairo would almost cost a man his life.

The Jews produced Jesus, and what have they become? Pariahs and fugitives amongst the nations of men. Who remembers them with any feeling of gratitude for that which they have given? A miserable formula, "the Jews who crucified Him," has taken the place amongst the devout of any memorial of the fact that they created the language, the thought, the habits of life, and the outlook of righteousness, in which He assumed the garb of humanity.

Is something of this sort to be the fate of India? To give a religion to the world may be a sufficient proof that one's past was not in vain, but evidently it is no sort of safeguard for the future. The process by which the peoples of a vast continent may become mere hewers of wood and drawers of water has already begun, is already well afoot. Their indigenous institutions are all in decay. Their prosperity is gone. Some portion or other of the immense agricultural area is perpetually under famine.

Their arts and industries are dead or dying. They have lapsed into mere customers for other men's cheap wares. Even their thought would seem to be mainly imitative. The orthodox is apt to tread the round of his own past eternally. The unorthodox is as apt to harness himself to the foreign present, with an equal blindness. In suicidal desperation, the would-be patriotic reiterate the war-cries of antagonistic sects, or moan for the advent of a new religion, as if, by introducing a fifth element of discord, the Indian peoples could reach unity. Nor does the education at present offered promise any solution of the problem. It is the minimum that is possible to the efficient clerk, and even that minimum is undergoing reduction rather than increase.

In spite of the absence of any theory of history that might elucidate the course of events in the East during the next two centuries, one truth reveals itself with perfect plainness. A nation becomes whatever she believes herself to be. She is made great, not by her relative superiority, but by her thought about herself. It becomes important therefore to ask—What conception of her own nature and power forms the inheritance of India?

As Roman Catholicism is but one element inhering in a great whole called Christianity, and as a man may well claim to be a good Christian without being a Catholic, so the religious system of Hinduism is only a fragment inhering in a vast social-industrial-economic scheme called the dharma, and a man may well and rightly be the servant of the dharma, without calling himself a Hindu. It is this dharma, in its large and non-sectarian activity, that determines the well-being of every child of the Indian soil. The word itself is an ancient name for national righteousness or national good.

It is true that the Brahman who bows before one who is net the rightful king is held many times accursed by Manu. It is true that the Bhagavad Gita is the only one of the world-gospels that turns on the duty of fighting for the true sovereign against usurpers. And yet it is also a fact that the person of the ruler is always a matter of singular indifference to the theocratic consciousness. It has been hitherto indeed a mere detail for military persons to fight out amongst themselves. The secret of so curious an attitude is reached when we discover that in the eyes of the Indian peasant, the sovereign himself is only the servant of the dharma. "If he uphold it, he will stay: if not, he will have to go," they all say when questioned. Little do they dream, alas! that themselves and their children and their children's children may be swept into oblivion also by that same failure to uphold!

Thus, whoever was the master that an Indian statesman served, whether Hindu, Muslim, or British sat upon the throne, it was the minister's duty, as the loyal and obedient child of an Asiatic race, to use all his influence in the best interests of his people and his country. It is this element in the national system that tends, with its great regard for agriculture, to rank the cow almost on a level with the human members of the commonwealth, making the Hindu sovereign forbid beef-eating within his frontiers.

It was this that made a certain prince, in despair, hand over his salt-mines to the British Government, rather than obey its mandate to tax this commodity to his people, and thus derive personal benefit from their misfortune. It was this that made it incumbent upon many of the chiefs in the old days to provide, not only salt, but also water and fruit free to their subjects, a kind of "noblesse oblige" that has left the wayside orchard outside every village in Kashmir, till that favoured land is almost like the happy island of Avilion, "fair with orchard lawns, and bowery hollows crowned with summer sea." It was this power of the dharma to safeguard the welfare of its people, through a law as binding upon the monarch as upon his subjects, that brought about the immense network of custom which regulated the relief of beggars, the use of water, the provisioning of pilgrimages, habits of sanitation, distribution of grazing-lands, the forest-rights of the peasant, and a thousand other matters of importance.

The mere fact that the king's personal devotions were offered in a mosque could not interfere with his acceptance of the system, in any important measure. It was the language of rule, dominating all rulers alike, by every detail of birth and upbringing, and by the very impossibility of imagining any deviation. Hence it could never be more than a question of time till some new prince had assimilated the whole, and Muslim cooperated actively with Hindu in the great task of enforcing and extending the essentials of the common weal. We may regret, but we cannot condone, the strange indolence by which the Indian people have permitted themselves to lose sight of these national and civic responsibilities of their ancient civilization, and become absorbed in its personal and domestic rites. Nor can we for one moment admit that this substitution of the trees for the forest deserves the name of orthodoxy,—faithfulness to the dharma.

It is, however, an essential weakness of theocratic rule that while it can tolerate any neighbour, it has no idea of dominating and unifying diverse elements round itself. The great mass of its subjects, too, see life indirectly through the nimbus of the supernatural. Instead of subordinating the priesthood in national affairs to the recognised leaders of the nation, exalting it only in its rightful capacity of influence upon the social and individual conscience, a theocracy is apt to require that its leaders move, encumbered by the counsels of the priests.

It was the Prophet's clear perception of these facts that gave its peculiar characteristics to Islam. He established a strong confraternity, and made subscription to a brief and concise formulae its sole condition of membership. But Arab blood was comparatively unmixed, and the greater part of Mohammed's work was done for him, in the close bond of consanguinity that united his central group. At one bound, and without any means save that power of personality which is the first demand of the theocratic method, he performed the double task of creating an all-absorbing consciousness of nationality, and carrying his people through the required emancipation of thought. To this day the great Semitised belt that divides Eastern Aryans and Mongolians from Europe, reminds us, whenever we look at the map, of the reality of his achievement. And the history of the origins of European learning remains to attest the enthusiasm of freedom which he conferred on the Saracenic intellect.

Geographical conditions impose upon India the same necessity of unification at all costs, and yet combine with other facts to make her the meeting-ground of all races. Especially is this the case in modern times, when the ocean has become a roadway instead of a boundary. She is almost a museum of races, creeds, and social formations, some hoary with age, some crude with excessive youth. Thus her problem is vastly more difficult than that of Arabia before the seventh century. Yet she contains in herself every element of self-recovery.

If the fact had been open to doubt before, the British rule, with its railways, its cheap postage, and its common language of affairs, would sufficiently have demonstrated the territorial unity of the country. We can see today that India's is an organic, and no mere mechanical, unity. "The North," it has been said, "produces prophets, the South priests." And it is true that her intellectual and discriminating faculty, her power of recognition and formulation, lies in the South; that Maratha, Muslim and Sikh, form her executive; while to Bengal, the country that has fought no battle for her own boundaries, falls the office of the heart, which will yet suffuse all the rest with the realisation of the vast inclusiveness of meaning of the great word "India." Historically the Indian unity is obvious. And if socially it appear doubtful, the country itself could set aside the doubt in an instant by grasping that intuition of nationality which alone is needed to give the spiritual impulse toward consolidation.

But the bare fact of an actual social, historical, and geographical unity, waiting for precipitation as a national consciousness, is not the only possession of India at the present crisis. She has a great past to return upon, and a clearly defined economy for model. Her traditions are unstained. There is no element of national life—art, poetry, literature, philosophy, science—in which she has not at some time been exceptionally strong. She has organised at least two empires of commanding character. In architecture, three of the most imposing styles in the world have been hers—the Dravidian in the South, the Buddhist across middle India from Orissa to Bombay, and the Indo-Saracenic in the North.

There can be little doubt that her next period will confront India with the necessity of introducing some community of ritual as between priest and people; and this of itself must create fresh architectural needs, a new architecture of the communal consciousness which would be sufficient to make the required appeal to the national imagination, and at the same time give the needed scope to the passion of democracy.

For in looking to the growth of a sentiment or nationality as the solution of Indian problems, we are of course turning away from kings and priests, and appealing to Woman and the People. A similar appeal, in the only form possible to the unmixed theocracy of that day, was made by Buddhism; and the whole history of India, from the Christian era onwards, is the story of the education of the popular consciousness, by the unifying and ameliorating influence of Hinduism, as it was then thrown open. Today, if we adopt, moral and intellectual tests as the criteria of civilization, we can hardly refuse to admit that in such issues the East has been more successful than the West. In strength of family ties; in sweetness and decorum of family life; in widespread understanding of the place of the personal development in the scheme of religion as a whole; in power of enjoyment of leisure, without gross physical accompaniments; in dignity, frugality, continuous industry without aggressive activity; in artistic appreciation of work done and doing: and above all in the ability to concentrate the whole faculty at will, even the poorest classes in India, whatever their religion, will compare favourably with many who are far above them in the West. Such are some of the results of the Buddhist period.

The Mughal Empire fell into decay and failed, simply because it did not understand how to base itself on a great popular conception of Indian unity. It could neither assimilate the whole of the religious impulse of India, nor yet detach itself completely from it. Hence, as a government, it succeeded neither in rooting itself permanently, nor in creating that circuit of national energy which alone could have given it endurance. Nevertheless, it contributed invaluable elements to the national life of the future, and it is difficult to see how that life could hope to organise itself without its memorable preliminary experiment.

The foreign character of the English period produced, as its first effect, a wide sense of bewilderment and unrest, which gave birth to a hundred projected panaceas. There were social reformers, who thought that by a programme more purely destructive than they then realised, their Motherland would be best served. And while we may deprecate the form taken by their zeal, we can but admit that no other testimony could have been given to the living energy of the race which would have been so convincing. If Indian civilization had really been stationary, as is so sapiently supposed by the West, the embers could hardly have leaped into such flame, at the bare touch of new ideas. If, on the other hand, the country had accepted the superficial theory, and run agate in the endeavour to reform itself, we could not thereafter have conceived of India as possessing sufficient depth and stability to make hope possible. Meanwhile the reformers have not failed to bring forth fruit. They have produced groups of persons who represent what is valuable in Western thought and habits, without necessarily being denationalised, and they have demonstrated once for all the fact that India contains sufficient forces of restitution within herself to be completely independent of foreign advice and criticism.

Next came political agitators, who seemed to think that by entire deference to an alien idea their country would be saved. There can be no doubt that here also a valuable contribution had been made. The foreign idea can never save India—indeed, the use of the word "politics" in the present state of the country may strike some of us as a painful insincerity—but at the same time, the mastery and assimilation of the foreigners' method is an absolute necessity. The education of the people, also, to a knowledge of their common interests, and the throwing of a net of friendship and mutual intercourse all over the country, are great services.

Outside social and political movements, again, there are a hundred emancipations and revivals of religious centres, all of which are noteworthy symptoms of inherent vitality. And still a fourth school declares that the one question of India lies in the economic crisis, and that that once surmounted all will be well.

At this moment, however, a new suspicion is making itself heard, a suspicion that behind all these interpretations—the social reform, the political agitation, religious movements, and economic grievances—there stands a greater reality, dominating and coordinating the whole, the Indian national idea, of which each is a part. It begins to be thought that there is a religious idea that may be called Indian, but it is of no single sect; that there is a social idea, which is the property of no caste or group; that there is a historic evolution, in which all are united; that it is the thing within all these which alone is to be called "India." If this conception should prevail, it will be seen that social, political, economic, and religious workers have all alike helped to reveal it; but it can never be allowed that the whole problem is economic, grave as the last-mentioned feature of the situation undoubtedly is. It is not merely the status, but the very nature and character of the collective personality of a whole nation, occupying one of the largest areas in the world that has to be recaptured. In the days when ancient Egypt made an eternal impression on human civilisation, the personal belongings of her great nobles were no more than those of an Indian cowherd today. It was the sentiment of fraternity, the instinct of synthesis, the mind of coordination that was the secret of her power.

The distinctive spirituality of the modern world depends upon its ability to think of things as a whole, to treat immense masses of facts as units, to bring together many kinds of activity, and put them in true relation to one another. This is the reality of which map, census, and newspaper, even catalogue, museum and encyclopaedia, are but outer symbols. In proportion as she grasps this inner content will India rise to the height of her own possibilities.

The sacraments of a growing nationality would lay in new developments of her old art, a new application of her old power of learnedness, new and dynamic religious interpretations, and a new idealism in short, true child of the nation's own past, with which the young should throb and the old be reverent. The test of its success would be the combining of renewed local and individual vigour with a power of self-centralisation and self-expression hitherto unknown.

# Bibliography

Adas, Michael: *Machines as the Measure of Men: Science, Technology, and Ideologies of Western Dominance*, Cornell University Press, Ithaca, 1989.

Ahmad, Imtiaz: *State and Foreign Policy: India's Role in South Asia*, Vikas, New Delhi, 1993.

Ainslee T. Embree: *Imagining India: Essays on Indian History*, Oxford Univ. Press, Delhi, 1989.

Ames, Roger T.: *The Art of Rulership: A Study in Ancient Chinese Political Thought*, University of Hawaii Press, Honolulu, 1983.

Apte, V. M.: *Social and Religious Life in the Grihya Sutras*, Rawat Press, Bombay, 1954.

Archer, W. G.: *Kangra Painting*, Faber and Faber, London, 1956.

Artola, George T.: *The Banner of Kamadeva and other Topics of Sanskrit Literature and Indian Culture*, Popular Prakashan, Bombay, 1977.

Austin, Granville: *The Indian Constitution: Cornerstone of a Nation*, Clarendon Press, Oxford, 1966.

Baker, Christopher J.: *An Indian Rural Economy: The Tamiland Countryside*, Clarendon Press, Oxford, 1984.

Beach, Milo Cleveland: *The New Cambridge History of India, I.3: Mughal and Rajput Painting*, Cambridge University Press, Cambridge, 1992.

Bhardwaj, Surinder Mohan: *Hindu Places of Pilgrimage in India: A Study in Cultural Geography*, University of California Press, Berkeley, 1973.

Bhattacharjee, Arun: *Rajiv Gandhi: Life and Message*, Ashish, New Delhi, 1992.

Bowes, Pratima: *Hindu Intellectual Tradition,* Allied Publishers, New Delhi, 1977.

Bromley, David and Larry Shinn: *Krishna Consciousness in the West,* Bucknell University Press, Lewisburg, 1989.

Brown, Judith M.: *Modern India: The Origins of an Asian Democracy,* Oxford University Press, New York, 1994.

Cauquelin, J.: *Asian Values. Encounters with Diversity*, Surrey, Richmond, 2000.

Collect, S. D.: *The Life and Letter of Raju Rahmmohun Roy*, Kali Ram Press, Calcutta, 1962.

Cunningham, Joseph Davey: *History of the Sikhs, From the Origins of the Nation to the Battles of the Sutlej*, Sultan Chand, Delhi, 1955.

Das, M.N.: *India under Morley and Minto: Politics Behind Revolution, Repression, and Reforms*, Allen and Unwin, London, 1964.

De, Sushil Kumar: *Ancient Indian Erotics and Erotic Literature*, Firma K. L. Mukhopadhyay, Calcutta, 1959.

Dehejia, Vidya: *Antal and Her Path of Love: Poems of a Woman Saint from South India*, State University of New York Press, Albany, 1990.

Diwan, Paras: *Human Rights and the Law: Universal and Indian,* Deep and Deep, New Delhi, 1996.

Dixit, Prabla: *Communalism: A Struggle for Power*, Orient Longman, New Delhi, 1981.

Eno, Robert: *The Confucian Creation of Heaven: Philosophy and the Defense of Ritual Mastery*, SUNY Press, Albany, 1990.

Erickson, Erik H.: *Gandhi's Truth: On the Origins of Militant Nonviolence*, Norton, New York, 1970.

Farquhar, J. N.: *A Primer of Hinduism,* Faber & Faber, London, 1912.

Farrand, Livingston: *Traditions of the Quinalut Indians,* American Museum of Natural History, New York, 1902.

Gambhirananda, Swami: *Brahma Sutra Shamkar Bhasya,* Adavita Ashrama, Calcutta, 1977.

Heinsath, Charles: *Indian Nationalism and Hindu Social Reform*, Princeton University Press, Princeton, 1964.

Howard Schwartz: *Reimaging the Bible: The Storytelling of the Rabbis,* Oxford University Press, New York, 1998.

John Drew: *India and the Romantic Imagination,* Oxford Univ. Press, London, 1987.

John, Elsner: *Pilgrimage: Past and Present in the World Religions,* Harvard University Press, Cambridge, 1995.

Kapur, Rajiv: *Sikh Separatism: The Politics of Faith*, Vikas, New Delhi, 1987.

Lal, Vinay: *Fingerprinting Popular Culture: The Mythic and the Iconic in Indian Cinema*, Oxford, Delhi, 2006.

Lamba, B.: *Fauna of Corbett National Park,* ZSI, Calcutta, 1987.

Louis, Fischer: *Essential Gandhi: An Anthology of His Writings,* Vintage, New York, 1983.

MacDonell, Arthur Anthony: *History of Sanskrit Literature*, South Asia Books, Columbia, 1990.

Mahalingam, T.V.: *Administration and Social Life under Vijayanagar*, University of Madras, Madras, 1969.

Michael A. Sells: *Early Islamic Mysticism: Sufi, Quran, Miraj, Poetic and Theological Writings*, Paulist Press, New York, 1996.

Misra, Satya Swarup: *The Aryan Problem: A Linguistic Approach*, Munshiram Manoharlal, New Delhi, 1992.

Morris M. Faierstein: *Jewish Mystical Autobiographies: Books of Visions and Book of Secrets*, Paulist Press, New York, 1999.

Narasimhan, C.V.: *The Mahabharata: An English Version Based on Selected Verses*, Columbia University Press, New York, 1965.

Organ, Troy W.: *Hinduism: Its Historical Development,* Barron's Educational Series, New York, 1974.

Piatigorsky, Alexander: *The Buddhist Philosophy of Thought,* Rowman & Allenheld, London, 1984.

Potter, Karl: *Guide to Indian Philosophy*, G.K. Hall, Boston, 1988.

Prajnanananda, Swami: *Schools of Indian Philosophical Thought,* Firma K. L. Mukhopadhyay, Calcutta, 1973.

Ranade, R. D.: *Mysticism in Maharashtra*, MacMillan, Delhi, 1933.

Reuven, H.: *The Classic Midrash: Tannaitic Commentaries on the Bible*, Paulist Press, New York, 1995.

Rudolf Otto: *Mysticism East and West: A Comparative Analysis of the Nature of Mysticism*, MacMillan, New York, 1969.

Sankaia, H.D.: *Aspects of Indian History and Archeology*, B.R. Publishing, Delhi, 1977.

Sivaramamurti, C.: *Sri Lakshmi in Indian Art and Thought*, Kanak, New Delhi, 1982.

Thapar, Romila: *Ashoka and the Decline of the Mauryas*, Oxford University Press, London, 1961.

Thomas, P.: *Kama Kalpa or the Hindu Ritual of Love,* D. B. Taraporevala Sons, Bombay, 1960.

Thompson, Edward: *The Making of the Indian Princes*, Oxford University Press, London, 1943.

Tobias, Michael: *A Day in the Life of India,* Collins Publishers San Francisco, San Francisco, 1996.

Trimingham, J.: *Sufi Orders in Islam*, Oxford University Press, New York, 1998.

Walters, Donald: *The Path: Autobiography of a Western Yogi (Swami Kriyananda),* Ananda Publications, Nevada City, 1977.

Wells, Oliver: *Salish Weaving Primitive and Modern,* Oliver Wells, Sardis, 1970.

Zimmer, Heinrich. *The Art of Indian Asia*, Pantheon, New York, 1955.

Zion, Bokser: *Abraham Isaac Kook: The Lights of Penitence*, Paulist Press, New York, 1978.

# Index

## H



## I



## J



## K



## L

## S



## T



## U



## V

❑❑❑